Approaching Home Automation

A Guide to Using X-10 Technology

Second Edition

Bill Berner - Craig Elliott

Approaching, Inc.
Chicago • San Francisco

Library of Congress Cataloging in Publication Data

Approaching Home Automation: A Guide to Using X-10 Technology /

Bill Berner...Craig Elliott. — 2nd ed.

p. cm.

ISBN 1-881911-01-2 (soft cover)

1. Electronics

Library of Congress Card Catalog Number 95-083517

Cover design by Dale Engelbert

Interior illustrations by Brian Maggi

Printed in the United States of America

Preface

The advent of electronics has brought us many incredible technologies. We take calculators, digital watches, and personal computers for granted in our everyday lives. As these silicon marvels came into being, one of the applications thought to be imminent was the "automated home." The idea was to use electronics to control lights and appliances, monitor security, and make life in general more comfortable. In fact, Steve Wozniak's open design of the Apple II computer was largely to facilitate the development of home-control devices. Woz was confident that one of the major applications for his new personal computer would be home automation.

It never really happened.

Sure, you can buy an electric iron that shuts off if it hasn't been moved for a period of time, and if you watch enough late-night TV, you can purchase devices that will turn lights on and off at the sound of clapping hands, but the dream of home automation is largely unrealized.

The big question is, "Why?" Simple, inexpensive, and readily available, the X-10 system has been on the market since 1978 and provides an excellent means to implement many home-automation tasks. Other technologies have promised marvelous cutting-edge features that will surpass X-10. Until that happens (and don't hold your breath), X-10 provides a wonderful mechanism to explore home automation inexpensively—today.

This technology was invented in the late 1970s by a company called X-10 and distributed by BSR, Inc. Just as important was X-10's licensing of technology to literally hundreds of other electronics manufacturers for inclusion in their products. The combination of products from the X-10 company and others makes this the most widely used home-automation system in the world.

The second edition of this book is designed to give you an understanding of what X-10 is all about. It describes the components of an X-10 system and provides design guidelines to create a useful, functional automated home. We've extended this edition to cover all of the latest X-10 technology and additional products that will help deliver on the promise of home automation. You'll also find good ideas from the readers of our first edition on new products and interesting ways to use them.

All items described in this book were available from X-10 (USA), Inc. and its distributors at the time of publication. You'll find other products with similar (if not identical) features from other manufacturers. Most of the information applies to those products, but check the product manuals for differences.

We've also included a technical overview, a troubleshooting section, a list of X-10– compatible manufacturers by chapter, and other information we thought might be helpful.

We also give safety guidelines when discussing electrical equipment. All of the products described in this book are listed with the Underwriters Laboratories for product quality and safety, but you still need to use common sense. The X-10 products in this book require about the same electrical skills needed to install a dimmer control. But that still means dealing with potentially lethal electricity. Contact a qualified electrician if you have any questions or doubts. It's a relatively inexpensive way to gain peace of mind.

We'd like to thank Dave Rye, Vice President and Technical Manager of X-10 (USA) Inc. Dave is an expert in the field of home automation, with more than 15 years of experience, and has written many articles on the subject. His expert advice and review added unique value to this book. We're convinced he knows everything.

We also would like to thank Jim Berner (two of them), Dave Lenkaitis, Dan Torres, Lisa Elliott, and Bill Scheffler for their efforts in reviewing, editing, and generally keeping us honest. Special thanks goes to Alexandra Boettcher, our copy editor, who's been a tremendous asset.

We were amazed at the lack of information that was available about X-10 and its applications. It's not difficult, just not very well known.

Most of all, we think this stuff is fun—and getting better. That's why we wrote the second edition.

We hope you like it.

Contents

1 Concepts 9

Overview 9
Basics 9
Controllers 11
Modules 12
Compatibility 15

2 Controllers 17

Overview 17
Maxi Controller 18
Mini Controller 21
Sundowner 24
Mini Timer 26
Using the Mini Timer for Timed Events 28
Home Automation Interface 36
Telephone Transponder 38
Remote Control and Wireless Transceiver 44
Compatible Products 54

3 Controlling Lights 63

Overview 63
Lamp Module 63
Screw-In Remote Controlled Dimmer Module 66
Wall Switch Module 68
Three-Way Wall Switch Module 71
Motion Detector 74
Troubleshooting 84
Applications 85
Compatible Products 86

4 Controlling Appliances 91
Overview 91
Appliance Modules 91
Two- and Three-Pin Appliance Modules 92
Wall Receptacle Module 94
Thermostat Set-Back Controller 96
Heavy-Duty Appliance Module 100
Universal Module 101
Compatible Products 110

5 Home Security 113
Overview 113
Home Security Basics 113
Powerflash Burglar Alarm Interface 116
Supervised Home Security System 120
Home Security Options 130
Using the Supervised Security System 134
Compatible Products 137

6 Windows 139
Overview 139
Setup 140
Creating a Unit List 147
Defining Scenes 150
Creating Schedules 156
Downloading Commands to the Interface 162
Creating Reports 163
Compatible Products 165

7 Apple Macintosh.....167

Overview.....167
Setup.....168
Getting Started.....170
Testing the Interface.....172
Creating and Using a Module Icon.....174
Setting Up Timed Events.....180
Setting the Base Housecode.....190
Configuring and Customizing.....193
Instant X-10.....200
Summary.....202

8 DOS.....203

Overview.....203
Setup.....204
Entering Module Information.....209
Erasing Module Information.....213
Controlling Modules.....213
Setting Timed Events.....218
Saving, Printing, Exiting, and Other Activities.....222

A Technical Overview.....227

Overview.....227
How It Works.....227

B Troubleshooting.....233

Overview.....233
Things Don't Work at All.....233
Things Don't Work Right.....235

C Troubleshooting Equipment.....237

Overview.....237
Testing Controllers.....237
Testing Modules.....238
Phase Coupling.....239
Signal Amplification.....239

Glossary 241

Index 247

1 Concepts

Overview

This chapter explains the concepts you'll need to understand before you begin automating your house. Because we know you're eager to get started, we've kept this introductory chapter as short as possible, but it does contain important information, and you should read it carefully before continuing.

First you'll learn about the basic components of a home-automation system: **controllers** and **modules.** Next you'll learn how controllers communicate with modules by sending **commands** to them. You'll learn about the specific commands you can use, and how controllers can send commands to particular modules by using the module's **address.**

When you've finished this chapter, you should have a solid understanding of **X-10 Home Automation** components and their operation, and you should be ready to learn about the different kinds of controllers and modules that you can use to build your system.

Basics

You need two types of devices to automate your home: controllers and modules. Modules are adapters that you connect to light switches, lamps, appliances, or other devices that you want to control. Controllers send commands to modules to control the device attached to the module.

The diagram below shows the simplest X-10 configuration: a single controller sending commands to a single module. The controller shown here is used to turn the lamp on and off, and to dim or brighten it.

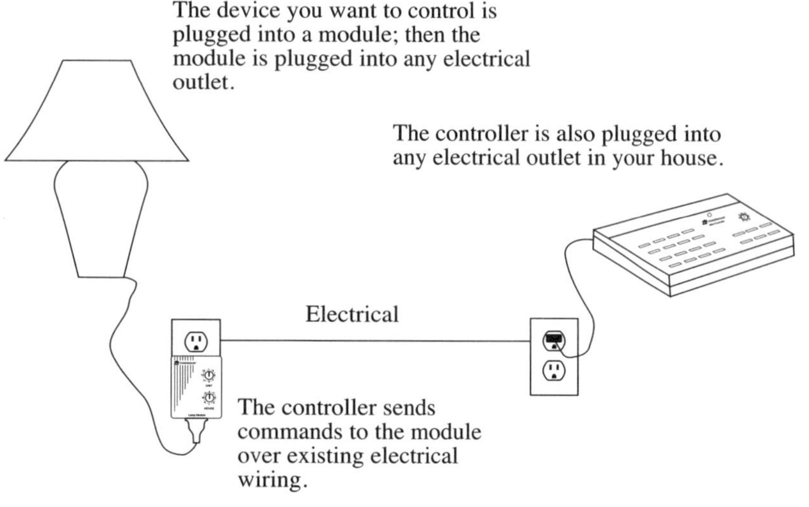

You can buy modules to control just about anything: lights, appliances, sprinklers, security systems—even draperies. In general, any controller can be used to control any of the modules, and we often will use the term **device** to refer generically to something that can be attached to an X-10 module. A complete description of the most popular controllers is given in Chapter 2, "Controllers," beginning on page 17. Modules you can use to control lights are in Chapter 3, "Controlling Lights," beginning on page 63, and modules that control appliances are described in Chapter 4, "Controlling Appliances," beginning on page 91.

You may be asking, "Why not just turn the lamp on and off by hand?" That's a good question. In fact, there will be times when you'll want to turn the light on and off by hand, and you'll still be able to do that once you're using X-10 controllers and modules. But if you've ever stumbled through a dark house to find a light switch, or left a garage light on all night (or all week), or been startled by a noise in the middle of the night, or gone on vacation and worried about your house looking empty, then an X-10 system can be an inexpensive way to make your life a whole lot easier.

At this point, you're probably thinking, "Well, that's all great, but I'll bet it's a pain in the neck to set up the system." Wrong. X-10 controllers and modules communicate over the existing electrical wiring in your home, so you don't need to install new wiring. You just plug modules and controllers into existing electrical outlets. The X-10 devices can send commands over the same wire that carries electricity throughout the house (without disrupting your electrical service in any way, of course).

The technology behind all this is a little complex, and you certainly don't have to understand it to use X-10 products. But if you're curious, see Appendix A, "Technical Overview," beginning on page 227.

Controllers

You've already learned that there are two components to every X-10 system: controllers and modules. You also know that controllers send commands to modules and that modules execute those commands to control the devices attached to them.

When you want to control a device, you push one or more buttons on the face of the controller. (Or, if you are using the Home Automation Interface, you enter commands at your computer.) When you push a button, the controller sends a command to the module or modules that you've selected, and the modules control the devices attached to them.

This section describes the commands that controllers use to communicate with modules. There are two types of commands: **address commands** and **function commands.** Address commands identify the modules that you want to control. Function commands tell the modules what to do.

Address Commands

Each X-10 module has a specific address, which you'll learn more about in the next section. X-10 controllers use these addresses to send function commands to a particular module. This is how an X-10 controller can turn on a light in the living room without turning on every other device in the house at the same time.

When the controller sends an address command, the module or modules with that address "wake up" and begin listening for a function command. As soon as they "hear" the function command, they perform that function.

Function Commands

Here's a description of the different X-10 function commands:

ON/OFF You can use X-10 controllers and modules to turn lights, appliances, and other devices on and off.

DIM/BRIGHT You also can use X-10 controllers to dim incandescent lights—even lights without a dimmer control.

ALL LIGHTS ON Some controllers allow you to turn on all of the lights in the house with a single button. This is especially useful in an emergency—for example, when you suspect that someone is breaking in. With ALL LIGHTS ON, you can turn on every light in the system at once, possibly scaring away the intruder.

ALL UNITS OFF Controllers that support ALL LIGHTS ON also support ALL UNITS OFF. This turns off all of the devices attached to modules with the same Housecode (more about Housecodes later). ALL UNITS OFF provides a convenient way to turn off all of the lights in the house after you're in bed, or to make sure that you've turned off all appliances before leaving town.

Modules

Modules are adapters that you install between the device you want to control and the source of electricity for the device. For example, the Lamp Module is a small interface box that you plug a lamp into. Then you plug the Lamp Module into an electrical outlet. Because the Lamp Module sits between the source of electricity (the outlet) and the device (the lamp), it can control the device by regulating the amount of electricity the device receives.

Other modules replace standard light switches and control the lights that the switches turn on and off. Still others can be used to control low-voltage electrical devices, such as lawn sprinklers and outdoor lighting.

In the previous section, we introduced the concept of the module address, which controllers use to send function commands to specific modules or groups of modules.

X-10 addresses are similar to the addresses that the post office uses to deliver mail. The post office can identify an individual house because each house has a unique address: a street number and name, a city, a state, and a zip code. X-10 addresses are a little simpler than postal addresses because they have only two components: a **Housecode** and a **Unit Code.**

You set the Housecode and Unit Code of a module by adjusting two dials on the front of the module. Typical dials are shown below.

Each dial has 16 different settings. The Housecode is selected from the letters A through P, and the Unit Code is selected from the numbers 1 through 16. The address of the module is simply its Housecode followed by its Unit Code. So, for example, the address of the module shown above is A1.

Because there are 16 different Housecodes and 16 different Unit Codes, there are 16 x 16 = 256 possible addresses. That should be more than enough for the average home. You also can assign two or more modules the same address if you want to control them simultaneously. For example, you might have two porch lights that you want to go on and off at the same time. In that case, you can assign both modules the same address.

In general, you can assign addresses to modules however you want, but there are some guidelines that you might want to follow to make your system easier to use. We'll give a few suggestions here.

- Select devices that you *always* want to control at the same time and give them the same address (the same Unit Code and Housecode).

By assigning the same address to all of the modules in a group, you will be able to turn all of them on or off simply by pushing a single button on the controller. In addition, you'll be able to create **timed events** to control all of these modules with either a Mini Timer or a Home Automation Interface (see Chapter 2, "Controllers").

- Select devices that you *occasionally* will want to control simultaneously and give them the same Housecode.

This will allow you to control the group of devices with the ALL LIGHTS ON and ALL UNITS OFF commands. For example, you might have 10 different lights in your home. By giving all of them the same Housecode, you can turn off all of them at night from a single controller on your nightstand. But, at the same time, you might have other devices—for example, a stereo or an outdoor porch light—that you *don't* want to turn off when you go to bed. In that case, you'd assign these lights and appliances a *different* Housecode from that for the rest of the lights, so that the ALL UNITS OFF command would not turn them off.

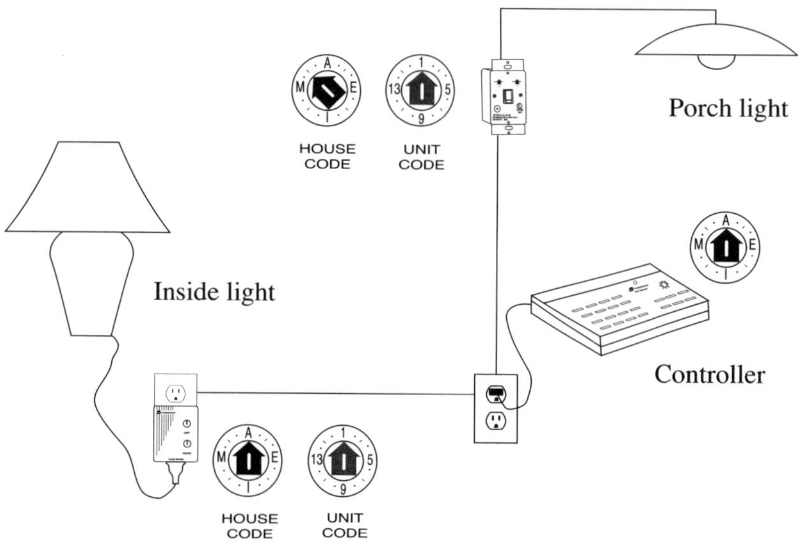

In the diagram above, the ALL UNITS OFF button on the controller will turn off the inside light, but not the porch light. That's because the porch light has a different Housecode.

Also, the buttons on a controller will send commands to only one Housecode. You must adjust a dial on the controller to send commands to modules with a different Housecode. By grouping modules with similar functions, you can control the entire group with a single controller. For example, if you have five sprinkler heads in the yard and 10 lights in the house, you could have one controller next to your bed for controlling all lights and another on the porch for controlling all sprinklers.

Compatibility

The set of commands described in this chapter, and the method for transmitting them over standard electrical wire, were established in the late 1970s by a company named X-10 (USA), Inc. Literally thousands of X-10–compatible home-automation products are in use today.

This book provides detailed information on the products that are manufactured by X-10 (USA), Inc. In addition, at the end of each chapter, you'll find information (including phone numbers) about companies that manufacture compatible products for that particular solution. Generally, because these products all use the same standard set of commands, you can mix and match products from different vendors in the same system. For example, you can use a Radio Shack controller with an X-10 (USA), Inc. Lamp Module.

A word of warning: Although two products from different vendors may do exactly the same thing, their names are liable to be quite different. Occasionally, you might have trouble deciding whether you're buying the right thing. In this book, we use the names established by X-10 (USA), Inc. If you're not sure whether a similar product is compatible, you may be able to find out by asking a knowledgeable salesperson. If that doesn't work, try calling the manufacturer.

2 *Controllers*

Overview

Chapter 1 explained the basic concepts of X-10 home automation: Controllers send commands to modules, and the modules execute the commands, turning devices on or off, dimming lamps, and so on. This chapter describes the different kinds of controllers that you can use for your X-10 system.

Each section talks about a different controller. The section begins with a drawing of the controller and an explanation of its major components. Once you've become familiar with X-10 technology and products, you should be able to answer most of your controller-related questions just by looking at these diagrams. Later in the section, we list the important features that distinguish one controller from another and make some controllers more appropriate for a particular application. We also provide suggestions for using each controller in your home.

Once you've read this chapter, you should be able to select the controller or controllers most appropriate for your system and your plans. You also should know which controllers you can use to add features to your system in the future.

Maxi Controller

Overview

The Maxi Controller is a general-purpose controller that can be used to control up to 16 devices. Here's a diagram of the Maxi Controller with a description of the major components.

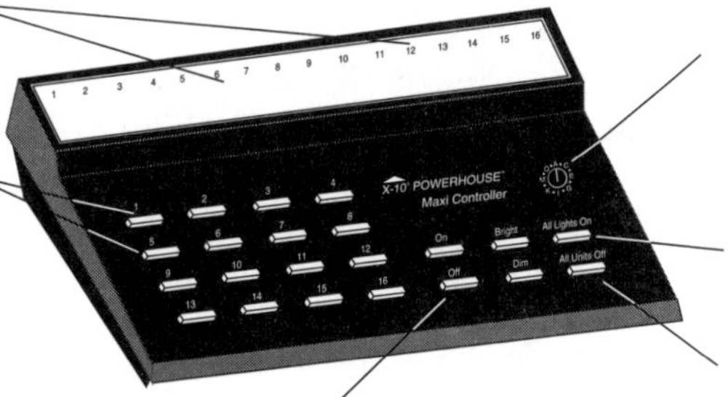

Write the names of devices you're controlling at the top of the console for quick reference.

Click one or more of the 16 **Unit Code buttons** to identify the Unit Codes of the modules you want to control.

Set the Housecode here. Make sure that it matches the setting on the modules that you want to control.

Press ALL LIGHTS ON to turn on all lights.

Press ALL UNITS OFF to turn off all modules with the same Housecode as the Maxi Controller, including Appliance Modules.

After selecting one or more devices, press ON, OFF, BRIGHT, or DIM to control the selected device or devices.

Using the Maxi Controller

Using the Maxi Controller is easy. Here's what you'll do:

Plug the Maxi Controller into any electrical outlet.

Don't forget this step, or the Maxi Controller won't be able to send commands, and nothing will work.

Set the Housecode on the Maxi Controller to the same setting as the Housecode on the module or modules that you want to control.

With the Maxi Controller, or any other controller, you can send commands *only* to modules that have the same Housecode as the controller. This means that you can control only 16 devices (with distinct Unit Codes) at a time. You can, of course, control more than

16 devices by assigning the same Unit Code to more than one module.

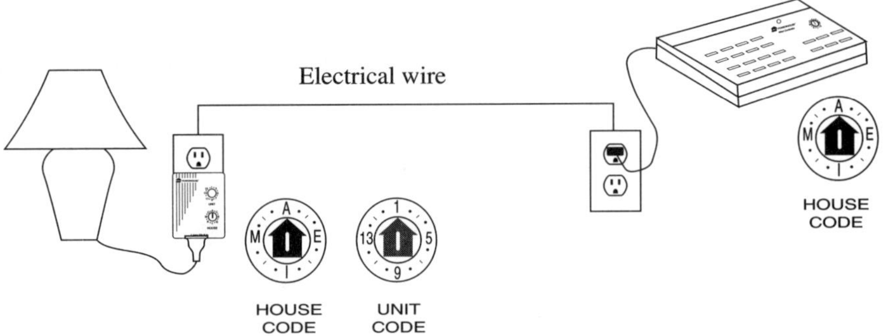

The Housecode on the controller *must* match the Housecode on the module. A controller set to Housecode A, like the one shown above, will not turn on a module with a Housecode other than "A." For example, it would not turn on the module shown below, which is set to Housecode O. For that module, you would have to use a controller set to Housecode O, like the one shown below.

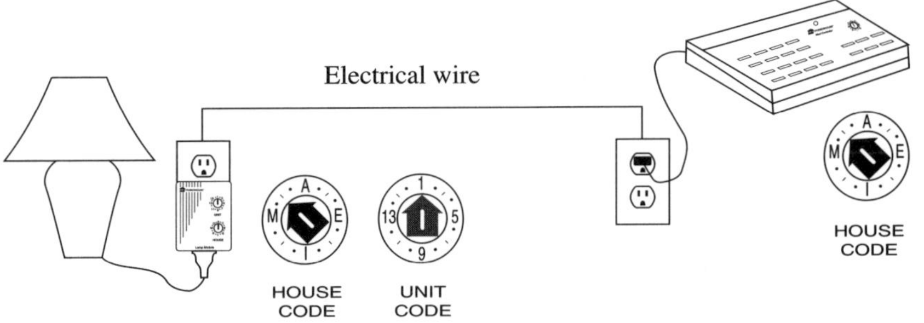

You can change the Housecode by inserting a small screwdriver into the dial in the upper-right corner of the controller and turning to the desired Housecode.

Press one or more Unit Code buttons to send address commands to the modules you want to control.

You'll select the modules that you want to control by pressing the appropriate Unit Code buttons. For example, if you want to turn off a lamp that is connected to a module with the Unit Code set to 10, then you'll press the button marked "10." When you do this, the controller will send an address command that consists of the Housecode you've set on the Maxi Controller plus the Unit Code corresponding to the button that you press. This will cause any modules with that address to "listen" for the next function command.

Note that you can press more than one Unit Code button. For example, if you want to turn off two space heaters that have Unit Codes 3 and 4, you'll press the button marked "3" and then the one marked "4." When the first module sees the first address command with Unit Code 3, it will wake up and ignore the next address command with Unit Code 4, while continuing to listen for a function command. By pressing multiple Unit Code buttons before pressing a function command button, you can control groups of modules, which is an important feature of the Maxi Controller.

Next choose the function commands that you want to send to the module(s).

You'll send function commands to the selected modules by pressing the ON, OFF, DIM, or BRIGHT buttons. Note that you can dim or brighten only lamps that are connected to Lamp Modules or Wall Switch Modules.

That's it! That's all you need to know to control individual devices or groups of devices with the Maxi Controller.

ALL LIGHTS ON and ALL UNITS OFF

There are times when you might want to turn on all lights with the same Housecode at once, or turn off all devices with the same Housecode at once. Here's how you'll use these additional features:

Make sure that the Housecode on the Maxi Controller is the same as the Housecode on the modules you want to control.

You can change the Housecode by inserting a small screwdriver into the dial in the upper-right corner of the controller and turning to the desired Housecode.

Press ALL LIGHTS ON or ALL UNITS OFF.

You'll press ALL LIGHTS ON to turn on all lights connected to Lamp Modules and Wall Switch Modules that have the same Housecode as the Maxi Controller.

ALL UNITS OFF works like ALL LIGHTS ON, but it turns off all modules that have the same Housecode as the Maxi Controller, including Appliance Modules.

It's important to remember that controllers can control only modules that use the same Housecode that the controller uses.

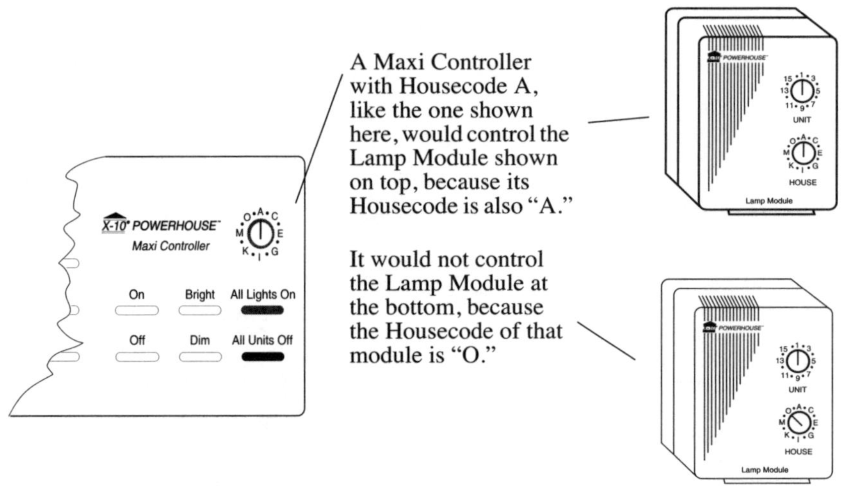

Comparing the Maxi Controller With Other Controllers

The Maxi Controller is perfect when you are home and able to turn appliances, lights, and other devices on and off. For example, it lets you turn off lights from your bedside before going to sleep, or turn off basement or garage lights from inside the house.

The Maxi Controller cannot be used for timed events. For example, you can't set the Maxi Controller to turn sprinklers on and off at a specified time every day. For this type of control, you'll need to purchase either a Mini Timer or a Home Automation Interface. The Home Automation Interface works in conjunction with a personal computer; the Mini Timer doesn't require a computer. Both controllers are described later in this chapter.

Mini Controller

Overview

Using a Mini Controller is a low-cost way to control up to eight modules. It can brighten or dim lights, and it can turn all lights on or all units off.

The Mini Controller is also ideal as a second controller used in conjunction with a Maxi Controller or a Home Automation Interface (described elsewhere in this chapter).

Here's a diagram of the Mini Controller, with a description of its major components.

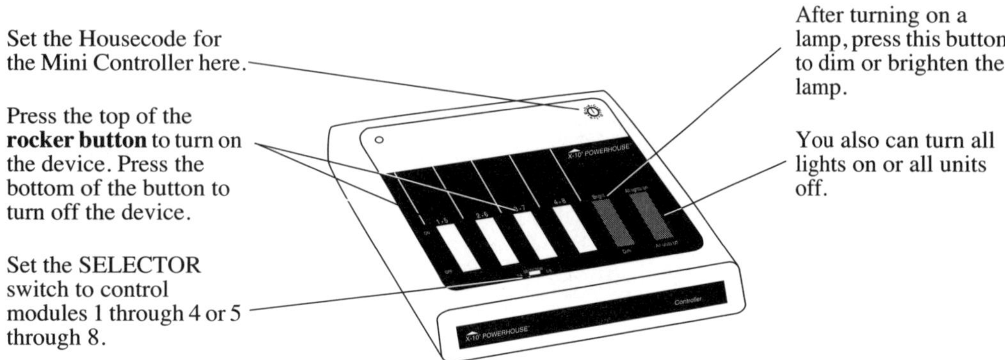

Using the Mini Controller

To use the Mini Controller, here's what you'll do:

Plug the Mini Controller into any electrical outlet.

If you forget this step, you won't be able to communicate with anything.

Make sure that the Housecode on the Mini Controller is the same as the Housecode on the modules you want to control.

Like any other controller, the Mini Controller will communicate only with modules that use the same Housecode. If the Housecodes are not the same, nothing will happen. If you have problems controlling a lamp, an appliance, or anything else, check the Housecode first.

Remember that you can change the Housecode by inserting a small screwdriver into the dial in the upper-right corner of the controller and turning to the desired Housecode.

Determine which module you want to control and set the SELECTOR switch appropriately.

The Mini Controller works differently than the Maxi Controller does. Remember that the Maxi Controller has separate Unit Code buttons and function command buttons. The Mini Controller has combined Unit Code and ON/OFF buttons—called "rocker buttons" because they rock back and forth. If you press one side of the button, the controller sends an address command followed by ON; if you press the other side, the controller sends an address command followed by OFF. The ON and OFF sides are labeled clearly on the controller so that you won't get confused.

Although the Mini Controller can control up to eight devices, it has only four rocker buttons. Each rocker button can control one of two Unit Codes, depending on how you have set the SELECTOR switch.

If you want to control a module with Unit Code 1 through 4, you'll push the SELECTOR switch to the left. You'll push the SELECTOR switch to the right to control a module with Unit Code 5 through 8.

Press the appropriate rocker button to turn the module on or off. Or press ALL LIGHTS ON or ALL UNITS OFF.

Each of the white buttons on the front of the Mini Controller is labeled with two numbers corresponding to the Unit Codes of the modules that the button controls. For example, the first button is labeled "1•5." If the SELECTOR switch is set to the left, this button will turn the module with Unit Code 1 on or off. If the SELECTOR switch is set to the right, the button will turn the module with Unit Code 5 on or off.

Instead of pressing one of the white buttons to turn an individual module on or off, you can press ALL LIGHTS ON to turn on all lights connected to Lamp Modules or Wall Switch Modules that have the same Housecode as the Mini Controller. Alternatively, you can press ALL UNITS OFF to turn off all devices connected to modules with the same Housecode as the Mini Controller.

Each rocker button on the Mini Controller turns modules both on and off. To turn a module on, press the top of the button. To turn a module off, press the bottom of the button. Remember that ALL LIGHTS ON and ALL UNITS OFF control only modules that have the same Housecode as the Mini Controller.

After you've turned on a light, press the BRIGHT/DIM button if you want to change the intensity of the light.

Remember that you can dim or brighten only lamps that you're controlling with either a Lamp Module or a Wall Switch Module. You even can dim or brighten lights that have been turned on using ALL LIGHTS ON.

Note that if you press more than one rocker button at the same time, you can turn on lights as a group and then dim or brighten them as a group. For example, if you press rocker buttons 1 and 2 simultaneously, the Mini Controller will send wake-up commands to modules 1 and 2, followed by ON. You then can change the intensity of both lamps by pressing DIM or BRIGHT.

That's it! That's really all you need to know to use the Mini Controller to control devices in your home.

Comparing the Mini Controller With Other Controllers

The Mini Controller is one of the least-expensive controllers, and is ideal if you want to turn a small number of modules on and off. The Mini Controller doesn't support timed events, so if you need to turn devices on and off at specific times throughout the day, the Mini Timer or the Home Automation Interface would be a better choice.

The Mini Controller works well for controlling small groups of lights or appliances. Here are some examples.

- Turn off a group of lights from your nightstand after going to bed.
- Turn on a group of lights when you walk in the front door at night.
- Turn individual sprinklers on and off from inside the house.
- Turn your computer, printer, and other peripherals on and off from your desk.

Sundowner

Overview

Think of the Sundowner as a Mini Controller that's smart enough to automatically turn on a group of up to four lights at dusk and automatically turn them off again at dawn. The Sundowner has a built-in photocell. Each night, when the sun goes down, the photocell in the Sundowner "triggers," causing the Sundowner to send a wake-up command to up to four X-10 addresses, followed by an ON command. In the morning, the photocell triggers as soon as the level of sunlight reaches a certain point, and the Sundowner then sends a wake-up command to the same group of lights, followed by an OFF command.

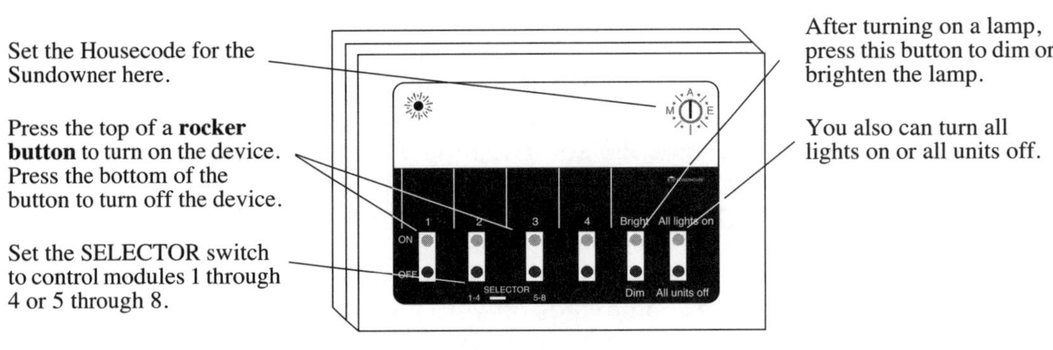

Here's a look at the bottom of the Sundowner, which has special controls for turning lights and appliances on and off automatically.

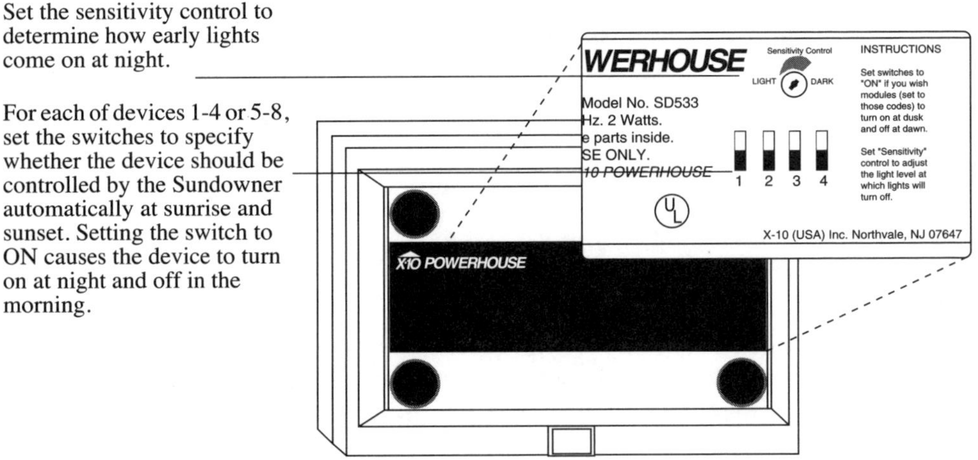

Comparing the Sundowner to Other Controllers

Using the Sundowner is an ideal way to control lights that you want to turn on every night—for example, porch lights, yard lights, and even landscape lighting. The Sundowner costs about the same as a Maxi Controller, so the trade-off is between the number of units you can control (eight for the Sundowner, 16 for the Maxi Controller) and the ability to automatically turn lights on and off at night.

You also might compare the Sundowner to the Mini Timer or the Home Automation Interface, both of which are capable of sending "timed events," which take place at the same time every day or every week. The big difference between the Sundowner and these other controllers is that the Sundowner sends commands only at dusk and dawn. Depending on what you want to control, this may not work. For example, someone going fishing couldn't use the Sundowner as an alarm clock because he might have to get up before dawn. The Mini Timer probably would be a better choice in that case.

Likewise, the Sundowner is better for some applications precisely because it sends commands only at dusk and dawn. For example, if you use a Home Automation Interface to turn on a porch light every evening, you need to reprogram the interface continuously as days become longer or shorter throughout the year. This could be annoying after a while, making the Sundowner a reasonably priced addition to your automation system.

Of course, if you can afford it, the best solution probably is to have one of each: a Sundowner for lights that should go on at dusk and off at dawn every day, a Mini Timer that you can set next to your bed and use as an alarm clock, and a Home Automation Interface for those other modules that you want to control at odd intervals and odd times, such as yard sprinklers, exhaust fans, appliances, and so on.

Mini Timer

Overview

The Mini Timer combines the features of the Mini Controller and an alarm clock, allowing you to control modules both manually and using **timed events**. For example, you can use the Mini Timer to automatically turn outdoor lights on every evening and off every morning.

Here is a diagram of the Mini Timer, with a description of its major components.

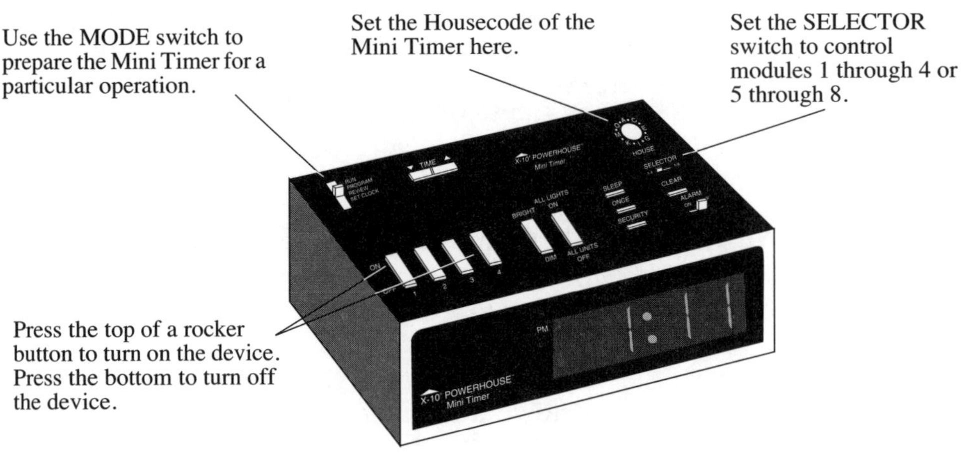

Using the Mini Timer for Manual Control

In manual mode, you use the Mini Timer the same way that you use the Mini Controller. Here's an overview of the steps, in case you've forgotten:

- Choose a Housecode and set it using the dial in the upper-right corner of the control panel.
- Set the SELECTOR switch to control modules 1 through 4 or 5 through 8.
- To turn on a device, press the top of the rocker button that corresponds to the Unit Code of the device that you want to control; to turn off a device, press the bottom of the rocker button.
- Once you have turned on a lamp, you can brighten or dim it by pressing the top or the bottom of the BRIGHT/DIM rocker button.
- You also can use the ALL LIGHTS ON and ALL UNITS OFF buttons to control all modules with the same Housecode as the Mini Timer.

Remember that pressing a rocker button turns on or off *all* devices that have the same Housecode as the Mini Timer and the same Unit Code as the rocker button. This allows you to control multiple lamps, appliances, or other devices at the same time.

If you still are not sure how to use the Mini Timer to control devices manually, review the steps outlined in the Mini Controller section. The steps for controlling modules with these two controllers are identical and are given in more detail in the Mini Controller section. The next section describes how to use the Mini Timer to create timed events.

Using the Mini Timer for Timed Events

Overview

You can use the Mini Timer to create timed events, which gives you the power to automate your home in many useful ways. For example, you can create a timed event to turn on your bedroom light at 6:00 AM every morning to help you wake up.

Setting the Clock

Before doing anything else, you'll need to set the clock on the Mini Timer. Until you do this, your timed events won't happen at the right time!

Here's how to set the clock:

Plug the Mini Timer into a standard electrical outlet.

When you plug in the Mini Timer, the display will flash.

Next you'll tell the Mini Timer that you want to set the clock. You'll do this by using the MODE switch, in the upper-left corner of the Mini Timer control panel.

Set the MODE switch to CLOCK SET.

Refer to the diagram at the beginning of this section if you have trouble locating the MODE switch.

Now you're ready to set the time.

Set the time by pressing the rocker button marked "TIME."

To advance the time, you'll press the side of the rocker button marked "▲." To move the time back, you'll press the side of the button marked "▼." Note that pressing the button and releasing it quickly moves the time slowly; pressing and holding the button moves the time rapidly. Also note that the PM indicator light comes on for PM times and turns off for AM times. Be sure that you have correctly set the time for AM or PM. This will be very important when you set the Mini Timer to turn devices on automatically. You wouldn't want it to brew the coffee at 6:00 PM or turn on the porch light at 6:00 AM.

Now that you've set the time correctly, you'll need to change the mode of the Mini Timer so that it's ready to work.

Set the MODE switch to RUN.

Setting Timed Events

Now the clock is set, and you've learned to use the Mini Timer to control modules manually. The real power of the Mini Timer, however, is its ability to use timed events to control modules automatically at different times throughout the day.

The procedures outlined here will allow you to turn a module (or a group of modules) with the same Unit Code on or off automatically. For example, you can turn on the porch light at 6:00 PM every day.

You can create timed events for only one group of four modules. You can choose from modules with Unit Codes 1 through 4 or 5 through 8. You'll choose which group you want to control by using the SELECTOR switch on the face of the Mini Timer.

In other words, you cannot set timed events for both sets of Unit Codes at the same time. For example, if the Housecode on the Mini Timer is "A," you can create timed events for modules with addresses A1, A2, A3, and A4 *or* modules A5, A6, A7, and A8. But you cannot simultaneously control modules from both groups.

In fact, if you program timed events for the modules in one group and then change the SELECTOR switch setting, the events you've programmed will occur for the modules in the other group. For example, let's say that you control a porch light with a module that uses Unit Code 1 and a space heater with a module that uses Unit Code 5. If you set the SELECTOR switch to 1-4 and program an event to turn on the porch light at 6:00 AM every day, and then move the SELECTOR switch to 5-8, the space heater, not the porch light, will come on at 6:00 AM every day. This kind of mistake could be dangerous, and you should be sure you understand how the Mini Timer works before you use it to create timed events.

You also should know that you can create only two "on" times and two "off" times for each of the four Unit Codes in the group you've chosen. While this may be enough for many home-automation systems, you'll need to use a Home Automation Interface if you want to program more than two "on" times or two "off" times.

To create timed events, you'll first put the Mini Timer into PROG SET mode, short for Program Set mode.

Set the MODE switch to PROG SET.

When the Mini Timer is in Program Set mode, the display will show you the events that already have been programmed. If you have not programmed any events, the display will show "12:00."

Next you'll need to set the time at which you want the event to take place.

Use the TIME button to set the time of the event. Pressing ▼ moves the time back. Pressing ▲ moves the time forward.

Note that the PM indicator turns on for PM times and off for AM times. Be sure that you have correctly set the time for AM or PM.

You also must set the SELECTOR switch appropriately for the module or modules that you want to control.

Set the SELECTOR switch to 1-4 or 5-8, depending on the Unit Code of the module you want to control.

Note that if you set the SELECTOR switch to 1-4, create timed events, and then change the SELECTOR switch to 5-8, events that you created for modules with Unit Code 1 will occur for modules with Unit Code 5, events that you created for modules with Unit Code 2 will occur for modules with Unit Code 6, and so on.

For example, let's say that you control a lamp with a module set to Unit Code 2 and a space heater with a module set to Unit Code 6. If you set the SELECTOR switch to 1-4 and program events for the lamp, and then change the SELECTOR switch to 5-8, all of the events that you programmed for the lamp will happen for the heater.

Next you'll program the event.

Press ON or OFF on the rocker button that corresponds to the Unit Code of the module you want to control.

For example, if you want to turn on the module with Unit Code 1, first set the SELECTOR switch to 1-4 and then press ON for the rocker button labeled 1•5.

Now you can program additional events by following these steps:

- Set the time for the event.
- Press ON or OFF for the Unit Code of the module you want to control.

If "18:88" appears on the display, the memory for the selected Unit Code is full. You must clear one of the currently stored events before setting a new one. See "Reviewing Timed Events" on page 33.

Once you have finished setting events, you'll need to reset the MODE switch for normal operation. If you do not, the Mini Timer won't execute any timed events.

When you have finished programming events, set the MODE switch to RUN.

Setting the Wake-Up Alarm

When you set the Mini Timer to control a module with Unit Code 1 or 5, you can set a buzzer to go off as well. To do this, create an event for Unit Code 1 or 5 by following the instructions above. Then set the WAKE UP switch to IN. You can deactivate the wake-up buzzer by setting the WAKE UP switch to OUT.

You should consider the wake-up alarm feature when you decide which modules you want to assign Unit Code 1 or 5 and which SELECTOR setting you want to use for the Mini Timer. For example, if you plan to use the wake-up alarm, you should assign Unit Code 1 or 5 to devices that you want to turn on when you wake up, such as a coffee pot. You should assign these devices Unit Code 1 or Unit Code 5, depending on how you have set the SELECTOR switch.

Note that when the buzzer sounds, pressing any button on the Mini Timer activates the "snooze" feature, which turns the buzzer off for

10 minutes. After this 10-minute period, the buzzer sounds again. It goes off automatically after it has sounded for 10 minutes. If you want to turn off the buzzer permanently, just set the WAKE UP switch to OUT.

You can temporarily suspend timed events for modules with Unit Code 1 or 5 by setting the MODE switch to CLOCK SET and the WAKE UP switch to OUT. This is useful when you want to turn off timed events for a short period of time. For example, if you normally program the light in your bedroom to turn on at 6:00 AM, you can suspend this event after a late night simply by setting the MODE switch to CLOCK SET and the WAKE UP switch to OUT. Note that when you do this, you still can use the rocker buttons on the front of the Mini Timer to control devices manually.

At this point, you know all you need to know to set up timed events with the Mini Timer. The sections that follow give details about advanced features of the Mini Timer. Before reading these sections, you might want to try out what you've already learned.

One-Time Timed Events

Sometimes you might want to set a timed event to happen only once. For example, you might set the porch light to turn on at midnight on a particular day because you know you're going to get home late. You'll do this by using the Once mode.

To specify that an event happen only once, press ONCE within four seconds of setting a timed event.

The timed event will occur at the specified time within the next 24-hour period and then be cleared from the Mini Timer's memory.

Security Mode

One of the benefits of being able to set timed events is that you can give your home a lived-in look, even when you're not there. By using the Security mode, you can enhance the lived-in look by having timed events occur at slightly different times every day. For example, if you set the porch light to go on at 6:00 PM every day and then set Security mode, the light will come on at 6:00 PM the first day and at a random time between 6:00 PM and 7:00 PM every day after that.

To activate Security mode, press SECURITY within four seconds of setting a timed event.

Sleep Mode

Occasionally, you might want to turn a module on or off after a specific amount of time. For example, you might want to listen to the radio while falling asleep and have the radio turn off automatically after 15 minutes. You can do this by using the Sleep mode.

Press ON for the module you want to control. Then, within four seconds, press SLEEP once for each 15 minutes you want the module to remain on.

For example, assume that your radio is connected to an Appliance Module set to Unit Code 1. If you want the radio to play for 30 minutes and then turn off, press ON for the rocker button marked "1•5," and then press SLEEP twice within four seconds (2 x 15 minutes = 30 minutes).

You also can use the Sleep mode to turn on a device. Here's how:

Press OFF for the module you want to control. Then, within four seconds, press SLEEP once for each 15 minutes you want the module to remain off.

For example, assume once more that your radio is connected to an Appliance Module set to Unit Code 1. If you want to take a nap for 45 minutes and then have the radio turn on, simply press OFF for the rocker button marked "1•5" and then press SLEEP three times (3 x 15 minutes = 45 minutes) within four seconds.

Sleep mode is the last of the advanced Mini Timer features. The rest of this section covers reviewing, modifying, and deleting timed events.

Reviewing Timed Events

There are two reasons that you'll need to know how to review timed events: to confirm the events that you've already set and to clear previously defined events.

First you'll learn how to review the events that you've already set; but to do that, you'll need to set the mode.

Set the MODE switch to PROG REVIEW.

PROG REVIEW, as you may have guessed, stands for Program Review. Now you can check events for each of your devices.

Press either ON (to review On events) or OFF (to review Off events) for the rocker button of the device whose timed events you want to confirm.

For example, if you want to check the time when the module or modules with Unit Code 1 will go on, press ON for the rocker button marked "1•5." After you press the button, the time of the event is displayed. If there is no event set for that Unit Code, "0:00" will be displayed. Note that if two events are set (for example, if the module is set to go on at 6:00 AM and 6:00 PM), you'll need to press the Unit Code button twice to see both times.

You can review events for more than one Unit Code simply by pressing more rocker buttons. When you're finished, you'll need to change the mode back to RUN, or the Mini Timer won't execute your timed events.

Once you've reviewed the settings you are interested in, set the MODE switch to RUN.

Clearing Events

Sometimes you'll want to clear events from the Mini Timer's memory to make room for new timed events or to deactivate old events. To clear events, you'll first have to change the mode.

Set the MODE switch to PROG REVIEW.

Next you'll select the event you want to clear.

Select the event you want to clear by pressing ON or OFF for the appropriate rocker button until the event is displayed.

Note that if two events are set for the Unit Code whose event you want to clear, you'll need to ensure that the correct one is displayed before continuing; otherwise, you'll clear the wrong event.

Once the event is displayed, it's easy to clear.

Press CLEAR to remove the event from the Mini Timer's memory.

You can repeat this procedure for as many events as you want to clear. When you have finished, you'll need to reset the mode.

When you have finished clearing events, set the MODE switch to RUN.

Remember that you can create only two On events and two Off events for each Unit Code. If you try to create a timed event when there are already two events programmed for that Unit Code, the display will show "18:88." Before creating this new event, you must use the procedure outlined above to remove one of the existing events.

Installing the Backup Battery

If you do not install a backup battery in your Mini Timer, and the power goes off for some reason (say, during a thunderstorm), you will lose the clock setting and any timed events that you've set.

Here's how to install the backup battery:

Open the battery compartment cover.

The battery compartment cover is located on the back of the Mini Timer.

Connect a nine-volt battery to the battery contact inside the compartment. Then replace the battery compartment cover.

Once you've installed the battery, you'll look at the front of the Mini Timer. To the right of the display, there will be an LED indicator labeled "Battery Sentinel." When the LED comes on, that means the battery is weak and should be replaced.

Comparing the Mini Timer With Other Controllers

The key feature of the Mini Timer is that it supports timed events. If you need to turn devices on and off automatically at specific times during the day or night, then the Mini Timer might be for you. The key question to ask yourself is, "Are there devices that I want to turn off or on at the same time *every* day?"

Here are some situations that might require the functionality of the Mini Timer:

- Turning on an outside porch light at dusk every evening
- Turning on a coffee maker first thing every morning
- Turning "grow lights" on and off at the same time every day
- Controlling sprinkler systems, outdoor lights, or other low-voltage electrical devices
- Turning a "bug zapper" on every night and off every morning

If you decide that you need a controller that supports timed events, you'll have to choose between a Home Automation Interface and a Mini Timer. (Well, you don't *have* to choose: One of the authors owns three Home Automation Interfaces and one Mini Timer!) The biggest factor in your decision should be whether you have a personal computer. If you do, you should almost certainly purchase the Home Automation Interface.

The Home Automation Interface can control modules with any address—that is, any combination of Housecode and Unit Code. The interface can store up to 128 timed events. In comparison, the Mini Timer can control only modules with the same Housecode it uses and control only one group of four modules with that Housecode: either those with Unit Codes 1 through 4 or 5 through 8. In addition, it can store only two On and two Off events for each module.

Note that in the previous paragraph, we used the term *modules* to mean modules with unique addresses. Naturally, you can control more than four modules with the Mini Timer if some of them share the same Unit Code. For example, you could control any number of lights if each of them was connected to a module set to Unit Code 1.

Home Automation Interface

Overview

The Home Automation Interface is used with a personal computer to control up to 256 X-10 modules (or more, if some modules share the same address). It comes with software and a cable for connecting it to your computer. Detailed information about using the interface with a Macintosh computer is given in Chapter 7, "Apple Macintosh," on page 167. Information about using the interface with an IBM PC or compatible running DOS is given in Chapter 8, "DOS," on page 203. Information about using the interface with an IBM PC or compatible running Windows 3.1 or Windows 95 is given in Chapter 6, "Windows," on page 139. Versions are also available for the Apple II, the Commodore 64, and the Commodore 128 computers.

Here is a diagram of the interface, with a description of the major components.

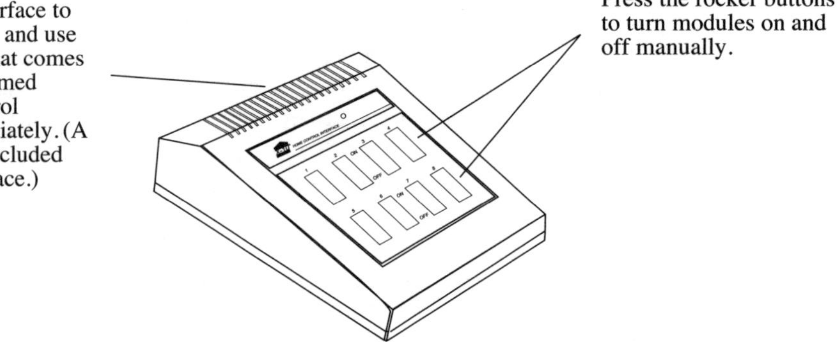

Using the Interface for Manual Control

You can use the interface to control up to eight modules manually simply by pressing a rocker button. You control modules manually with the interface in the same way that you control them with the Mini Controller. If you are not sure how the rocker buttons work, refer to the instructions for the Mini Controller on page 22.

Using the Interface for Timed Events

The real value of the interface comes when you use it with your computer. The software included with the interface allows you to set timed events for up to 256 modules. Unlike the Mini Timer, the interface lets you set timed events for modules that have *different* Housecodes. This gives you maximum flexibility.

For example, you can use the interface to create timed events for lights attached to Lamp Modules that use Housecode A, as well as for sprinklers attached to Universal Modules that use Housecode B. What's more, with a Macintosh computer, you can use a graphics package to create a floor plan of your house and then use the floor plan in conjunction with the interface software. This makes it easier to identify all of the modules in your system and review the timed events you've set for each module.

Comparing the Interface With Other Controllers

Like the Mini Timer, the big advantage of the Home Automation Interface is its ability to create timed events.

If you don't have a personal computer, the biggest drawback of the interface is certainly the requirement that you gain access to a PC to use it. If you already have a computer, though, the only drawback of the interface is that it's more expensive than the Mini Timer (but probably not too much more—shop around!).

The interface is definitely the most flexible controller described in this book. Using the software that comes with it, you can set up to 128 timed events, and each can correspond to a module with a unique address. That's a lot. In addition, the interface is the only controller that allows you to control modules that have different Housecodes.

The interface makes an ideal foundation for almost any home-automation system. You can use it to set up timed events for *all* modules in the system and then use other controllers to add functionality. For example, you can use a Telephone Transponder to control devices when you're away from home and a remote control to turn off the TV without leaving your favorite chair.

Telephone Transponder

Overview

The Telephone Transponder lets you control up to eight modules manually, using the rocker buttons on the front of the transponder. In addition, the Telephone Transponder can be used to control up to 10 devices remotely from *any* touch-tone telephone in the United States.

A diagram of the Telephone Transponder is shown below, with a description of the major components.

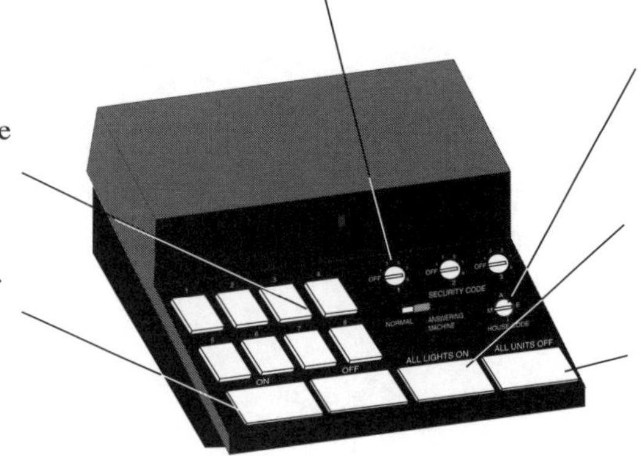

Using the Telephone Transponder for Manual Control

To manually control devices in your home, you'll use the Telephone Transponder exactly as you would the Maxi Controller. In case you've forgotten, here are the basic steps:

- Plug the Telephone Transponder into any electrical outlet.
- Set the Housecode on the Telephone Transponder so that it matches the Housecode on the module or modules you want to control.
- Select the module or modules you want to control by pressing the appropriate Unit Code buttons.
- Choose the function command that you want to send to the modules by pressing ON or OFF.
- Press ALL LIGHTS ON to turn on all lights attached to modules with the same Housecode as the Telephone Transponder. (ALL LIGHTS ON turns on only lights attached to Lamp Modules or Wall Switch Modules.)
- Press ALL UNITS OFF to turn off all devices attached to modules with the same Housecode as the Telephone

Transponder, including devices attached to Appliance Modules.

That's it! If things are still a little unclear, please see "Using the Maxi Controller" on page 18.

Using the Telephone Transponder for Remote Control

Now you know how to use the Telephone Transponder to control devices manually. The really nifty feature of the Telephone Transponder, though, is its ability to control devices remotely, from any touch-tone telephone in the United States. The following sections tell you how.

Setting the Security Code

You may want to set the security code before attaching the Telephone Transponder to your phone system. This helps to prevent ne'er-do-wells from calling and controlling devices in your house. It also prevents the unsuspecting from accidently turning devices on or off in your home when they call and end up talking to the Telephone Transponder instead of to you.

To set the security code, use a small screwdriver to turn the three dials marked "SECURITY CODE" on the face of the Telephone Transponder.

You can set a one-, two-, or three-digit security code. If you decide to set a one-digit code, be sure to use the Security Code dial labeled "1." If you decide on a two-digit code, use dials 1 and 2. For a three-digit code, you need to use all three dials.

The diagram below shows how the dials would be set for no security code, for a single-digit code, and for a three-digit code.

1 2 3
SECURITY CODE

No security code set. When you call, enter commands as soon as the Telephone Transponder answers the phone with three beeps.

1 2 3
SECURITY CODE

Here, the security code is 5. When the Telephone Transponder answers the phone with three beeps, press 5, then enter commands.

1 2 3
SECURITY CODE

Here, the security code is 8-6-5. When the Telephone Transponder answers the phone with three beeps, press 8-6-5, then enter commands.

Setting Up the Telephone Transponder

You're ready to set up the Telephone Transponder. By now the first step should be obvious.

Plug the Telephone Transponder into any electrical outlet.

The only other installation required is connecting the Telephone Transponder to a phone line so that it can accept incoming calls.

Connect the Telephone Transponder to a standard phone line by plugging the modular phone jack connector attached to the Telephone Transponder into any modular telephone jack.

This is **techno-speak** for "plug the Telephone Transponder into a telephone jack." If you don't have a spare telephone jack, you can either have one installed or buy a "coupling jack" to connect both the phone and the Telephone Transponder to the same telephone jack. You can find a coupling jack at most stores that sell telephones.

Setting the ANSWERING MACHINE Switch

If you have an answering machine, you still can use the Telephone Transponder, but you'll need to tell the transponder to expect an answering machine to answer the phone.

Set the switch in the center of the Telephone Transponder to ANSWERING MACHINE if you have one. Set the switch to NORMAL if you don't have an answering machine.

Operating the Telephone Transponder is a little different if you have an answering machine; the details are covered in the next section.

Remote Operation

To use the Telephone Transponder, the first thing to do is leave the house and phone home.

Call the phone number of the phone line to which you've attached the Telephone Transponder. Then wait for the Telephone Transponder to answer the phone.

When the Telephone Transponder answers, you'll hear three short beeps.

If you have an answering machine and you've set the ANSWERING MACHINE switch accordingly, the Telephone Transponder will sound three short beeps 30 seconds after the first ring, which probably will be *after* your answering machine message finishes. Be patient!

If you set a security code, enter it now. Otherwise, skip to the next instruction.

The Telephone Transponder will not do anything after you enter the security code.

Press the number on the phone keypad that corresponds to the Unit Code of the module or modules you want to control. Then press ✳ to turn on the devices, or press # to turn off the devices.

Note that you can control only modules with Unit Codes 1 through 10. To control a module with Unit Code 10, you'll press 0. After you enter a command, you should hear the characteristic three short beeps of the Telephone Transponder. After the three beeps, you can either enter another command or hang up the phone.

Flashing the Lights

There's one more feature of the Telephone Transponder that you should know about. Any lights connected to modules set to the same Unit Code as the third Security Code dial will flash on and off when the phone rings. This is a very useful feature for those who are hearing impaired. Even if you don't have a hearing impairment, this feature can be useful if you don't want to miss phone calls while you're outside at night or when the stereo is playing loudly.

That's it! You know how to use all of the features of the Telephone Transponder.

Comparing the Telephone Transponder With Other Controllers

You'll need a Telephone Transponder if you want to control devices when you're away from home. Here are some examples:

- To turn on a heater or air conditioner so the house is comfortable when you get home
- To ensure that appliances, such as a heater or an iron, are off when you're away from home
- To turn on lights for added security when you're away from home
- To turn sprinklers on and off when you're away from home

Because it lets you control devices remotely, the Telephone Transponder is ideal for people who have vacation homes. With the Telephone Transponder, you can adjust the heating or air conditioning in the vacation home before you arrive and ensure that you've turned off all appliances and lights when you leave.

If you don't need to control devices while you're away from home, you probably should purchase a different controller with features more suited to your needs.

Remote Control and Wireless Transceiver

Overview

Sometimes, using a controller that you have to plug into an electrical outlet is not the ideal solution. Say, for example, that you want to open the garage door and turn on the lights in the house when you pull into the driveway. In this case, you'd need to have a very long extension cord or take very short trips. Fortunately, there's a better solution: wireless controllers and transceivers for your home-automation system.

A wireless controller system really consists of two pieces: a remote control that runs on batteries and that you can carry with you, and a transceiver, which plugs into an electrical outlet, receives commands from the wireless remote, and transmits them across the electrical wiring in your home to control various devices. This is why the second piece is called a transceiver: because it TRANSmits and reCEIVES signals. Simple, eh?

Wireless remotes for your X-10 home-automation system come with many of the same conveniences (and a few problems) as do remote controls for televisions, videocassette recorders, and so on. The main benefit is that the remote doesn't have to be plugged into an electrical outlet to function properly, so you can carry it wherever you want. One obvious use was mentioned at the beginning of this section: using the remote to open your garage door and turn on lights in the house from the car as you pull into the driveway. Another advantage is that you can economize by purchasing a single wireless remote and using it from any room in the house, versus purchasing individual controllers for every room from which you want to be able to control devices.

One potential drawback is that, just like remotes for other appliances, wireless remotes for X-10 are easily misplaced by some people and probably should be avoided. You know who you are.

There are three wireless remotes to choose from, depending on your needs. The main differences between remote controls are size and the number of devices that can be controlled. The bigger the remote, the more devices it can control, but bigger remotes are also somewhat bulkier and more difficult to carry around. One of the remote controls is even designed with an adhesive back so that it can be attached to a wall and function as an extra light switch.

The standard remote control is ideal for carrying around the house and provides the most flexibility in controlling devices. There are eight rocker buttons on the front that can be used to control devices with either Unit Code 1 through 8, or 9 through 16. A diagram of the remote control is shown below.

Remote Control

Press the left side of a rocker button to turn on the device. Press the right side to turn off the device.

After turning on a lamp, press this button to dim or brighten it.

Set the SELECTOR switch to control modules 1 through 8 or 9 through 16.

Set the Housecode for the remote control here. Make sure that it matches the Housecode on the wireless transceiver and the modules that you want to control.

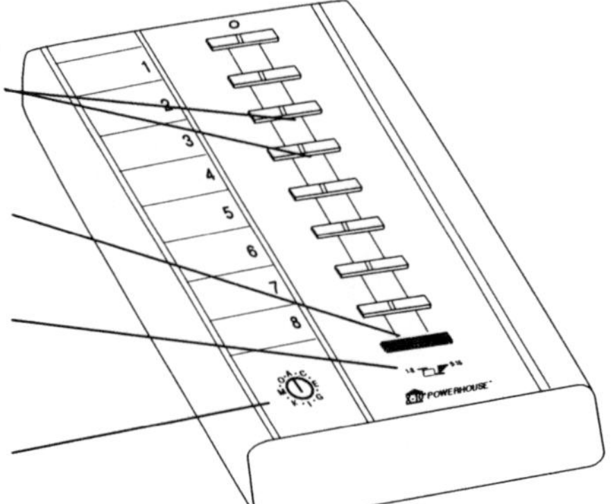

Key Chain Remote

The Key Chain Remote Control is more limited than the full-function remote because it can control only two devices. But it's much smaller than the standard remote and is more suited to being carried in a purse or a car. There are two buttons on the front that allow you to control devices with Unit Code 1 and 2 or 5 and 6, depending on the position of a SELECTOR switch located in the battery compartment (see diagram).

Key Chain Remote—Front

Press the top of a rocker button to turn on the device. Press the bottom to turn it off.

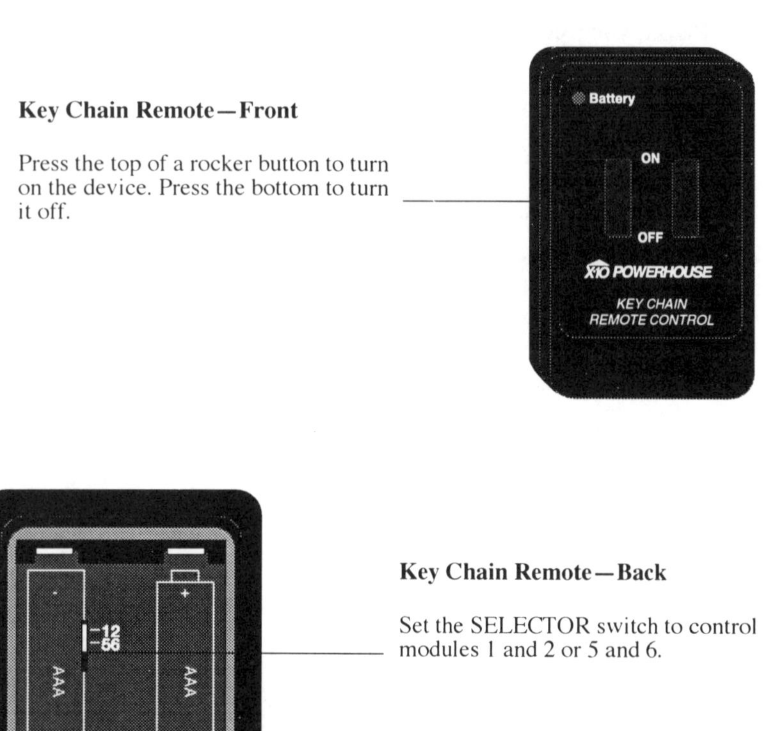

Key Chain Remote—Back

Set the SELECTOR switch to control modules 1 and 2 or 5 and 6.

Set the Housecode for the Key Chain Remote Control here. Make sure that it matches the Housecode on the wireless transceiver and the modules that you want to control.

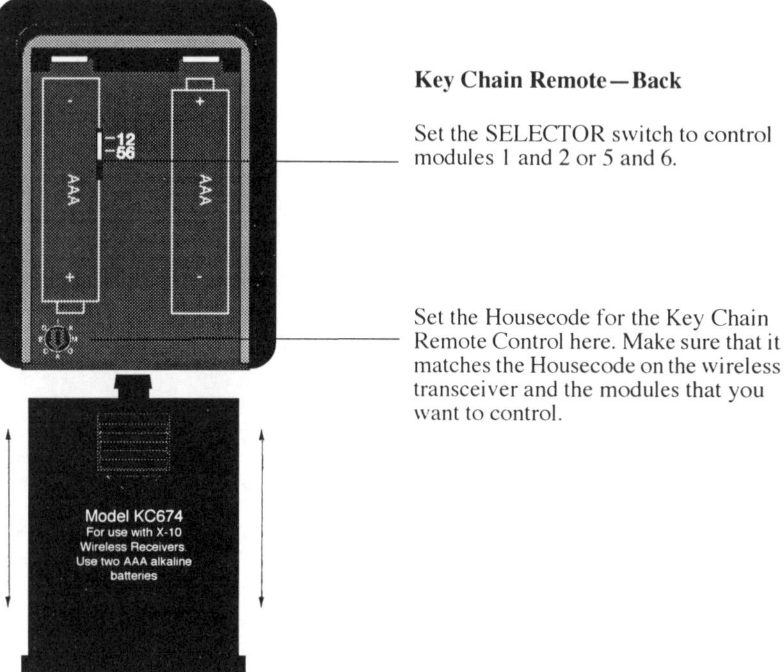

Your third option for a wireless remote control is the Wireless Wall Switch. This remote control includes an adhesive backing, which allows you to attach it to a wall and use it as a replacement wall switch for any X-10–controlled lights. The three rocker buttons on the front of the wireless wall switch can be used to control devices with Unit Codes 1 through 3, 5 through 7, 9 through 11, or 13 through 15. The SELECTOR switch is located on the back of the unit, in the battery compartment. You must remove the battery to access it.

After setting the Housecode and the SELECTOR switch on the back, just attach the Wireless Wall Switch to the wall and control up to three devices using the rocker buttons on the front.

Here's a diagram of the front of the Wireless Wall Switch.

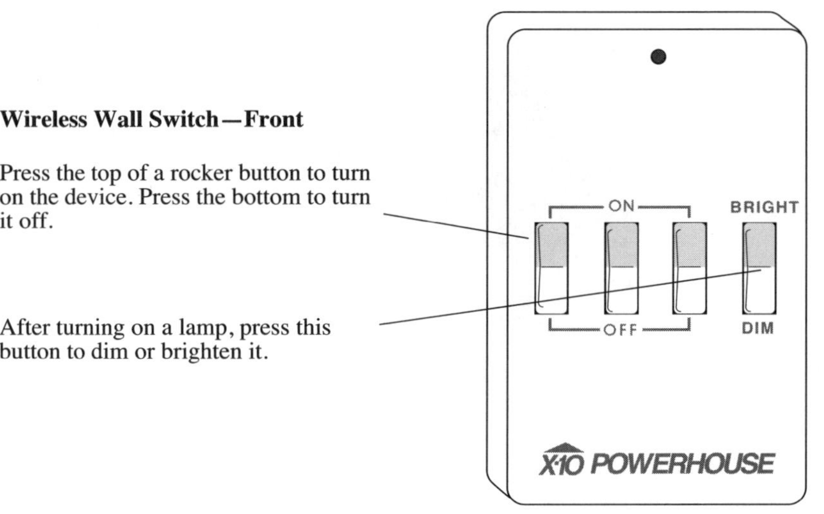

Wireless Wall Switch—Front

Press the top of a rocker button to turn on the device. Press the bottom to turn it off.

After turning on a lamp, press this button to dim or brighten it.

The diagram below shows the back of the Wireless Wall Switch with the battery compartment exposed.

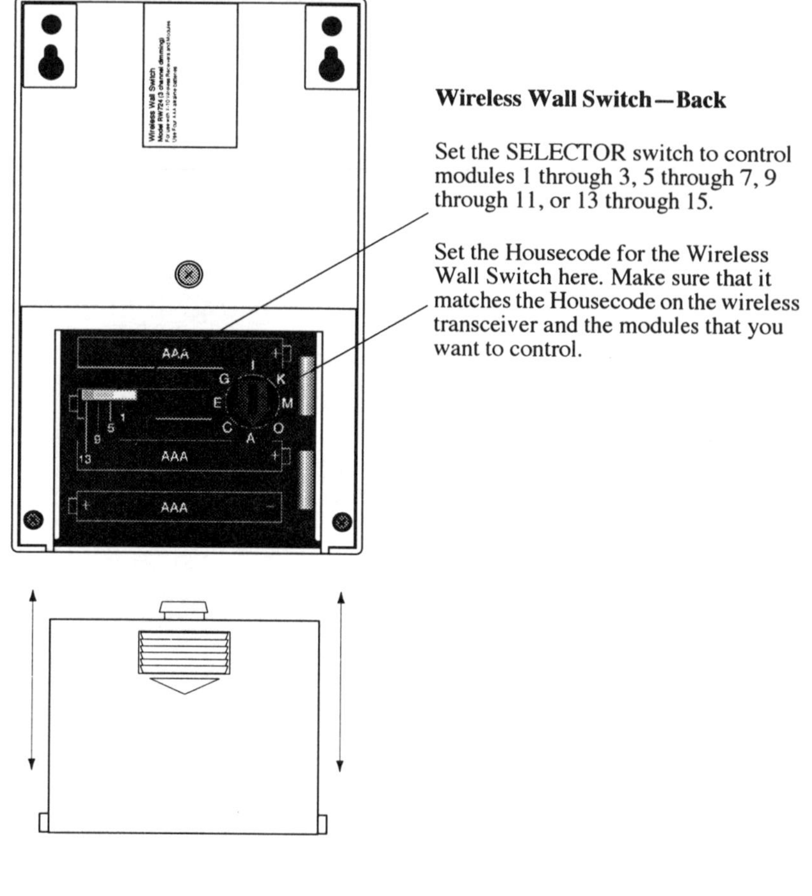

And here's a diagram showing the transceiver module with its most important components.

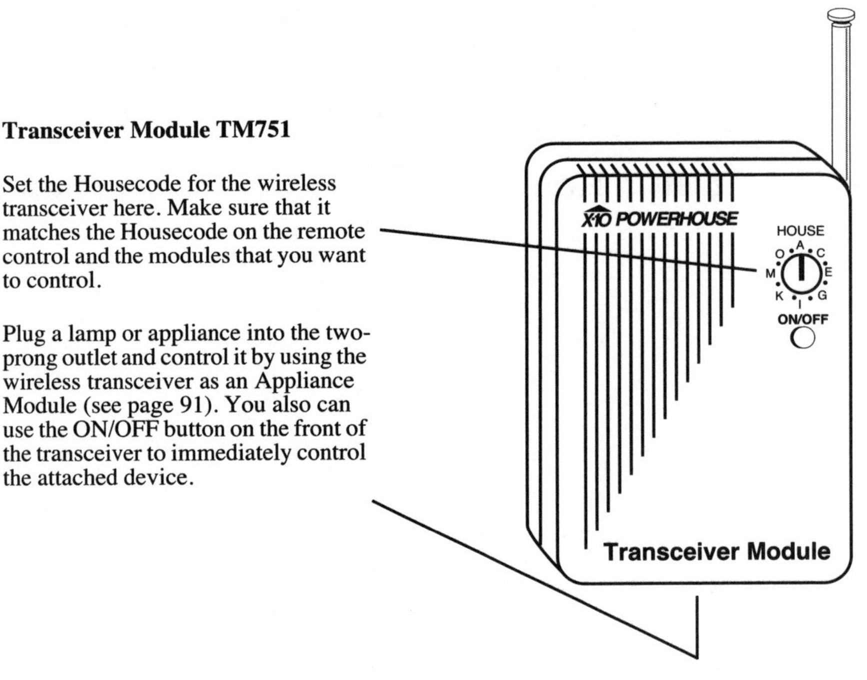

Although X-10 remote controls are similar to most TV remotes, there is one major difference. TV remote controls usually use **infrared (IR)** wireless technology, which requires that you be in the line of sight of the TV you want to control and that you point the remote control directly at the TV. So, for example, an infrared remote that works with a TV in the living room will probably do nothing if you carry it into the kitchen and start pushing buttons.

Infrared (IR)

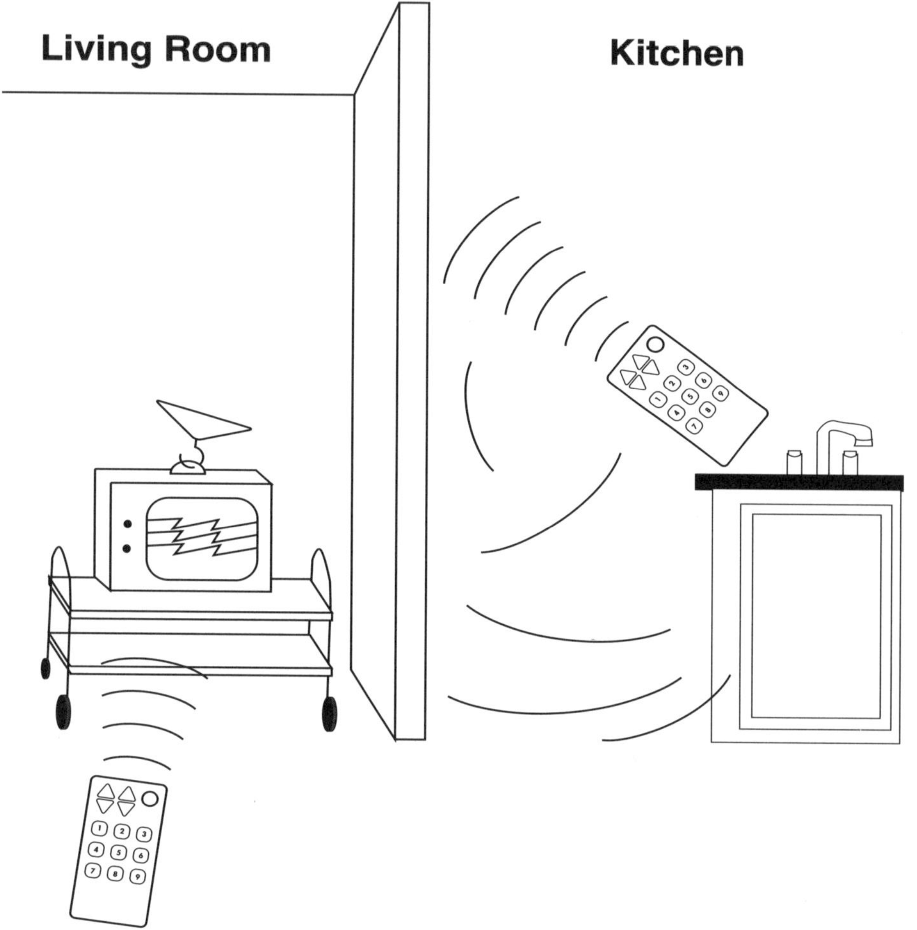

The X-10 remote controls use **radio frequency (RF)** technology that allows signals to travel greater distances and pass through walls and other obstructions. With RF technology, you can carry the remote control with you around the house and turn devices on and off simply by pressing a button. You even can use the remote control to open your garage door and turn on the house lights from your car as you pull into the driveway. In fact, you can extend the distance over which an X-10 wireless remote can communicate with a transceiver even further with a Smart RF Repeater, available from

X-10 (USA), Inc. See the "Compatible Products" section, beginning on page 54.

Radio Frequency (RF)

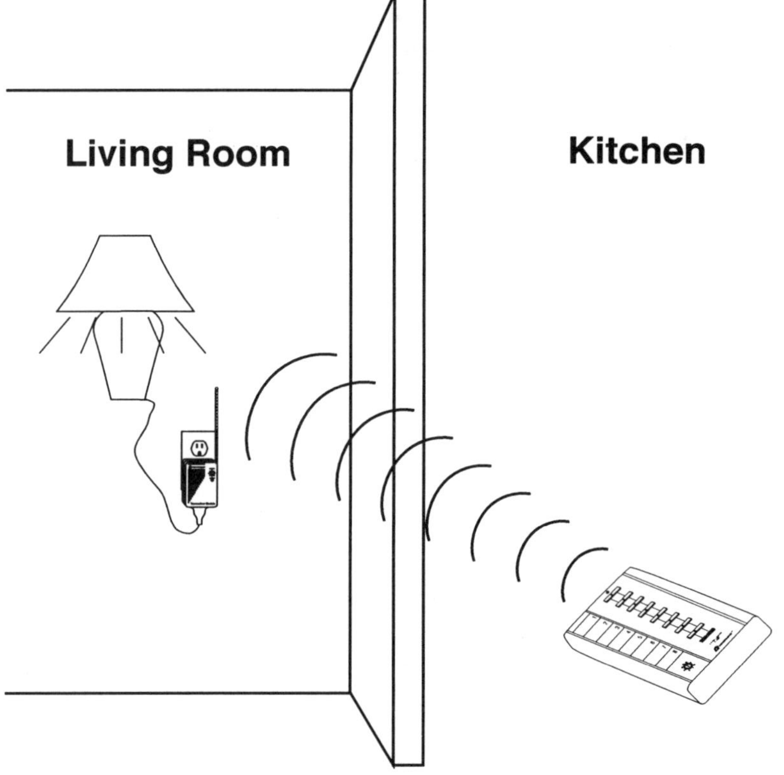

Setting Up a Wireless Remote Control System

The following instructions are general and can be applied to any of the three remote controls.

Install AAA batteries in the remote control. Then set the Housecode on the remote control to the same Housecode you've set on the wireless transceiver.

Note that the Housecode you choose also must be the Housecode of any modules you want to control with the remote control.

Set the SELECTOR switch on the remote control.

Each of the remote controls has a SELECTOR switch that lets you choose which modules you want to control with the remote.

This is necessary because the remotes are generally small, and it's not possible to put a lot of rocker buttons on them. Using a SELECTOR switch keeps the remotes small but still gives you a lot of flexibility. For example, the Key Chain Remote is so small that it has only two rocker buttons on the front. Still, the SELECTOR switch on the back lets you choose between using the buttons to control devices with Unit Code 1 and 2 or 5 and 6.

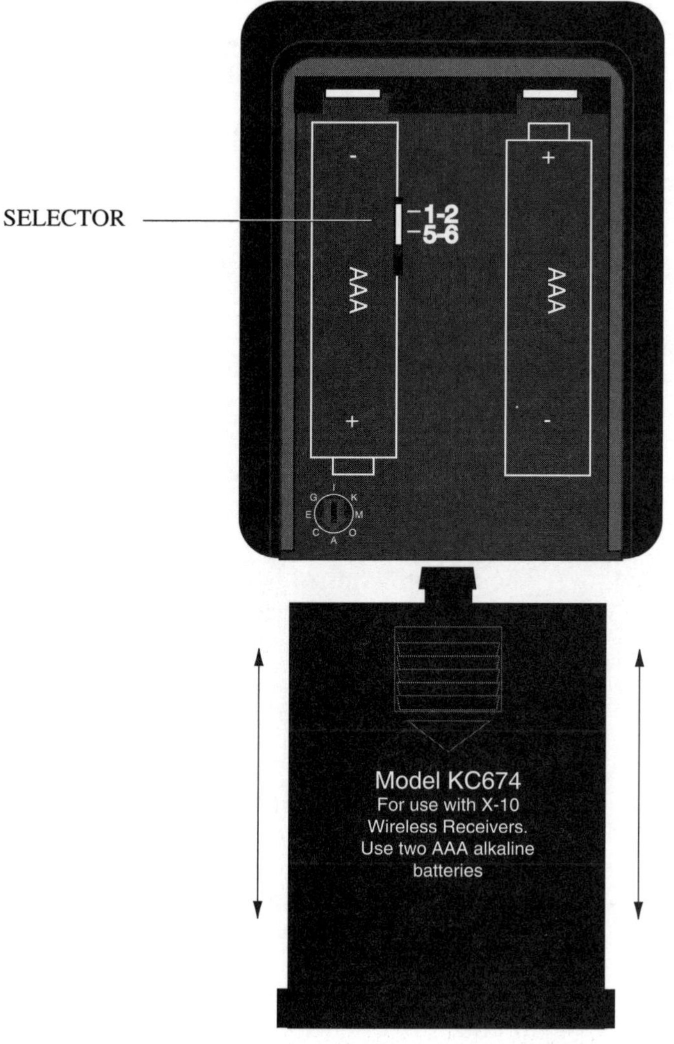

The SELECTOR switch for the X-10 module RT504, the largest remote, is located on the front. The SELECTOR switch for the Wall Switch Module and the Key Chain Remote both are located in the battery compartment. You have to remove the batteries to access them. This may be a consideration when you're deciding which remote to buy because it's obviously much easier to access the SELECTOR switch on the front. However, you also should consider that you're probably not going to be changing the SELECTOR switch setting frequently.

Setting Up the Transceiver Module

Plug the wireless transceiver into any standard electrical outlet. You also can use the Transceiver Module to control a device by attaching the device to the plug on the bottom of the Transceiver Module.

Note that a device plugged directly into the Transceiver Module will respond to commands sent to devices with Unit Code 1.

Using the Wireless Remote Control

You'll use the rocker buttons on the remote control to turn devices on and off, and to dim or brighten lamps.

Comparing the Remote Control With Other Controllers

The remote control is useful for someone who has trouble getting around. It's also a great solution for turning on lights from outside the house, even from the car as you're pulling into the driveway.

You also could use the remote control from your backyard to turn sprinkler systems on and off. This is very helpful if you have drip systems and need to check for faulty components by turning the sprinklers on and off frequently.

For information about using the X-10 Universal Module to control sprinkler systems and other low-voltage electrical devices, see the section called "Universal Module" on page 101.

The eight-button remote control could be used as the only controller in your system, especially if you don't need to create timed events. It has all the functionality of a Maxi Controller and more: It's transportable. But remember, there's no reason to limit yourself—you always can use *both* a Maxi Controller and a remote control in your home-automation system.

Compatible Products

Here's a list of X-10–compatible controllers that you can use to expand your system.

HomeTech Solutions

10570 S. De Anza Blvd.
Cupertino, CA 95014
Phone: (408) 257-4406

Mènage UCIX
The UCIX is a whole-house programmable controller that can send and receive X-10 powerline carrier signals. UCIX communicates with a TV, VCR, CD, and other devices that use remote controls with infrared signals. You can communicate with UCIX via a 32-key UHF remote control. UCIX has infrared emitters that transmit signals to a TV, VCR, CD player, and other devices that use infrared signals for remote control. UCIX learns the infrared codes it needs from an existing remote control. Once you've programmed the UCIX, you don't need the old remote controls. A single UCIX remote can perform all of the functions that now require a swarm of remotes. You can add special functions that aren't on existing remotes. For example, you can program a single button to turn down the volume on the TV, stop the VCR, and turn on the lights that lead to the telephone. Press the button again and reverse the process. Unlike remotes that use infrared signals, UHF can pass through walls. You can travel throughout your house and have control of the lights, TV, VCR, CD player, and anything else that has infrared or powerline carrier control.

Price: contact Home Tech Solutions

Intella-Home Inc.

P.O. Box 780392
Sebastian, FL 32958
Phone: (407) 589-0970

IntellaVoice
The IntellaVoice is a stand-alone X-10 Message Controller that provides voice annunciation for X-10–based home-automation systems. Owners create their own customer announcements to accompany key X-10 events. Patented voice-to-EEPROM storage can retain messages even without power. A built-in microphone and automatic gain circuits produce high-quality, natural voice reproduction. Up to eight nearly 10-second customer announcements can be recorded. The on-board processor monitors the power line, using the included X-10 TW523 interface, for key

event commands, then plays the correct announcement for that event.

Price: $379

JDS Technologies

16750 W. Bernardo Dr.
San Diego, CA 92127
Phone: (619) 487-8787
Fax: (619) 451-2799

TC100-C TeleCommand System 100
The TC100-C is a telephone-operated automation system that controls X-10–compatible devices from any touchtone telephone, including wireless and cellular phones. Its features include intercom, hold, call transfer, and dual password protection, and it has isolated contacts with battery backup for control of security systems—all programmable by phone.

Price: $375

TCM-2W TimeCommander
The TCM-2W is an advanced two-way automation system that's X-10–compatible. It has support for if-then conditional event control and can be used as a serial device with an IBM or compatible computer. Other features include an interactive on-screen display, stand-alone operation, optional Xpanders for infrared control of audio-video systems, and hard-wired inputs and outputs. You even can program, monitor, and control the TCM-2W remotely via modem. The package includes Event Manager software for DOS and Windows.

Price: $295

TCM-PLUS TimeCommander Plus
The TCM-PLUS is an advanced two-way automation system that's X-10–compatible. You can connect the TCM-PLUS to the serial port of an IBM or compatible computer. Event Manager software for DOS and Windows is included, allowing you to create if-then conditional statements along with timed event control sequences. The Event Manager software includes an interactive on-screen display and allows stand-alone operation—that is, the TCM-PLUS can be disconnected from the computer after you've programmed it. The TCM-PLUS includes 16 digital inputs, eight analog inputs, and eight relay outputs (expandable to 112 digital/40 analog/72 relay). The optional IR-Xpander allows infrared control of audio-video

systems. You even can program, monitor, and control the TCM-PLUS remotely via modem.

Price: $595

StarGate—Integrated Automation System
StarGate is an advanced, integrated automation system that's X-10–compatible. Its features include two-way control of X-10 devices; infrared and hard wired I/O; control by time/event, phone, computer, keypad, and wireless remote; user-programmable interactive voice response; intercom services; and advanced telephone functions such as multi-level remote access, auto dial, caller ID, distinctive ring, call hold, and call transfer. StarGate connects to IBM or compatible computers via a serial port. Stargate has 16 digital inputs, eight analog inputs, and eight relay outputs (expandable to 112 digital/40 analog/72 relay). You even can program, monitor, and control StarGate remotely via modem. StarGate has an expansion bus that will allow it to support multiple protocols in the future, including CeBus and LonWorks. Software for the Windows operating system is included.

Price: contact JDS Technologies

WristCommander—Wristwatch Telephone Controller
The WristCommander is a cordless telephone and wristwatch in one. It includes two rechargeable/interchangeable batteries and a scrambler for secure communications. It also provides intercom functions and can work in conjunction with the TeleCommand System 100, TimeCommander, or StarGate for convenient wireless control of X-10, IR, and other control functions.

Price: contact JDS Technologies

PC-T4000 Pocket Commander
The PC-T4000 is a pocket-size cordless telephone with a speakerphone-capable base unit. You can use it with the TeleCommand for wireless remote control of X-10 environments. Other features include 10-number memory, activation of multiple-command macros, and support for two or more base units at different locations in the home.

Price: $225

VC-50 HF VoiceCommander
The VC-50 is a programmable, voice-dialing speakerphone that can be used with a TeleCommand system for hands-free voice control of X-10 environments. Features include the ability to store 50 voice and 50 touch-tone commands (or telephone numbers) that can

control a single X-10 device or execute a multiple-command macro. The VC-50 can operate via speakerphone or handset, and includes inputs for an external microphone and a headset. It is compatible with most assistive switching devices.

Price: $295

IRX-10 IR-Xpander
The IRX-10 is an infrared controller/interface for control of audio-video systems from any X-10 controller. You can program the IRX-10 with a preset schedule or use any touch-tone telephone to control the IRX-10 immediately. It also can be connected to a TeleCommand system via the TimeCommander auxiliary port.

Price: $125

Leviton Manufacturing Company, Inc.

59-25 Little Neck Parkway
Little Neck, NY 11362
Phone: (718) 281-6488
Fax: (718) 631-6508

6325 Telephone Transponder
The 6325 provides touch-tone telephone control for up to 256 X-10 addresses. Security features include a three-digit access code. Other features include a human-voice response system for confirmation of codes that have been entered.

Price: $180

6308 Photocell Transmitter
The 6308 senses darkness and responds by sending ON commands to as many as four groups of DEC Switch Modules. It also will transmit OFF commands at a user-selected time or in response to daylight. The 6308 is weather-resistant and is mounted on a standard round electrical box.

Price: $75

6311-I (Ivory) 6311-W (White) Delux Wall-Mounted Programmable Transmitter
The 6311 maintains a seven-day schedule for control of X-10 devices using up to 63 program sequences. Each program sequence may include from one to 16 individual address codes. The 6311 also permits manual switching of all 256 available addresses without affecting programmed schedules. Battery backup provides 24 hours

of memory protection in case of power interruption. It can be surface-mounted on a standard single-gang wall box.

Price: $271

6312-I (Ivory) 6312-W (White) Basic Wall-Mounted Programmer
The 6312 carries out scheduling for up to four addresses and manual override for up to eight addresses, with up to two ON and two OFF commands per 24-hour period for each address. It permits random ON-OFF switching within programmed hours, and provides ALL LIGHTS ON security switching, DIM/BRIGHT rocker, LED time of day, and PRAM status readout. Other features include 10-hour battery backup. The 6312 is mounted using a single-gang wall box.

Price: $86.40

6313 Hand-Held Controller
The 6313 transmits radio command signals for dimming and switching up to 16 X-10 addresses. This unit is completely wireless, requires four AAA batteries, and must be used in conjunction with the 6314 Plug-in Transceiver.

Price: $28

6314 Plug-In Transceiver
The 6314 receives radio commands from the 6313 Hand-held Controller. It plugs into a standard 120-volt AC outlet and switches one controlled load plugged into itself. It relays radio command signals onto AC lines by converting them to powerline carrier commands for eight DEC addresses. Rated 120v 60Hz AC only.

Price: $44

6320 Manual Transmitter
The 6320 transmits X-10 signals by manual control to all 16 Unit Codes with Housecode selection dial for A-P on back. The console located under the hinged lid has buttons for ON, OFF, DIM/BRIGHTEN, ALL LIGHTS ON, and ALL UNITS OFF commands. The 6320 plugs into any 120-volt outlet.

Price: $43.20

6319-1, 6319-1A, 6319-2, 6319-2D, 6319-4, 6319-4D, 6319-4A Wall-Mounted Transmitters (Controllers)
The 6319 series consists of various controllers. Each product differs by the number of modules it will allow you to control, whether it has a button for ALL LIGHTS ON and ALL UNITS OFF, and so on. Specifics for each product in the series are given below. Up to four

Wall-mounted Transmitters can be ganged to control up to 16 addresses. All Wall-mounted Transmitters are packed in a single-gang Decora Wallplate and can be mounted in a standard single-gang wall box (the same opening that you have for a standard light switch). All are available in ivory and white. The 6319-1 provides manual ON/OFF switching commands to one address. The 6319-1A transmits ALL LIGHTS ON and ALL UNITS OFF signals to all addresses on the same letter code. The 6319-2 provides ON/OFF switching commands to two addresses. The 6319-2D provides ON/OFF control and dimming for one address. The 6319-4 provides manual ON/OFF control of four sequential addresses. The 6319-4D provides manual ON/OFF control plus dimming control for three sequential addresses. The 6319-4A provides manual ON/OFF control for three sequential addresses, plus ALL LIGHTS ON and ALL UNITS OFF commands for appropriate addresses.

Price: $80

6315 Dry Contact Transmitter
The 6315 monitors up to four dry-contact enclosures. It transmits ON and OFF command signals in response to contact closure or opening. This unit can be used, for example, to transmit ON commands to outdoor lighting when a dry-contact-equipped photocell senses dusk approaching. When the photocell detects dawn, the 6315 will respond by automatically turning off outdoor lighting. The transmitter can be installed in a standard single-gang wall box. Power to control side: 125v 60Hz AC only.

Price: $167.90

6316 Dry-Contact Transmitter
The 6316 monitors up to four dry-contact closures, transmitting ON and OFF command signals upon contact closures and no command signal upon contact opening. This unit can be used, for example, to send an OFF signal at the upper end of a heating, air-conditioning, or security lighting range, and an ON signal at the lower end of the range. It can maintain temperatures and lighting regimens in an unoccupied home and installs in a standard single-gang wall box. Power to control side: 125v 60Hz AC only.

Price: $167.90

6317 Passive Infrared Outdoor Transmitter
The 6317 switches its dual floodlights and up to four DEC switch modules in response to motion or darkness. It also can receive signals and permit manual override as needed.

Price: $70

6326 Interflash Controller
The 6326 automatically sends intermittent ON/OFF signals to all Switch Modules set to the same Unit Code and Housecode. It responds to a 6-24 volts DC input signal. When the DC input stops, all lights and appliances will remain on until turned off manually or by a controller. The 6326 is an ideal accompaniment for home-security systems. Rated: 125w 60Hz AC only.

Price: $122.60

Radio Shack Plug 'n Power

700 One Tandy Center
Fort Worth, TX 76102
Phone: (817) 878-4852
Fax: (817) 878-6508

Various Plug 'n Power Command Center and Remote Controller/ Timers
Radio Shack makes a complete line of X-10–compatible products. In many cases, the functionality of Radio Shack products is identical to that of X-10 products. You can obtain a catalog of Plug 'n Power products by contacting Radio Shack directly.

Prices: vary by product

Residential Control Systems, Inc.

3983 S. McCarran Blvd., Suite 190
Reno, NV 89502
Phone: (800) 952-2425
Fax: (916) 635-7668

4CUX10 X-10 4-Channel DPDT Relay Controller
The 4CUX10 is an X-10-compatible four-channel DPDT Relay Controller. Each output channel can be individually controlled by an X-10 ON or OFF command. The controller responds to standard X-10 ON and OFF commands to control the four relay channels. Each output channel corresponds to an X-10 Unit Code. Channel Unit Codes can be selected in four groups of sequential codes (1 through 4, 5 through 8, 9 through 12, and 13 through 16). Any standard Housecode can be selected. It does not respond to other X-10 commands. The controller connects to an X-10 Power Line Interface Module (TW523), not included. Included is an X-10 I/O connector that allows additional 4CUX10s to be cascaded without requiring additional PowerLine Interface Modules. Each relay has independent DPDT open-contact outputs rated at 2A, 30VDC. LEDs

indicate the status of each channel. The 4CUX10 controller is powered by an external 12VDC power transformer (included).

Price: $170

HVACX10 X-10-Compatible HVAC

The HVACX10 is an X-10-compatible controller that allows X-10 control of heating and air-conditioning systems. X-10 ON/OFF commands are used for "Heat" and "Cool" inputs to the controller, which in turn generates the appropriate outputs to the HVAC system. It works with either standard or heat pump systems. The controller responds to standard X-10 ON and OFF commands to control heating and air-conditioning systems. The controller responds to four sequential Unit Codes that are selectable in four groups (1 through 4, 5 through 8, 9 through 12, and 13 through 16). Any standard Housecode can be selected. The controller connects to an X-10 PowerLine Interface Module, model TW523 (not included). For standard gas/electric systems, the HVAC X-10 controller accepts X-10 commands for HEAT, COOL, and FAN. An unused channel can be used for AUX functions. The controller outputs to the HVAC system the appropriate control signals for gas valve or electric heatstrips, compressor, and fan controls. For heat pump systems, the HVACX10 controller accepts X-10 commands for HEAT (stage 1), HEAT (stage 2), COOL, and FAN. The controller outputs the appropriate control signals to the HVAC system for compressor, changeover valve, heatstrips, and fan controls. The HVACX10 controller is powered from the HVAC system to which it is connected (24VAC, 100MA max).

Price: $170

3 *Controlling Lights*

Overview

In this chapter, we'll show you how to use X-10 modules to control the lights in your home. By using an X-10 module connected to a lamp or replacing a light switch with an X-10 module, you can turn the lights on or off, and dim them to whatever brightness you want from anywhere in your home. For example, you can turn on lights in the garage without leaving your car, turn off all of the lights in your home using a single button at your bedside, or increase security when you're away by turning lights on and off at various times during the day. You'll find more suggestions in the section called "Applications" on page 85.

Although many variations exist, there are four main X-10 modules that you'll use to control lights in your home—the Lamp Module, the Screw-In Remote Controlled Dimmer Module, the Two-Way Wall Switch Module, and the Three-Way Wall Switch Module. Each is described later in this chapter. There is also a section on the Powerhouse Motion Detector that has a built-in controller driven by a motion detector or photocell to control two attached floodlights. This combination controller/module also can send signals to other Lamp or Appliance Modules.

By the end of this chapter, you'll be able to choose and install the best type of module for every light in your home.

Lamp Module

The Lamp Module is used to control the incandescent, free-standing lamps in your home. After plugging a lamp into the module and the module into an electrical outlet, you can use any X-10 controller to turn the lamp on and off, and dim it to any brightness.

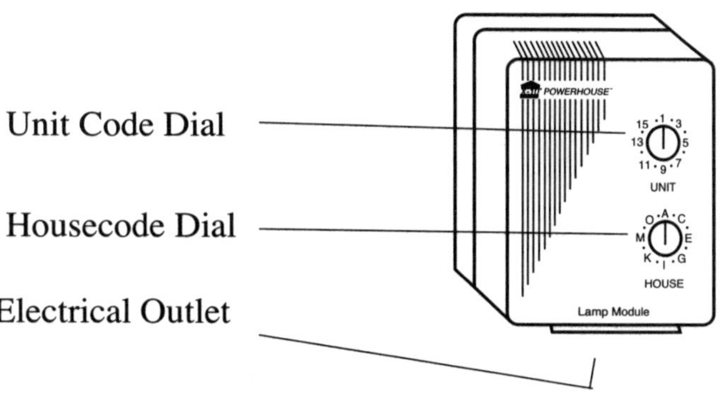

There are a few restrictions that you should observe when using the Lamp Module.

The Lamp Module should be used only with **incandescent** lamps. Most of the lamps in your home are probably incandescent lamps. You cannot use the Lamp Module to control **fluorescent** lamps. You generally can identify the fluorescent lamps in your home by the type of bulbs that they use. Incandescent lamps use standard, well, bulb-shaped bulbs. Fluorescent lights generally use either long, thin tubes or smaller, circular tubes. Another difference is that incandescent bulbs generate heat. They'll burn you if you touch them after they've been on awhile. Fluorescent bulbs in good working condition generate very little heat.

The Lamp Module works with lights that use up to 300 **watts** of electricity. Check the bulb in the lamp—it should display its power consumption. If a lamp uses two or more bulbs, you'll need to add the wattage of each bulb to determine whether the Lamp Module can be used to control the lamp. For example, you could use the module to control a lamp with two 150-watt bulbs (300 watts total), but not to control a lamp with two 200-watt bulbs (400 watts total). This restriction also applies if two lamps are plugged into a single module. Calculate the total wattage of all bulbs controlled by a single module to make sure that you don't exceed this limit.

The Lamp Module has no minimum wattage constraint and is easy to install and use.

Set the Housecode dial on the module to the same letter as the Housecode on the controller you plan to use with it.

This step ensures that the Lamp Module and the controller will communicate correctly. As your system gets more sophisticated, you'll use more than one Housecode. For now just use "A."

Set the Unit Code to an unused number from 1 to 16. Because this is your first module, use "1."

By setting a unique Unit Code for each module, you'll be able to control the lamp attached to the module. If you set two Lamp Modules to the same Unit Code, they will be controlled at the same time with the same commands.

Plug the lamp into the bottom of the Lamp Module.

Plug the Lamp Module into an unswitched electrical outlet.

An unswitched electrical outlet is simply one that isn't controlled by a wall switch of any type. The Lamp Module can work with a switched outlet, but it won't work if you turn off the switch, and we don't recommend it.

Make sure that any switch on the lamp itself is in the ON position.

An X-10 Lamp Module can't control a lamp whose switch has been turned off.

That's it! Try it.

Make sure that the controller is plugged into an unswitched outlet. Push "1" and then ON.

Some controllers have a single rocker switch that's used to select a Unit Code and turn the module on or off. Refer to Chapter 2 if you've forgotten how they work.

The lamp should turn on.

Press "1." Then press DIM and hold it.

The lamp should gradually become dimmer as you hold down the DIM button. Try BRIGHT and OFF. Lamp Modules respond to ALL LIGHTS ON and ALL UNITS OFF commands as well.

Another feature of X-10 modules is their local control capability. If you're standing next to the lamp and don't want to walk to the controller you simply can turn the lamp's switch off and then on again, and the lamp will turn on. Be sure to leave the lamp switch on so that you can control it using a controller.

If things aren't working, make sure that the Housecode on the module matches the one on the controller, and that you've set the Unit Code to "1." Make sure that the outlets you're using are unswitched. If that doesn't help, see Appendix B, "Troubleshooting," on page 233.

Screw-In Remote Controlled Dimmer Module

The Screw-In Remote Controlled Dimmer Module contains the same electronics and performs exactly the same function as the Lamp Module, but it's in a form that allows it to be screwed directly into a light socket with a bulb, instead of being plugged into an electrical outlet. If you just finished reading the Lamp Module section, you'll find this incredibly boring—it's almost identical. If not, jam ahead and you'll find out exactly what you need to make it work.

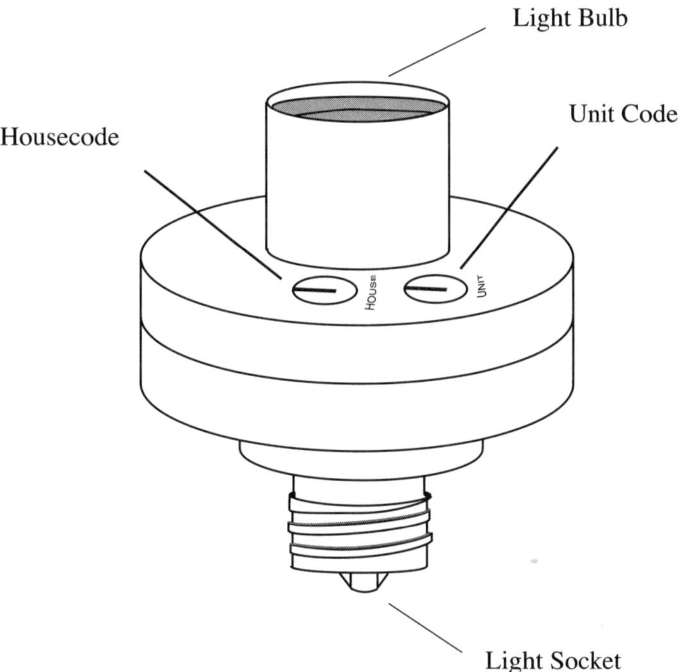

As with the Lamp Module, there are a few restrictions that you should observe when using the Screw-In Remote Controlled Dimmer Module.

The Screw-In Remote Controlled Dimmer Module should be used only with **incandescent** lamps. Almost all bulbs that are used in screw-in fixtures are incandescent. The exception is a relatively new type of fluorescent circular tubes that is designed as an energy-saving replacement for a standard light bulb. You cannot use the Screw-In Module to control **fluorescent** lamps.

Incandescent bulbs also differ from fluorescent bulbs in that they generate heat. They are hot to the touch after they've been on awhile. Fluorescent bulbs in good working condition generate very little heat.

The Screw-In Remote Controlled Dimmer Module can be used for lights that use up to 300 **watts** of electricity. The bulb that you're using should display its power consumption. The Screw-In Remote Controlled Dimmer Module has no minimum wattage constraint and is easy to install and use.

Set the Housecode dial on the module to the same letter as the controller you plan to use with it.

The Screw-In Remote Controlled Dimmer Module and the appropriate controller now should be communicating correctly. As your system gets more sophisticated, you will use more than one Housecode. For now just use "A."

Set the Unit Code to an unused number from 1 to 16. Because this is your first module, use "1."

By setting a unique Unit Code for each module, you'll be able to individually control the lamp that is attached to it. If you set two Screw-In Modules to the same unit number, they'll be controlled at the same time with the same commands.

Screw a light bulb into the bottom of the Screw-In Remote Controlled Dimmer Module. Screw the module and the light bulb into the light socket where they will be used.

Make sure that any switch on the lamp itself is in the ON position.

An X-10 Screw-In Remote Controlled Dimmer Module can't control a light bulb that has been turned off at its switch.

That's it!

Now try it.

Make sure that the controller is plugged into an unswitched outlet. Push "1" and then ON.

Some controllers have a single rocker switch to select a Unit Code and turn it on or off. Refer to the Chapter 2 if you've forgotten how they work.

The light bulb should turn on.

Now press "1" and then DIM and hold it.

The light bulb should gradually become more dim the longer that you hold down the DIM button. Try BRIGHT and OFF. Screw-In Remote Controlled Dimmer Modules respond to ALL LIGHTS ON and ALL UNITS OFF commands as well.

Another feature of X-10 modules is their local control ability. If the light bulb is controlled by a wall switch, you can control the bulb by turning the switch off and then on again; the bulb will turn on. Be sure to leave the bulb's switch on so that you can control it from a controller as well.

Wall Switch Module

The Wall Switch Module performs the same functions as the Lamp Module but replaces an existing built-in wall light switch, allowing you to remotely turn the lights on and off or dim them. The light switch is rated at 500 watts maximum and 60 watts minimum. Once again, a Wall Switch Module can be used only with incandescent lights. This module also can function as a regular light switch to turn lights on and off; you must use a controller to dim the lights.

The slide switch under the main push-button can be used to turn off the connected lights. It also turns off the X-10 module so that the light can't be turned on or off remotely—a safety feature required by Underwriters Laboratories. You also can use the slide switch to keep a light off or to turn off the power to the light before you change the bulb.

You'll use the Two-Way Wall Switch Module when only one existing wall switch controls a light. If two switches can control a light (one by each door, perhaps) you'll need to use the Three-Way Wall Switch Module. If only one switch controls a light or lights, it's connected to the circuit by two wires. If a switch is connected by three wires, it's usually a three way wall switch.

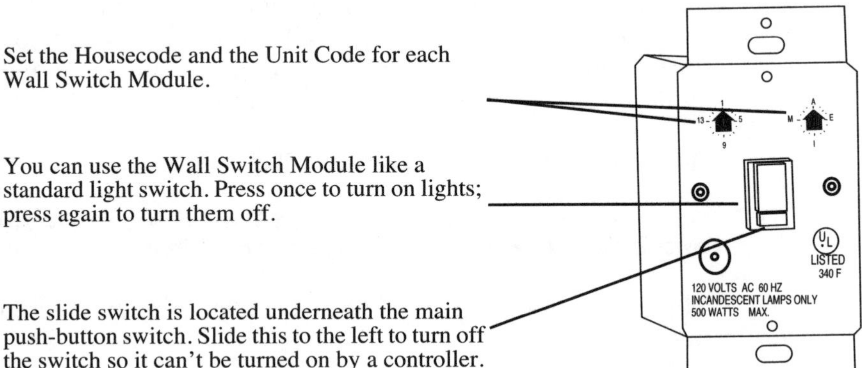

Installing a Wall Switch Module

WARNING! Installing a Wall Switch Module requires knowledge and experience in electrical wiring. If you're unfamiliar with electrical wiring, please consult a qualified electrician. Household electricity can be lethal.

Use a small screwdriver to set the Housecode to the same letter as you are using on the controller. To begin, use "A."

The Wall Switch Module is now ready to receive commands from the controller.

Set the Unit Code to an unused number from 1 to 16.

It's good to keep a list of the Housecode and Unit Code numbers for all of your modules so that you can keep track of them as your system grows.

Turn off the power at the circuit breaker or fuse box.

WARNING! Household electrical current can be deadly. Hire an electrician if you're not completely familiar with the installation of electrical switches.

Remove the existing wall plate and the old wall switch from the electrical box.

If more than two wires are connected to the switch, there's a good possibility that you have a three-way wall switch—that is, a light controlled by more than one wall switch. If there are more than two wires connecting the switch, leave them connected and put the switch back together. Then proceed to the next section.

Remove the two wires from the switch.

Connect the two wires on the Wall Switch Module (black and blue) using the wire nuts provided.

Make sure that all of the exposed metal wire is covered by the wire nut.

Reinstall the Wall Switch Module in the electrical box.

Make a note of the Housecode and the Unit Code.

Replace the cover plate.

Turn the power back on at the main circuit breaker.

That's it!

To test your Wall Switch Module:

Slide the switch underneath the push-button all the way to the right.

When this slide switch is moved to the left, it turns off the light and stops the Wall Switch Module's ability to receive commands from a controller. Use this feature whenever you're replacing the bulb. Sometimes this slide switch is inadvertently turned off, so this is the first place to look when troubleshooting your Wall Switch Module.

Press the Unit Code for the Wall Switch Module and the ON button on the controller.

Let there be light!

Press the push-button on the Wall Switch Module to check local operation.

One push of the button will turn off the light. The next will turn it on. Dimming is available only at the controller, not at the switch itself.

If you are having problems, see Appendix B, "Troubleshooting," on page 233.

Three-Way Wall Switch Module

The Three-Way Wall Switch Module can be used wherever lights are controlled by two or more switches. The Three-Way Switch includes two units that replace all of the switches that you currently have. The Three-Way Switch Module also is rated at 500-watts maximum and 60 watts minimum. The maximum is calculated the same way as the Two-Way Wall Switch Module.

The Three-Way Switch Module comes with two light switches, which replace the two switches that you're currently using to control a single light.

One switch contains an X-10 module that receives commands. This is called the Master Switch. The other acts as a normal three way switch; it's called the Companion Switch. They must be used together.

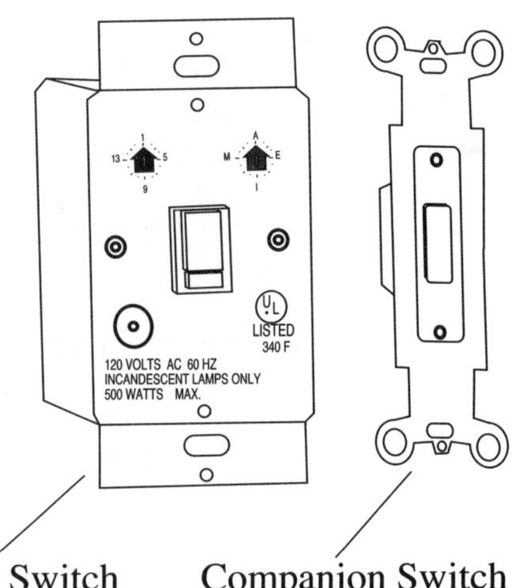

If you have a light that's controlled by more than two existing wall switches, you can purchase additional companion switches. Only one Master Switch is needed, no matter how many wall switches are included on the circuit.

Installing a Three-Way Wall Switch Module

Installing a Three-Way Wall Switch Module requires knowledge and experience in electrical wiring. Instructions are given here for a couple of common wire color codes. Your home may or may not follow these conventions. If you are unfamiliar with electrical wiring, please consult a qualified electrician. Household electricity can be lethal.

Use a small screwdriver to set the Housecode to the same letter you are using on the controller. To begin, use "A."

The Three-Way Wall Switch Module is now ready to receive commands from the controller.

Set the Unit Code to an unused number from 1 to 16.

It's good to make a list of the Housecode and Unit Code numbers for all your modules so that you can keep track of them as your system grows.

Turn off the power at the circuit breaker box.

WARNING! Household electrical current can be deadly. Hire an electrician if you're not completely familiar with the installation of electrical switches.

Select one of the existing switches. Either switch is fine, but if one is in an electrical box by itself, use it to install the X-10 Master Switch. Because the Master Switch is larger than the Companion Switch, it requires more room in the electrical box.

Remove the existing wall plate and the old wall switch from the electrical box.

Write down the color of each wire and where it's connected.

If something doesn't work, then it's easy to put things back the way they were.

On the existing switch, remove the wire that is connected to a terminal that is a different color from the other two terminals.

The terminals are the screws that the wires attach to.

Using a wire nut, connect this wire to the blue wire on the Master Switch.

No bare metal should be exposed.

Remove the other two wires, called travellers, from the existing switch. If one is red, connect it to the red wire on the Master Switch.

Even if there are no red wires connected to the existing switch, write down the color of the wire that you connect to the X-10 Master Switch. It will be important when you connect the Companion Switch.

Install the Master Switch in the electrical box, but leave off the cover plate.

Now you'll install the smaller Companion Switch.

Remove the existing wall plate and the old wall switch from the electrical box.

Write down the color of each wire and where it's connected.

On the existing switch remove the wire that is connected to a terminal that is a different color from the other two terminals

Using a wire nut, connect this wire to one of the two blue wires on the Companion Switch,

No bare metal should be exposed.

Connect the same color wire to the red wire on the Companion Switch that you connected to the red wire on the Master Switch.

Connect the remaining wire from the existing switch to the second blue wire on the Companion Switch.

If there is a discrepancy in the wiring, a different standard may have been used, or worse, the wiring in your home may have been improperly installed. If your wiring is different from this description, reinstall the old switches and call an electrician.

If everything checks out:

Install the Companion Switch in the electrical box.

Install both cover plates.

Move the small slide switch under the push-button on the Master Switch to the center, or on, position.

Turn on the power at the main circuit breaker or fuse box.

That's it!

To test your Three-Way Wall Switch Module:

When the slide switch is moved to the left, it turns off the light and halts the Three-Way Wall Switch's ability to receive commands from a controller. Use this feature to make sure that nobody remotely turns on the light while you're replacing a light bulb. Sometimes this slide switch is inadvertently turned off, so this is the first place to look when troubleshooting the Three-Way Wall Switch Module.

Press the Unit Code for the Wall Switch and the ON button on the controller.

Let there be light!

Press the push-button on the Three-Way Wall Switch Module and the Companion Switch to check local operation.

Each push of the button will turn off the light, and the next will turn it on again. Dimming is available only at the controller, not at the switch itself.

If you have problems, see Appendix B, "Troubleshooting," on page 233.

Motion Detector

The X-10 Powerhouse Motion Detector uses an infrared sensor to detect moving objects by sensing the heat they generate or the small change in temperature they create when moving. When it detects heat (which is light in the infrared spectrum), it then acts as a controller, turning on its own two 150-watt-maximum floodlights. It then sends signals over the powerline to other modules that are listening to the same Housecode, turning them on and off for adjustable lengths of time.

The Powerhouse Motion Detector also contains a photocell that can be set to turn on its own lights and up to four other lights in your home at dusk and turn them off at daybreak.

This interesting combination of a light module and a controller is especially useful if you want to detect the approach of a person or a car. In response, self-contained floodlights and other X-10-connected lights and appliances will turn on automatically.

Installing the Powerhouse Motion Detector

The Powerhouse Motion Detector should be located at least six feet above and parallel to the ground. The detector's head should not be pointed directly at the ground. A position that is a key traffic intersection is best so that anyone approaching will pass through the range of the detector. It is best to position the detector so that movement passes across the path of the beam, not directly toward it.

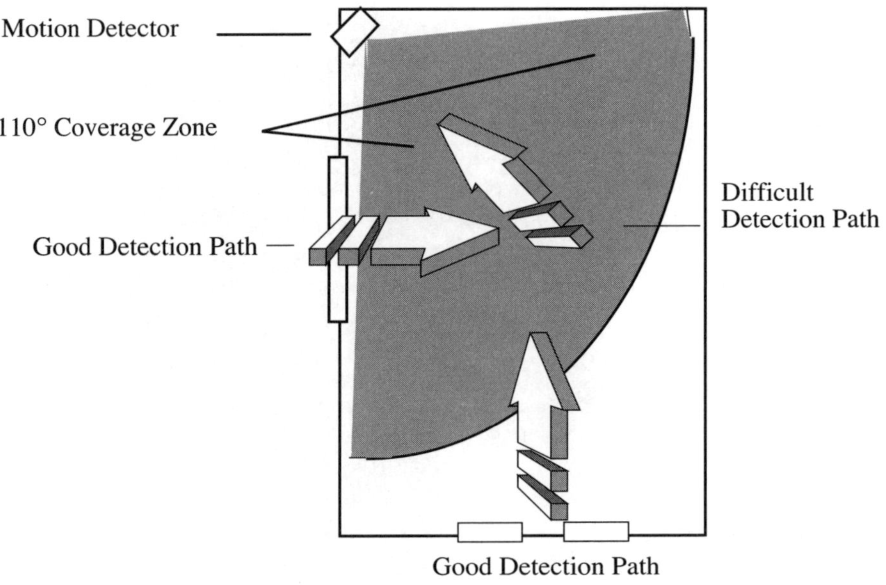

When installing a Powerhouse Motion Detector, there are several things to consider. First remember that this device detects heat. Heat from other sources can fool the detector into thinking that there is movement. The motion detector must be kept away from other floodlights, air-conditioning and heating vents, and direct sunlight. Swimming pools and glass that can create reflections also can trick the detector, so keep the detector head pointed away to help make it function more reliably.

You should place the Powerhouse X-10 Motion Detector on a standard, outdoor, round junction box. If the existing junction box at the installation location is rectangular, you should replace it or look for an adapter. Check at your local hardware store. Be sure to take the measurements of the existing junction box and the X-10 Motion Detector with you so that you can be sure to buy the correct adapter.

The X-10 Motion Detector can be connected to a junction box that is always on or one controlled by a standard switch. It should not be connected to a dimmer switch or an X-10 Two-Way Wall Switch that can be dimmed. Dimming can damage the unit!

If it is connected to a wall switch, the switch always must be left on. Turning off the wall switch will completely disable the Motion Detector.

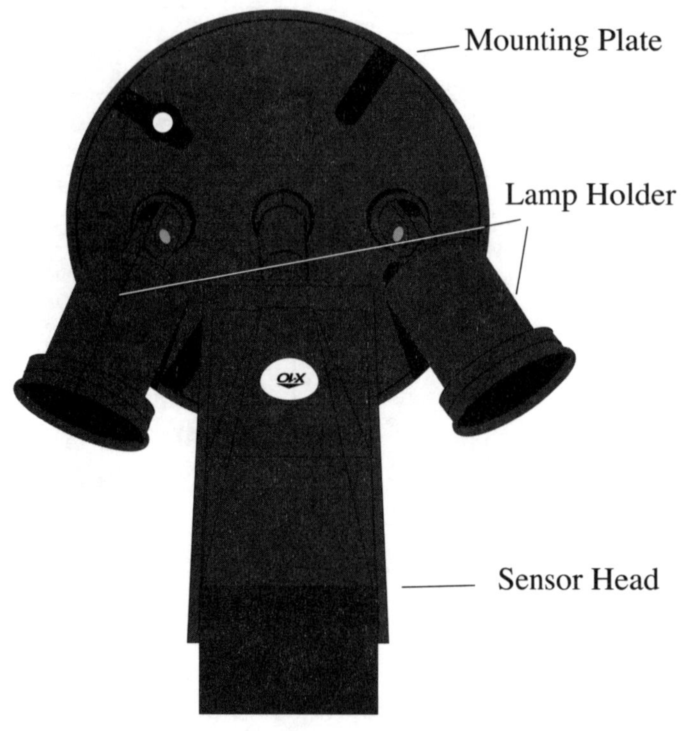

The Powerhouse Motion Detector is made of four main parts: the circular mounting plate (with three threaded holes), two lamp holders, and the sensor head. Also included are three locking rings, two mounting screws, a a large circular gasket, two smaller lamp gaskets, and several wire nuts.

First you must assemble the Motion Detector.

Screw each lamp holder into each of the outside holes in the circular mounting plate until they're tight against the plate surface.

Be sure that the black and white wires from the lamp holders are inserted through the holes in the circular mounting plate and are not pinched.

From the back of the mounting plate, screw a locking ring on the back of each of the lamp holders until finger tight.

Do not over-tighten! The mounting plate is not built to withstand extreme tightening, and finger tight is more than enough.

Screw the threaded end of the sensor head into the center hole of the circular mounting plate.

Again, make sure that all four wires from the sensor are through the center hole and not pinched.

Lock the sensor head with the third locking ring until finger tight.

You'll now wire the sensor head to the lamp holders.

Take the white wire from each of the lamp holders and one of the white wires (there are two) from the sensor head. Insert them into one of the provided wire nuts.

The three white wires all should fit in the wire nut.

Twist the wire nut just until it's secure.

No copper should be showing.

Take the black wire from each lamp holder and the blue wire from the sensor head, and insert them into a wire nut.

The two black wires and one blue wire all should fit into the wire nut.

Twist the wire nut until it's secure.

No copper should be showing.

The motion detector is ready to be mounted on the wall.

Turn off the power at the circuit breaker box.

WARNING! Household electrical current can be deadly. Hire an electrician if you're not completely familiar with the installation of electrical devices.

Place the gasket on the circular junction box and put the house wires through the gasket.

There should be a bare copper wire extending from the house or a green grounding screw on the circular electrical junction box.

Using a wire nut, attach the green ground wire connected to the motion detector's circular mounting plate to the bare copper house wire, or to the green grounding screw on the electrical junction box.

If no house grounding wire is supplied, and the electrical junction box doesn't have a grounded screw, you'll need to run a ground wire or consult an electrician. The system will operate without the ground connected, but it's not recommended.

Using a wire nut, connect the remaining white wire from the sensor head to your home wiring's white wire.

Twist it until finger tight.

No copper wire should be exposed.

Using a wire nut, connect the black wire from the sensor head to your home wiring's black wire.

Twist it until finger tight.

No copper wire should be exposed.

Tuck all the wires and wire nuts behind the circular mounting plate and position the two holes in the plate over the two holes in the circular electrical junction box.

Secure the circular mounting plate to the circular junction box using the screws provided.

Make sure that no wires are caught in the edges.

Insert lamp gasket into each of the lamp holders.

Sometimes these come pre-installed, so check inside the lamp holders if you don't see them.

The supplied lamp holders are capable of handling a maximum of one 150-watt bulb in each holder. Two 150-watt outdoor floodlights would be a good choice.

The Powerhouse Motion Detector is now mounted, but don't turn on the power yet!

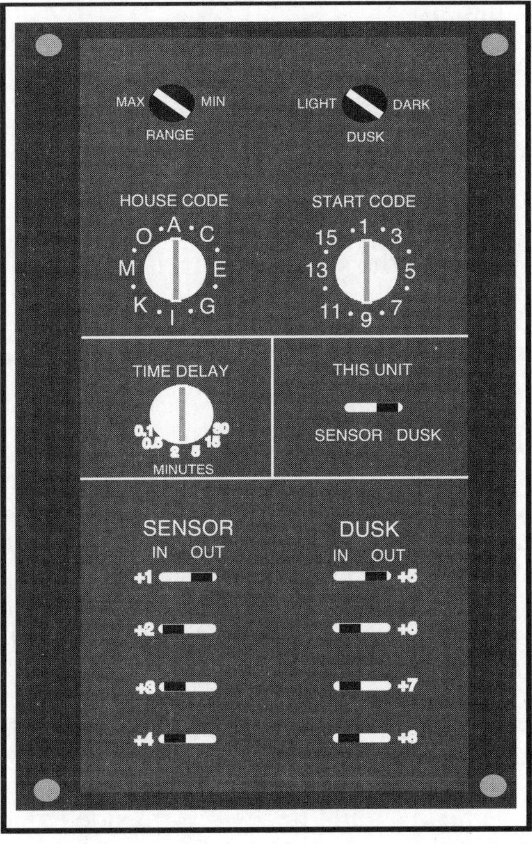

You're not quite ready. The motion detector has a number of different options and features that can be used. You must set it up so that it functions correctly. You'll need to access the hidden control panel.

Turn the small silver knob on the bottom of the sensor head to open the cover.

The cover will swing open to expose the interior controls. The first time you set up the system, you'll need to make sure that you're starting at a base level. Some controls can be manipulated by hand and some are more easily adjusted using a small, flat-bladed screwdriver. Have one handy before you begin.

Turn the DUSK control in the top-right corner clockwise, in the direction marked LIGHT.

This sets the sensor head to operate 24 hours a day and renders the built-in photocell non-functional. You'll start with it in this position to make sure that the other controls are set before you start using the photocell. Changes in the DUSK setting don't take effect for 10 minutes.

Turn the RANGE control in the upper-left corner clockwise, indicated by MAX on the control.

This sets the range of the infrared detector to its maximum.

The RANGE control is a sensitivity adjustment for the sensor head. Reducing the sensitivity of the sensor head can keep lights from going on when the wind blows or pets run by.

Turn the TIME DELAY control located in the center, to the left, to 0.1.

The TIME DELAY control sets the length of time that the lights will stay on after the infrared sensor is activated and motion has stopped. The dial is calibrated in minutes, so 0.1 equals six seconds (or 1/10 minute), 0.5 equals 30 seconds (half a minute), and then two minutes, five minutes, and 15 minutes, accordingly. For example, if someone walked in front of the sensor when the TIME DELAY was set at 0.5, the lights would stay on for 30 seconds after all motion in the area had stopped.

Point the sensor head in the direction that will best cover the intended area.

The head should be level from side to side and not be pointed directly toward the late afternoon sun.

The more the sensor head is pointed toward the ground, the smaller the effective range will be.

Position the sensor head parallel to the ground to maximize the coverage area.

Position the lamp holders and floodlights to light the optimum area.

If the floodlights are positioned too close to the sensor head, they can interfere with its operation.

Turn on the electricity and wait one minute.

The system has a built-in delay when the power is turned on to allow you to exit the area before the motion sensor is activated. Always remember this power-on delay when making adjustments.

Walk through the area covered by the motion detector.

As you move, the floodlights should turn on and stay on for six seconds (0.1 minute) after you stop moving or exit the area. Test the range by walking and stopping in different areas until you can determine the approximate range. Adjust the height and direction of the sensor head until the correct area is covered.

Tighten the locking nut on the sensor head to hold the correct position.

You have set the controls for the motion detector and built-in floodlights. Now you'll set up the control of other lights and appliances using the motion detector.

Additional Settings

The THIS UNIT switch allows you to use the photocell capability, rather than the motion-detecting capability to control the built-in floodlights. If you set the THIS UNIT switch to SENSOR, the motion detector controls the built-in lights. If you set it to DUSK, the floodlights come on at dusk and turn off at dawn, and aren't affected by motion. This switch just sets the method of control for the built-in lights. Other modules controlled by the motion detector can be controlled by using light detection (photocell) and motion detection simultaneously.

The DUSK control adjusts the amount of light required to turn on and off the light on the motion detector and other modules that it controls. The index mark (*) is a good place to start with this control. Turn the control toward DARK if the Motion Detector turns on too early in the evening. Turn it toward LIGHT if the motion detector turns on too late in the morning.

RANGE CONTROL adjusts the sensitivity of the motion detector to movement. Start in the center between MIN and MAX and adjust in small increments until the appropriate sensitivity is attained. Turn the control toward MIN if false alarms are too frequent.

Controlling Other Devices Using Motion Detection

The X-10 Powerhouse Motion Detector can be used to turn on and off other lights or appliances connected to X-10 modules in your home. The action will take place when light is sensed, or at dawn and dusk, via the built-in light sensor. Remember that the motion detector may sense motion at unexpected times, so having it turn on a light right near your bed could be annoying. Don't use the motion detector to automatically turn on anything that might be dangerous, such as a coffee maker or a portable heater.

Four Unit Codes (all in the same Housecode) can be set to turn on when motion is detected.

Set the module's Housecode to the same letter as the motion detector's Housecode.

The motion detector requires that the four modules that are to be controlled must be in sequential order. For instance, if you set the START CODE to 1, the modules that can be controlled have Unit Codes 2, 3, 4, and 5. If you choose 5 as a START CODE, modules with Unit Codes 6, 7, 8, and 9 are controlled. Because there are only 16 Unit Codes, if you choose 14 as that START CODE, the motion detector will control modules with Unit Codes 15, 16, 1, and 2.

Set the START CODE to 3.

This does two things. First it sets the Unit Code of the motion detector to 3. Second it gives you the option to control other modules with Unit Codes 4, 5, 6, and 7 by using the SENSOR "+" slide switches to indicate which modules should be controlled. In order to indicate each of the modules, the labels +1, +2, +3, and +4 are used. This means beginning with the START CODE that you set on the START CODE dial you add one, two three or four to get the module that is being controlled. If the START CODE dial is set to 3, the +1 slide switch allows you to control or not control a module with Unit Code 4. START CODE of 3+1. Slide switch +3 will allow you to control a module with the Unit Code 6. START CODE of 3 +3.

Move the SENSOR slide switch to IN for each of the modules you'd like to control with the motion detector.

Move the SENSOR slide switch to OUT for each of the modules you don't want to control with the motion detector.

Controlling Other Devices by Light Detection

The next set of slide switches under the word DUSK are used to control additional modules via the light-sensitive photocell in the motion detector.

Modules with selected Unit Codes will turn on at dawn and off at dusk via the built-in light sensor. Don't use the motion detector to automatically turn on anything that might be dangerous, such as a coffee maker or a portable heater.

Four Unit Codes (all in the same Housecode) can be set to turn on when light is detected.

Set the module's Housecode to the same letter as the motion detector's Housecode.

The motion detector requires that the four modules that are to be controlled must be in sequential order and their Unit Codes must be 5 greater than the START CODE set on the START CODE Dial. For instance, if you set the START CODE to 1, the modules that can be controlled have Unit Codes 6, 7, 8, and 9. If you choose 5 as a START CODE, modules with Unit Codes 10, 11, 12, and 13 are controlled. Because there are only 16 Unit Codes, if you choose 10 as that START CODE, the motion detector will control modules with Unit Codes 15, 16, 1, and 2.

Set the START CODE to 3.

There is only one START CODE dial, so this must be the same as the START CODE set for controlling other modules by motion detection. Once the START CODE dial is set, it may be easier to reset module Unit Codes to fit the scheme than to change the Start Code.

This gives you the option to control modules with Unit Codes 8, 9, 10, and 11 by using the SENSOR slide switches to indicate which modules should be controlled. In order to indicate each of the modules, the labels +5, +6, +7, and +8 are used. This means that, beginning with the START CODE that you set on the START CODE dial, you add five, six, seven or eight to get the module that is being controlled. If the START CODE dial is set to 3, the +5 slide switch allows you to control a module with Unit Code 8. START CODE 3+5. Slide Switch +7 will allow you to control a module with the Unit Code 10. START CODE of 3 +7.

Move the DUSK slide switch to IN for each of the modules that you'd like to control with the motion detector.

Move the DUSK slide switch to OUT for each of the modules that you don't want to control with the motion detector.

Because there is only one START CODE dial, you must coordinate your module Unit Codes to work with the START CODE and the "+" numbering system.

The modules controlled by the SENSOR and DUSK switches are independent of the THIS UNIT switch. The THIS UNIT switch sets only the method of control (motion if set to SENSOR or light if set to DUSK) for the floodlights built into the motion detector itself. The additional modules controlled will work with both sensors simultaneously and are unaffected by the THIS UNIT switch.

Troubleshooting

If the Light Doesn't Turn On...

Check to make sure that the motion detector has power. If it's contr^lled by a wall switch, confirm that the wall switch is on.

Check the setting of the DUSK control. Set it at the index mark (*). You must wait for 10 minutes for any change in the DUSK control to take effect.

Confirm that the THIS UNIT switch is in the right setting. Use SENSOR for motion detection and DUSK for light detection only.

If The Light Won't Turn Off...

Turn off the power at the circuit breaker and wait 10 seconds.

Set RANGE to MAX.

Set the DUSK control to LIGHT.

Se the TIME DELAY to 0.1 minutes.

Set THIS UNIT switch to SENSOR.

Turn on the power at the circuit breaker.

After you've turned it on, the motion detector will delay for one minute while you get out of the way. Don't begin the next steps until one minute has passed.

Walk past the motion detector.

The lights should still be on (since that's how they were before the power was shut off).

Make sure that there is no movement in the sensor area for at least 10 seconds. The lights should turn off.

Now you can reset the other controls one at a time. Start with RANGE, adjusting it very slightly until the appropriate sensitivity is attained. Adjust DUSK and then TIME DELAY in a similar manner.

Applications

Now that everything is installed, you already may have begun to think of ways to use your X-10 light control system. To help you, we're including a few suggestions and strategies here.

Before you start to hook up your Lamp Modules, think about the way you presently use lights in your home. Which ones are used most frequently? Which light switches are the furthest from the light source? When do you find yourself walking through a dark room to get to a light switch? Which room is the most uncomfortable to walk in without lights? Are there lights that you'd like to dim? The answers to questions like these will help you decide which lights need modules first.

Security. You can increase the security of your home with your X-10-home control system. Use an X-10 Mini Timer or Home Automation Interface to turn the lights on and off at intervals while you're away from home. You also can use any X-10 controller with an ALL LIGHTS ON button to turn on all lights in your home from your bed if you suspect there is an intruder. Using special controllers described in the Burglar Alarm chapter, you can have all lights in your home flash if entry or movement is detected. This can thwart a robbery before it ever happens—the best kind of protection.

Safety. Use an X-10 controller to switch off lights remotely. For example, you can turn basement or garage lights on or off without walking downstairs or outside in the dark. With a Wireless Remote Control System, you can turn on selected lights as you drive up to your home. Use a Mini Timer to turn your front porch light or pool light off and on automatically every night—even when you're out of town—to avoid dangerous situations on your property and possible liability for negligence.

Convenience. You also can use Lamp Modules and a Mini Timer or Home Automation Interface to turn plant grow lights or aquarium lights on and off every day.

Sometimes it might even make sense to turn off a particular light at a certain time every day. For example, you might have an outdoor light or a game room light that no one ever seems to remember to turn off. You can solve the problem with an X-10 Mini Timer by setting it to turn off the light every night at a certain time—say, midnight—after everyone is normally asleep. If the light's already off when the Mini Timer tries to turn it off, that's not a problem—the module will simply ignore the command.

Compatible Products

Radio Shack Plug 'n Power

700 One Tandy Center
Fort Worth, TX 76102
Phone: (817) 878-4852
Fax: (817) 878-6508

Various X-10—compatible lamp modules and switches.
Radio Shack makes a complete line of X-10—compatible products. In many cases, the functionality of the Radio Shack products is identical to that of the X-10 products.

Price: varies by product

Leviton Manufacturing Company, Inc.

59-25 Little Neck Parkway
Little Neck, NY 11362
Phone: (718) 281-6488
Fax: (718) 631-6508

6381-W Incandescent Switch Module
A single-pole switch controls incandescent lighting, with full-range manual dimming and switching capabilities, as well as remote switching and dimming capabilities from controllers. Equipped with radio/TV interference filter. Includes matching wallplate. Rated: 500 watts maximum, 60 watts minimum 120V AC. Brown, Ivory (-I), White (-W), Almond (-A), or Gray (-GY).

Price: $49.10

6383 Three-Way Incandescent Dimming Master Module
A three-way switch with same features as No. 6381. Also functions manually as a standard three-way switch installation. Used in conjunction with one or more Cat. No. 6294 Slave Units. Two-gang

installation of these dimming units requires a derating to 400 watts per unit. Three-gang (or more) installation requires derating to 300 watts per unit. Brown, Ivory (-I), White (-W), Almond (-A), or Gray (-GY).

Price: $93.20

6381-U Low-Voltage Switch Module
Manual and remote switching and full-range dimming. Also controls ceiling fans. 500 VA inductive, 4A motor. Brown, Ivory (-I), White (-W), Almond (-A), or Gray (-GY).

Price: $69.20

6383-U Three-Way Low-Voltage Switch Module
Same functions as 6381-U. For use in three-way switching applications. Brown, Ivory (-I), White (-W), Almond (-A), or Gray (-GY).

Price: $104.50

6291-WI Wall Switch Module
Same as Cat. No. 6381 but does not respond to DIM/BRIGHT commands. For use with fluorescent lighting, switch-controlled appliances, or high-wattage incandescent lighting where dimming is not required. Rated 20A 120V AC. Neutral wire required.

Price: $61.90

6293-WI Three-Way Master Module
Three-way switch with same features as No. 6291. Used in conjunction with one or more Cat. No. 6294 Slave Units. Also functions manually as a standard three-way 20A 120V AC switch installation. Ivory and white.

Price: $87.10

6294 Four-Way Slave Unit Switch Module
Provides manual and remote ON/OFF control. For use only in conjunction with DEC Cat. No. 6293 and 6383 Three-way master control modules as an additional slave switch. Provides three-way, four-way, or higher switching capabilities. Cannot be used for any other purpose. Brown, ivory, white, almond, and gray. Specify color, as this unit will not accept snap-on covers and frames.

Price: $26.40

6290 2400-watt Dimmer Module
Full-range dimming unit can be easily surface-mounted to control entire circuits or selected incandescent loads. Responds to ALL LIGHTS ON/ALL OFF, ON/OFF, and DIM/BRIGHTEN commands from controllers. Supplied in metal box with terminal strip wiring. Rated 2400 watts, 2400 VA, 120V AC incandescent, inductive, and resistive.

Price: $512.20

6375 Fixture Relay Module
This switch module can be mounted at a fluorescent fixture by using adhesive strips. Responds to ON/OFF and ALL LIGHTS ON/ALL UNITS OFF commands from controllers. Equipped with leads for easy installation. Rated: 5A 125V AC. Resistive or inductive only.

Price: $62.70

6376 Incandescent Dimming Fixture Relay Module
This switch module can be mounted at fixture by using adhesive strips. Responds to ON/OFF, ALL LIGHTS ON/ALL UNITS OFF, and DIM/BRIGHT commands from controllers. Equipped with leads for easy installation. Rated 300 watts 120V AC. Incandescent only.

Price: $62.70

PowerLine Control, Inc.

9031 Earthbound Ave.
Northward, CA 91325
Phone: (818) 701-9831
Fax: (818) 701-1506

MM4L, MM4A, MM4C Multi-Module
The PCS Multi-Module lets you plug more than one module into a standard wall outlet and also eliminates the problem of burned-out modules. If you exceed the capacity of a standard module, the module will be destroyed. Every Multi-Module is fully protected by a resettable breaker. The Lamp Multi-Module (MM4L) lets you control any combination of lights up to 1200watts from any combination of four outlets. The Appliance Multi-Module (MM4A) can control any combination of appliance loads up to 15 Amps from any combination of four outlets. The Lamp/Appliance Multi-

Module has two lamp and two appliance modules. The maximum total load is 10 Amps.

Price: $79

4 *Controlling Appliances*

Overview

This chapter will give you an overview of the X-10 modules available to control appliances and help you decide which ones are best for you. Appliances generally are described as all "nonlight" electrical devices. Typical applications are coffee makers, air conditioners, heaters, attic fans, and pool equipment. Appliance Modules are available for 110-volt two- and three-pin plugs, as well as for 220-volt appliances.

Generally, 220-volt systems are used for appliances with high energy demands such as air conditioners, shop equipment, pool filters, and the like. Appliances that use 220 volts can be identified by the type of plug they use. In the United States, 220-volt systems usually have plugs with three prongs that are angled differently than those on standard 110-volt systems. As always, if you have any questions, consult an electrician.

The Thermostat Setback Controller works in conjunction with an Appliance Module to control virtually any central heating and air-conditioning system.

There is also a specialized type of module, called a Universal Module, for appliances that operate on **low voltage** (up to 30 volts) such as sprinkler systems, low voltage electric motors, and low-voltage outdoor lights.

All of these modules are covered in this chapter, and when you've finished it, you'll be able to choose the module you need and install it in your home.

You're probably starting to get some ideas...

Appliance Modules

Appliance Modules differ from Lamp Modules in a couple of basic ways. Appliance Modules don't respond to the DIM command. This is extremely important to know because most appliances don't respond well to the low-voltages that result when a Light Module receives a DIM command. When a DIM command is sent, the module lowers the amount of electricity delivered to the appliance. Electric motors can be severely damaged if you attempt to run them on less than the appropriate voltage. This problem in not unique to X-10 systems; you never should operate an appliance on any type of dimmer switch.

Take care to ensure that a remotely controlled heating appliance does not come into contact with flammable material. Fire could result. It also is possible to turn on an appliance remotely without realizing it and leave it on for an extended period of time. This, too, is a dangerous situation. Don't let these potential problems discourage you from using Appliance Modules, though. With a little planning and common sense, you can ensure that your system will be safe.

For example, if you turn on your coffee maker in the morning at 7:00 AM with a Mini Timer or a Home Automation Interface, be sure to send an OFF command at 9:00 AM. If you remembered to turn off the coffee maker manually, the command will have no effect. If you forgot to turn the coffee maker off, the X-10 system will do it for you. You also could use the Telephone Transponder to call home from wherever you are and put your mind at ease by sending an OFF command to the module. A well-planned X-10 system can help prevent accidents in your home.

Two- and Three-Pin Appliance Modules

The X-10 Appliance Module is rated at 15A resistive load. This is the equivalent of about 1800 watts for items such as coffee makers, slow cookers, and electric blankets. Check the manufacturer's tag on your appliance to ensure that it's within the guidelines. A typical appliance such as a coffee maker might have "120V≈/900W" stamped on the bottom or listed in the owner's manual. This indicates that the coffee maker runs on standard household current of 120 volts and draws 900 watts of power, about half of the 1800-watt capacity of an Appliance Module.

An Appliance Module also can be used for lights, but then the DIM command and the ALL LIGHTS ON commands will not work. The 1800-watt rating for resistive loads cannot be translated to more capacity for large or multiple lights. Because of the way incandescent lamps "start up," an Appliance Module can be used to control lamps with up to a 500-watt total capacity. When you use an Appliance Module to control an incandescent lamp, it won't respond to DIM or ALL LIGHTS ON commands.

Appliance Modules also can be used for fluorescent lamps, but again, they won't respond to DIM or ALL LIGHTS ON commands.

The X-10 Appliance Module is rated at 1/3 horsepower for electrical motors. This is sufficient for most fans, sump pumps, and air conditioners, but be sure to check the listing for each appliance you plan to control.

It is very important to check each appliance against the rated capacity of the module before installing it. Severely overloaded modules can be fire hazards.

There are Appliance Modules with two-pin and three-pin grounded connections. Each works with standard 110-volt appliances and has a polarized connection (that means you can plug in the appliance only one way). You always can use a two-pin appliance in a Three-Pin Appliance Module, but never cut off a ground pin on a three-pin appliance in order to use it with a Two-Pin Appliance Module.

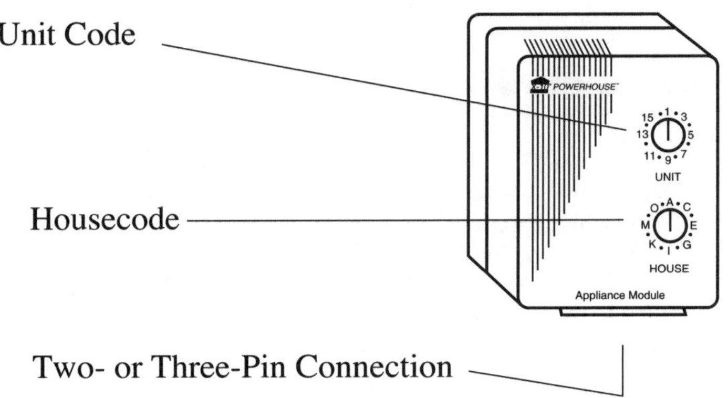

Appliance Modules are very easy to set up:

Set the Housecode dial to the same setting as the Housecode on the controller that you plan to use. For now, use "A."

Set the Unit Code to a unique number (one that isn't being used by any other module).

Plug the appliance into the module (the outlet is on the bottom of the module).

The connection is "polarized," meaning that some appliance plugs will fit in only one way. If the plug doesn't fit easily, turn it over.

Plug the Appliance Module into a nonswitched outlet (one that isn't controlled by a wall switch).

Bingo!

Test it using your controller. Make sure that the appliance's local switch is on. Control will now be at the Appliance Module.

Press ON for the Unit Code that you assigned.

The appliance will turn on.

Another feature of X-10 modules is their "local control" ability. If you are standing next to an appliance and don't want to walk to the controller, you simply can turn the appliance's switch off and then on again, and the appliance will turn on. Make sure to leave the switch on when you're done so that you can turn it on and off using the controller.

Wall Receptacle Module

The Appliance Module described above lets you control most appliances, but it isn't always esthetically pleasing to have the module protruding from the wall. The Wall Receptacle Module incorporates the same electronics, but uses a replacement receptacle that will fit in a standard electrical box. Except for the Housecode and Unit Code dials on the front, the module looks exactly like a regular outlet. This module provides one outlet (on the top) that's controlled via X-10 and one outlet (on the bottom) that acts as a standard electrical outlet. The bottom outlet is not affected by any X-10 commands.

The Wall Receptacle Module is rated at a full 15A (1800-watt) load. Unlike the Appliance Module, it's not restricted to 500 watts for lamps. It also can handle a two-horsepower motor.

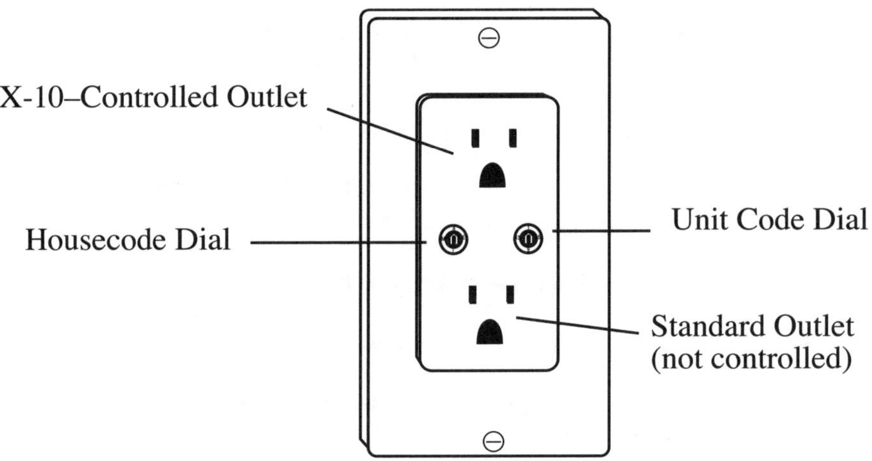

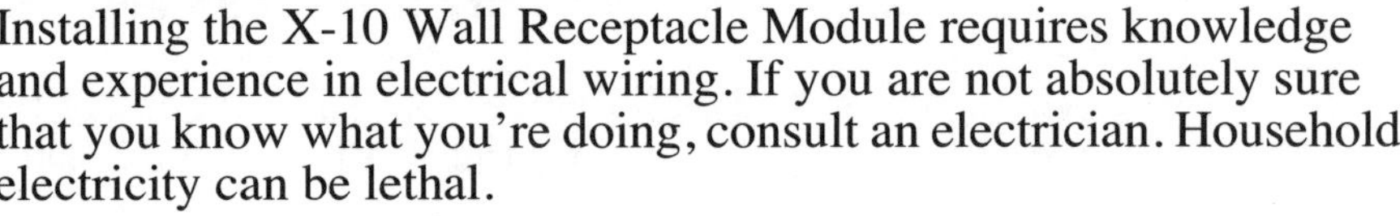

Installing the X-10 Wall Receptacle Module requires knowledge and experience in electrical wiring. If you are not absolutely sure that you know what you're doing, consult an electrician. Household electricity can be lethal.

Turn off the power at the circuit breaker or fuse box.

No kidding, really.

Remove the existing wall plate and the old outlet from the electrical box.

Write down the colors of the wires and where they're connected.

If something doesn't work, then you'll know how to put it back together.

Connect the white and black wires on the Wall Receptacle Module, black to black and white to white, using the wire nuts.

Make sure that there's no bare metal exposed on the wires.

Connect the green wire to the green or bare ground wire, or to the metal box itself.

Install the Wall Receptacle Module in the electrical box and replace the screws to hold it in.

Set the Housecode to the same letter as for the controller you will be using.

Set the Unit Code to a unique number (one that isn't being used by another X-10 module).

The Wall Receptacle Module is now ready to receive commands from the controller.

Make a note of the Unit Code and Housecode settings.

Replace the cover plate with the new one provided.

Turn on the power at the circuit breaker or fuse box.

That's all there is to it. To test the module:

Plug an appliance into the controlled (top) outlet.

At the controller, press the Unit Code and ON or OFF.

Make sure that the appliance you want to control is always left on. Control is now handled by the Wall Receptacle Module.

Another feature of X-10 modules is their "local control" ability. If you're standing next to an appliance and don't want to walk to the controller, you simply can turn the appliances's switch off and then on again, and the appliance will turn on.

Thermostat Set-Back Controller

The Thermostat Set-back Controller works with any household thermostat to regulate the heat and air conditioning. Household temperature regulation can dramatically reduce your utility bills and allow you to maintain a comfortable environment.

The Thermostat Set-back Controller works in conjunction with an Appliance Module or a Wall Receptacle Module and a Mini Timer or a Home Automation Interface. It allows you to regulate the temperature appropriately at different times of the day without touching the thermostat. If you also use a Telephone Transponder as a controller, you also can dial in from any touch-tone phone and adjust the temperature in your home.

The Thermostat Set-back Controller attaches to the wall directly under the existing thermostat. It “fools” it by adding a predetermined amount of heat. The thermostat then thinks that the room is warmer than it actually is, and is set back 5, 10 or 15 degrees, depending on how you’ve set the Thermostat Set-back Controller. This stops the heater from coming on until the room reaches a lower temperature.

In the summer, you can use the controller in the opposite way. Set the thermostat for the highest temperature that you want the room to attain, and the additional heat supplied by the Thermostat Set-back Controller fools the thermostat into thinking the room is warmer than it actually is. This turns on the air conditioning, to cool off the house before you get home.

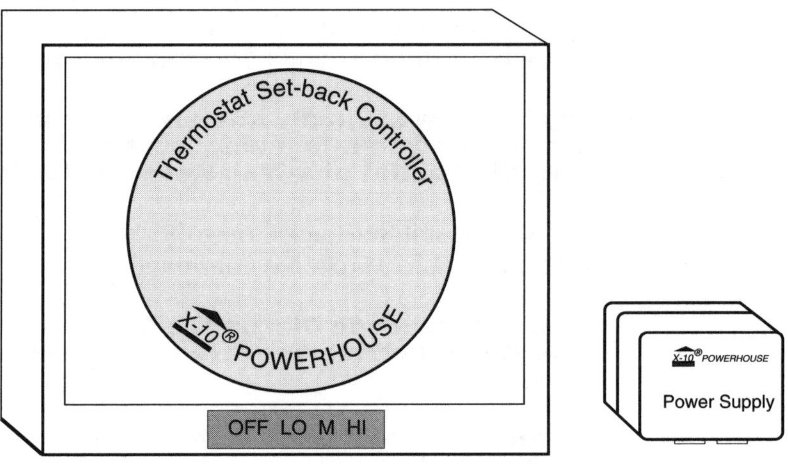

To mount and hook up the Thermostat Set-back Controller, you’ll need wire strippers and a small, standard screwdriver.

Remove the front cover and use the provided mounting screws to attach the Thermostat Set-back Controller to the wall about a-quarter inch below the existing thermostat that you want to control.

Adhesive-backed tape is included with the Thermostat Set-back Controller, but should be used only for temporary mounting. Be sure to use the provided mounting screws to secure it permanently.

Replace the front cover.

Check for the location of the nearest electrical outlet. You'll be running the provided wire from the controller to the outlet. Plot a direct path that won't be obtrusive.

Attach the connected wire down the wall using wire staples or the adhesive backing provided.

Run the wire along the floor or baseboard to the electrical outlet.

If you need more wire to reach the outlet, be sure to use a similar gauge (thickness) of wire.

Strip half an inch of plastic insulation from the end of the wire to expose two bare ends.

Connect the ends of the wire to the screw terminal on the Power Supply using a small, standard screwdriver.

The wire will not come off as easily if you wrap it starting on the left side of the screw terminal contact, wrapping it over the top in a clockwise fashion as you tighten the screw (clockwise).

Plug the Power Supply into an Appliance Module, and then plug the module into a electrical outlet or the upper, controlled outlet of a Wall Receptacle Module.

The Thermostat Set-back Controller now is attached to the electrical system and able to receive commands.

Set the Housecode Dial on the Appliance Module or the Wall Receptacle to the same letter as for the controller you plan to use.

Set the Unit Code to a number that is not being used by another module.

The Thermostat Set-back Controller is now ready to receive commands. First you'll set it to use less heat during the winter while you're away or asleep.

Set your existing thermostat to the warmest temperature that you want your home to be while you're there.

The heater will maintain this temperature when the Appliance Module or Wall Receptacle, and thus the Thermostat Set-back Controller, is off.

Set the SELECTOR switch on the bottom front of the Thermostat Set-back Controller to the desired amount of temperature reduction.

Lo (Low) reduces the temperature by approximately 5° F.

M (Medium) reduces the temperature by approximately 10° F.

Hi (High) reduces the temperature by approximately 15° F.

The Lo, M, or Hi setting will reduce the temperature of your home by these amounts when the Appliance Module or Wall Receptacle is on. Suppose you set the thermostat to 70° F and then set the Thermostat Set-back Controller to M (Medium or 10°). When the Appliance Module or Wall Receptacle is on, the house temperature will be 60° F. When the Appliance Module or Wall Receptacle is off, the temperature will rise to the thermostat setting of 70°. In this scenario, you would set the Mini Timer or Home Automation Interface to turn on the module while you're away and turn it off just before you get home.

For air conditioning, you take the opposite approach.

Set the existing thermostat to the warmest temperature you would like your house to reach while you are not there.

80° F might be a reasonable temperature.

Set the Selector Switch on the bottom front of the Thermostat Set-back Controller to the desired amount of temperature reduction.

Lo (Low) will reduce the temperature by approximately 5° F.

M (Medium) will reduce the temperature by approximately 10° F.

Hi (High) will reduce the temperature by approximately 15° F.

Lo, M, or Hi settings will reduce the temperature of your home by these amounts when the Appliance Module or Wall Receptacle is on. If you set the thermostat to 80° F and then set the Thermostat Set-back Controller to M (Medium or 10°) when the Appliance Module or Wall Receptacle is on, the house temperature will be 70° F. When the Appliance Module or Wall Receptacle Module is off, the temperature will rise to the existing thermostat setting of 80°. In this scenario, you would set the Mini Timer or Home Automation Interface to turn on the module while you're at home and turn it off just before you leave.

Heavy-Duty Appliance Module

Not all appliances run on 110 volts. Many air conditioners, pool pumps, pool sweeps, and hot-water heaters require 220 volts of electricity. X-10 provides two different modules that operate almost identically to the 110-volt version, but have additional capacity and load limits for larger appliances.

Heavy-Duty Appliance Modules work only with single- or split-phase systems, not with three-phase wiring (as is sometimes found in apartment buildings).

⚠ If you're not sure what type of system you have, please consult a qualified electrician. You don't want to mess around with 220-volt systems.

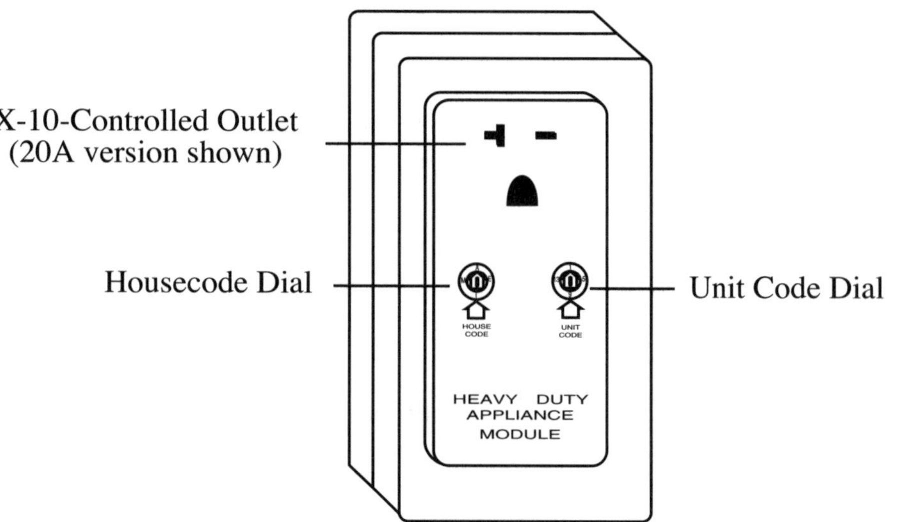

To use the Heavy-Duty Appliance Module, first determine the amperage rating of the appliance. If it is 15A or less, use the 15A Module. If it is 20A or less, use the 20A Heavy-Duty Appliance Module. This information should be somewhere on the appliance or in the owner's manual. You also should note the type of plug on the appliance.

Both of these modules are designed for single- and split-phase 110/220-volt systems. This is the most common wiring system found in most homes. Some apartments use three-phase systems. These modules will NOT work on three-phase systems.

Set the Housecode to the same letter at which you've set the controller.

The Heavy-Duty Appliance Module is now ready to receive commands sent by the controller.

Set the Unit Code to a unique number (one that isn't being used by any other module).

Note that you *can* use the same Unit Code for more than one module. But be aware that modules using the same Unit Code will respond to the same commands, turning the devices on and off simultaneously.

Plug the appliance into the outlet on the front of the module.

Plug the Heavy-Duty Appliance Module into a non-switched 220-volt outlet (one that isn't controlled by a wall switch).

Bingo!

Test it using the controller. Make sure that the appliance's local switch is on. Control will now be at the Appliance Module.

Press ON for the Unit Code that you assigned.

On comes the appliance.

The Heavy-Duty Appliance Module does not respond to the ALL LIGHTS ON command, but does respond to the ALL UNITS OFF command. If you don't want your 220-volt appliance to be turned off when an ALL UNITS OFF command is set, you may want to put it on a separate Housecode. When you go to bed at night, you could press ALL UNITS OFF to shut down all of the Light and Appliance Modules on one Housecode without turning off the air conditioning and other 220-volt appliances.

Heavy-Duty Appliance Modules don't have a local control feature. You must use a controller to operate the attached appliances.

Universal Module

X-10 and other manufacturers have created modules to handle lights and appliances that run on 110 or 220 volts. There are many other devices that run on low voltages that don't plug into a standard outlet. For these devices, X-10 has a special module, the Universal

Module. The Universal Module has two screw terminal contacts on the bottom front of the module. Light or Appliance Modules turn off the device that's plugged into it, while the Universal Module opens and closes the circuit between these two contacts, thus turning on or off any device that is properly attached to them. The CONTINUOUS/MOMENTARY slide switch allows you to tell the Universal Module whether to keep the contacts closed until it hears an OFF, or to close them for half a second and then reopen them.

The Universal Module also contains a **sounder** that will beep when an ON command is sent to its Housecode and Unit Code. It can be used whether or not you use the screw terminal contacts to control a low-voltage device. This is useful if you would like to be audibly alerted when the contacts are closed and the low-voltage device is on.

In fact, this module can be used just as an annunciator or sounder is for other modules. For example, you might want to know if an Appliance Module in another room is on. By setting the Housecode and the Unit Code of the Universal Module to the same Housecode and Unit Code as the Appliance Module, the sounder will sound either continuously or for three or four beeps, depending on how you set the MOMENTARY/CONTINUOUS slide switch.

The Universal Module is technically built to handle voltages up to 110-volt, 15A loads (500 watts for lights) and 1/3 horsepower inductive for motors, but the contacts are exposed and they are not insulated from being touched. If any voltage higher than 30 volts AC is switched through the Universal Module, the module must be placed in a locked, inaccessible place for safety. THIS IS CRITICAL! It is recommended that the Universal Module be used only for voltages up to 30 volts.

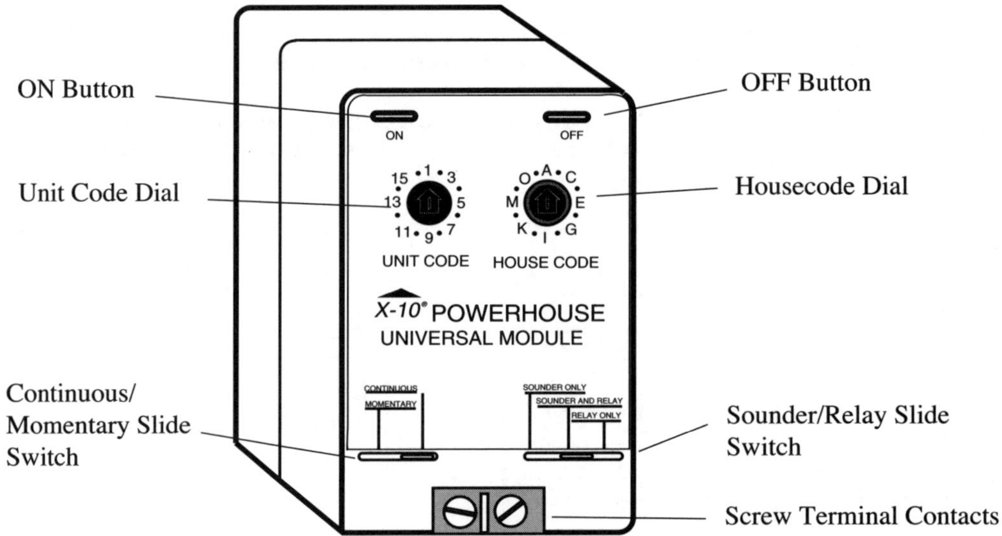

The Universal Module is relatively simple to set up, but can have many different options. In the first example, we'll explain how to set up a low-voltage sprinkler, and the same techniques can be applied to many other low-voltage devices.

Set the Housecode letter to the same one as for your controller. For now use "A."

Set the Unit Code to a number that isn't presently being used by another module.

You can think of the Universal Module just as you would a simple switch. In fact, you'll hook it up as if it were a switch. A sprinkler system can be controlled by using an **electric valve** powered by a low-voltage power source (a 24-volt power supply in this example). When both contacts on the electric valve are connected to both wires on the power supply, and it is plugged in and turned on, the electric valve opens and allows water to flow to the sprinklers. It wouldn't make much sense to install a fancy electric valve if you had to plug and unplug the power supply when you wanted to start and stop the sprinkler. That's where the Universal Module comes in.

This example uses an electric valve, a power supply (specified by the electric valve manufacturer), the appropriate gauge wire, and a Universal Module. Because there are many different types of electric valves, you'll need to check the specific requirements of the valve. The concepts, however, are the same. Make sure you use the recommended type of wire and power supply.

Run one wire from the power supply (either is fine) directly to one contact on the electric valve.

Run the second wire from the power supply to either of the screw terminals on the Universal Module.

Run a third wire from the unoccupied screw terminal on the Universal Module to the electric valve and connect it to the empty connection.

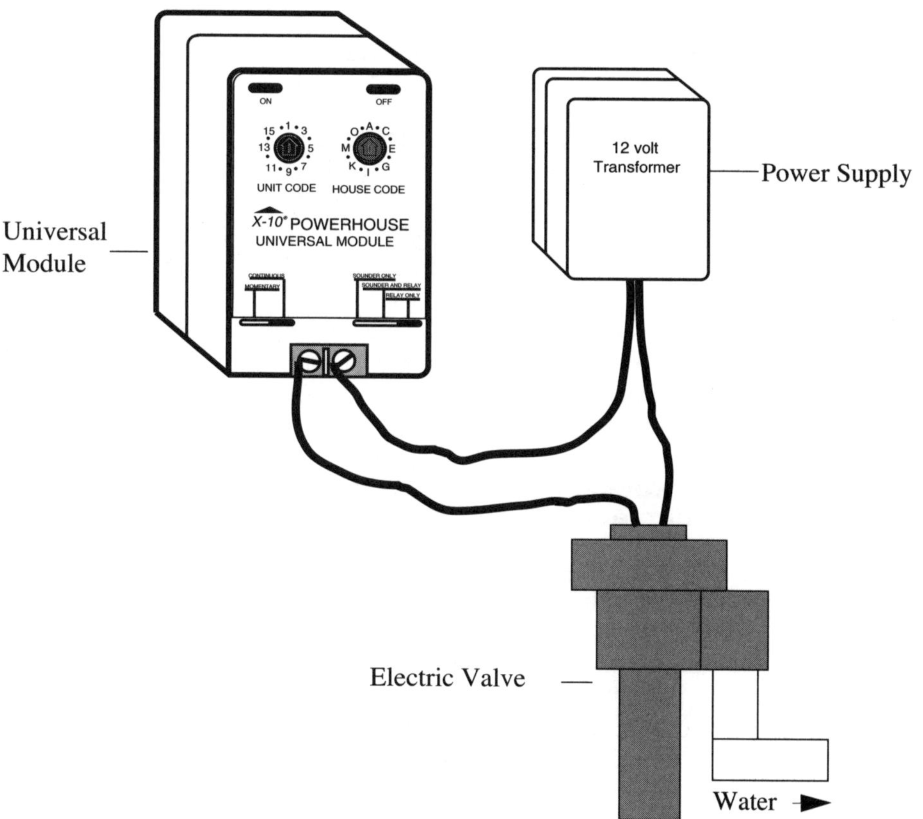

The Universal Module now can open and close the circuit between its two contacts and thus can connect and disconnect one of the wires to the electric valve. That's all there is to wiring the Universal Module.

There are a number of different options to set with the slide switches.

Move the CONTINUOUS/MOMENTARY slide switch to the CONTINUOUS position.

When the Universal Module receives an ON command and is set to CONTINUOUS, it will close the circuit between its two contacts (turn on the low-voltage device) and keep it closed (on) until it receives an OFF command. If the slide switch is set to MOMENTARY and the Universal Module receives an ON, command it will close the contacts (and turn on the low-voltage device) for about half a second and then open the contacts (turn off the device), leaving them open. MOMENTARY is used in the second example, when an electric garage door opener that operates with the push of a button is being controlled. The Universal Module set to MOMENTARY would close the circuit and then open it half a second later, simulating the push of a button. You'll see how this works in the second example.

For the sprinkler application, CONTINUOUS is the appropriate setting, unless you're in a drought area and want to water your lawn for only half a second!

The Universal Module also has a built-in sounder that can beep in conjunction with the closing of the contacts, by itself, or not at all. With some applications, it may be helpful to hear an audible tone when the Universal Module receives an ON command. If the CONTINUOUS/MOMENTARY slide switch is set to CONTINUOUS, the sounder will beep constantly until it receives an OFF command. A MOMENTARY setting will make the sounder beep three or four times and stop.

It would be annoying to have the sounder beep the entire time that the sprinkler is on, so you'll turn it off.

Set the SOUNDER/RELAY slide switch to RELAY ONLY.

Now you'll give it a try.

Plug the power supply and the Universal Module into their respective electrical outlets.

The Universal Module has ON and OFF buttons on the top for testing and local control. Try these first.

Push the ON button on the Universal Module.

The electric valve will open and the sprinkler will turn on.

Press the OFF button on the Universal Module.

The electric valve will close and the sprinkler will stop. Now test the Universal Module with the controller. As you can imagine, this works particularly well with controllers such as the Mini Timer and the Home Automation Interface. With these controllers, you can set up timed events to take place at certain times of the day or, in the case of the Home Automation Interface, a unique schedule for each day of the week. Try it with the controller.

From a controller with the same Housecode, push the Unit Code and the ON button.

On come the sprinklers.

Because X-10 is an **open loop system**, meaning that there's no confirmation that a command was received, sometimes it's a good idea to send commands a second time. In the case of a sprinkler system, this is a very good idea. If the Mini Timer sends the OFF command to the Universal Module, telling it to shut off the sprinklers, and for some reason the command isn't received (cosmic rays, perhaps?), you could have a swamp in your yard before you know it. An easy way to help avoid this is by sending one OFF command and then another again in a few minutes. If the module is off, it won't do a thing, but if it is still was on accidentally, you will have avoided a big problem.

The Universal Module can be used to add functionality to your electric garage door opener.

A typical electric garage door opener uses a device called a **momentary switch** to signal the electric motor that opens and closes the door. The momentary switch looks and acts much like the button for a doorbell.

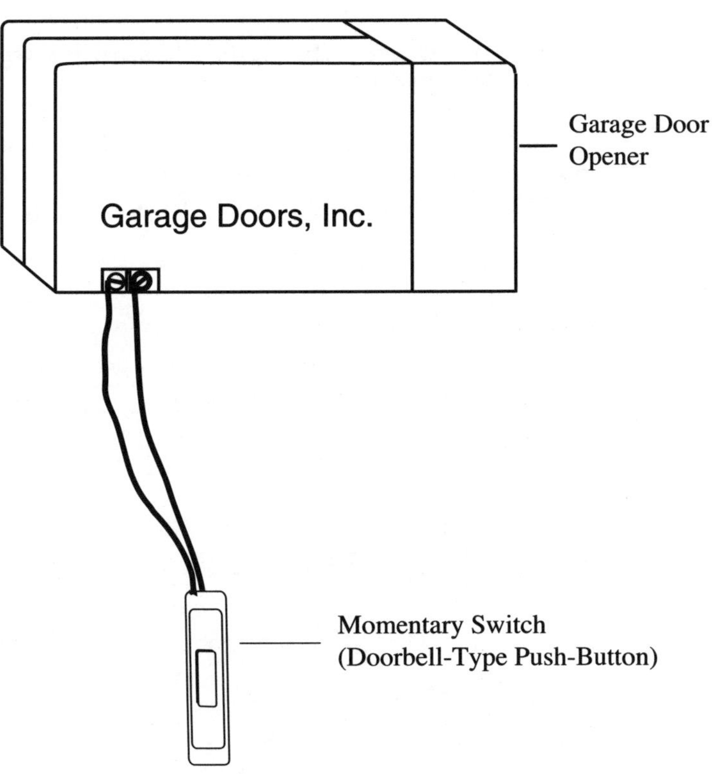

In this example, the Universal Module will act as an additional momentary switch so that you also can use X-10 controllers to open or close the door. If your present garage door doesn't have a remote control, a combination of a Universal Module and a Wireless Remote Control (see "Remote Control and Wireless Transceiver" on page 44) will give you this feature. Even if your present garage door opener has a remote control, by using X-10 modules and a Wireless Remote Control, you can consolidate the X-10 system and garage door opener in one remote control. Now when you pull into your driveway, you can use an X-10 Wireless Remote Control to open or close your garage door, turn on your lights, and control appropriate appliances.

Different garage door openers have specific requirements, so be sure to read the owner's manuals to make sure that the following example will work with your door. Most modern garage doors have a safety feature that won't allow the door to close if an object is in its way. By using a Universal Module as described below, you should not disable any safety features. However, be sure to test the door thoroughly to make sure that all safety features are working after you add X-10 features.

Let's get started.

Locate the button that you presently use to open and close the garage door.

It'll have two wires attached that connect when the button is pushed and disconnect when the button is released. You'll add the Universal Module as an additional switch for the garage door opener.

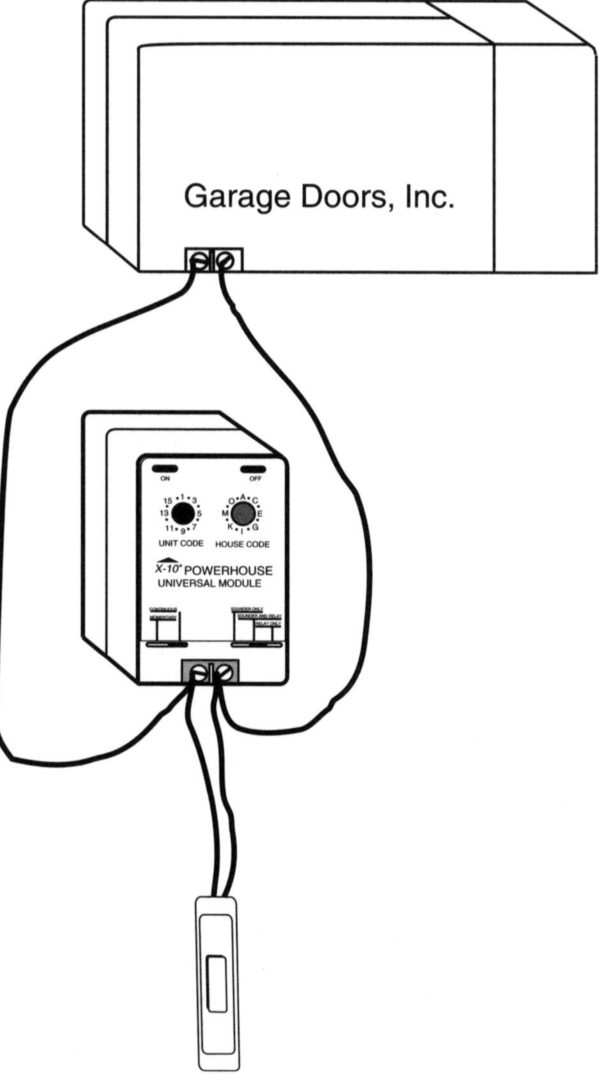

Disconnect the wires from the present push-button.

If you need to cut the wires, be sure to leave enough to make a connection. The Universal Module you'll add will act as another button for the system.

Find the two wires that went to the push-button and attach them to the screw terminals on the Universal Module.

You'll probably need to extend the wires so that they'll reach the Universal Module (which must be plugged into an electrical outlet).

Now you'll reattach the push-button, so that it'll work for local control.

Run one wire from each of the screw terminal contacts to the connection on the push-button. Do not disconnect the wires that already are attached to the screw terminal contacts.

Each terminal on the Universal Module will have two wires connected: one to the garage door and one to the push-button.

Now you'll set the slide switches.

You'll use the MOMENTARY/CONTINUOUS slide switch to make the Universal Module simulate the push of a button.

Move the MOMENTARY/CONTINUOUS slide switch to MOMENTARY.

It might be wise to have a warning sound when the garage door is being opened or closed. You will use the SOUNDER/RELAY switch to turn on the sounder.

Move the SOUNDER/RELAY slide switch to SOUNDER & RELAY.

Now the sounder will beep three or four times every time the Universal Module hears an ON command and closes the circuit between the screw terminal contacts.

The circuit now can be closed using either the push-button or the Universal Module. Give it a try.

Push the Universal Module's Unit Code ON from any controller set to the same Housecode.

The garage door will go up or down, depending on its position when you started.

Neat, huh?

Push the original garage door opener push-button.

It also should work as it did before.

Compatible Products

Leviton Manufacturing Company, Inc.

59-25 Little Neck Parkway
Little Neck, NY 11362
Phone: (718) 281-6488
Fax: (718) 631-6508

5371-I Double Pole Switch Module
Switch Module responds to ON/OFF and ALL LIGHTS OFF commands from controllers and also functions as a standard wall switch. Ideal for switching pool pumps, central air-conditioning units, and other large household loads. Matching wallplate included. Rated 20A 250V 2HP. Ivory only.

Price: $118.80

6227, 6280 Wall Receptacle Module
Duplex receptacle with top outlet responding to command signals and bottom outlet continuously live. Lights and appliances plugged into this module can be manually operated without the use of a controller. 15A, 125V AC. Brown, ivory, and white. 6280 has same features; both outlets controlled.

Price: $36.10

6296, 6297, 6298 Single Wall Receptacle Modules
Single receptacles provide ON/OFF control in response to command signals. All fit into standard wall boxes and include matching wallplate. Brown, ivory, or white. 6296: 15A, 120V, 60Hz, AC only NEMA 5-20R. 6297: 15A, 250V, 60 Hz, AC only, NEMA 6-15R. 6298: 20A, 250V, 60Hz, AC only, NEMA 6-20R.

Prices: $63.50-$80.90

Radio Shack Plug ’n Power

700 One Tandy Center
Fort Worth, TX 76102
Phone: (817) 878-4852
Fax: (817) 878-6508

Plug ’n Power Modules
X-10–compatible modules. Radio Shack makes a complete line of X-10-compatible products. In many cases, the functionality of Radio Shack products is identical to that of X-10 products.

Prices: vary by product

5 *Home Security*

Overview

In the previous chapters, you've seen the flexibility of X-10 technology and the variety of applications in which it's used. Another important application of home-control technology is home security. You've already seen how you can use controllers and light modules to light your home manually when you hear a suspicious noise. By installing sensors that sense the opening of a door or window, or detect the presence of an intruder, you can achieve the same results—*automatically*.

First we'll explain some general terms, devices, and strategies common to any home security system.

Then we'll describe the Powerflash Interface, a device that you can use to implement a simple security system with your existing X-10 system, or to integrate an existing alarm system with X-10 modules.

Most controllers and modules use the existing electrical wires in your house to send commands back and forth. In a security system installation, electrical outlets may not be conveniently placed near areas you want to protect. We'll describe the Supervised Wireless Security System, a complete security system that uses **radio frequencies** to communicate between **sensors** and the Base Receiver. This system takes the wiring hassles out of home security.

At the end of the chapter, you'll find answers to commonly asked questions and a comparison of the available components.

After reading this chapter, you should understand the applications for each of the components and be able to use them to design a professional-quality security system that's integrated with the other X-10 modules and controllers in your home.

Home Security Basics

All home security systems are made up of three components: sensors that detect a change (such as the opening of a window), **receivers** that monitor the sensors and initiate actions based on their status, and **alarms** that create a sound or otherwise alert you to the sensor's change in status.

There are many different types of sensors, most of which can be integrated into an X-10 security system. One of the most common is the **magnetic contact switch.** This switch makes a reliable connection between two wires that make up a **circuit,** or circle, of wire. You can imagine the problems that might occur if you attempted to get two wires to meet and separate consistently if the bare ends were exposed. It might work once or twice, but it would not be reliable.

A magnetic contact switch makes this connection much more reliable—it attaches and detaches two wires via magnets. Instead of moving the wires together and apart, the magnetic contact switch uses a magnet on one end and a magnetically sensitive switch on the other. As the magnet approaches the two contacts on the switch, they are pulled together and the circuit is complete. This type of magnetic contact switch is called a **normally closed** contact switch. In its normal state, with a magnet acting on it, it is closed, and the wires are together.

Normally Closed Magnetic Contact Switch

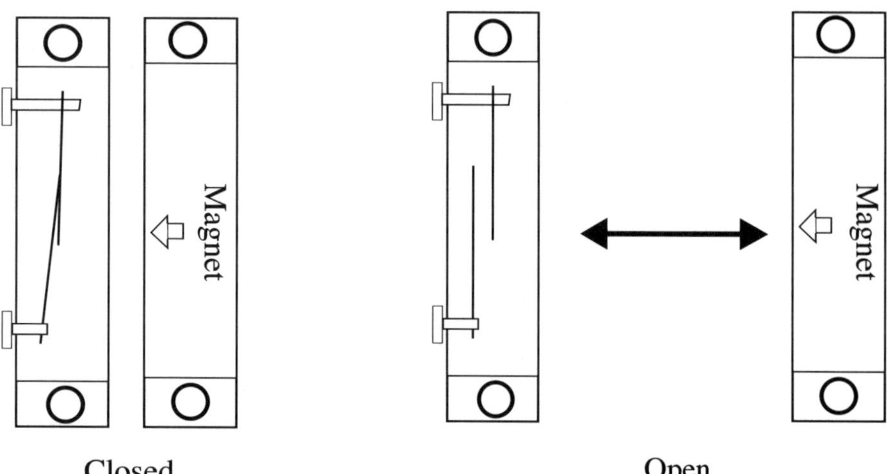

When the magnet is moved away—for example, when a door or window is opened—the circuit opens and the wires are disconnected.

In cases when you generally want the circuit to be disconnected, with the wires unattached, you would use a **normally open** switch. When the magnet moves away from this type of switch, the contacts are pushed together and the circuit is closed.

Normally Open Magnetic Contact Switch

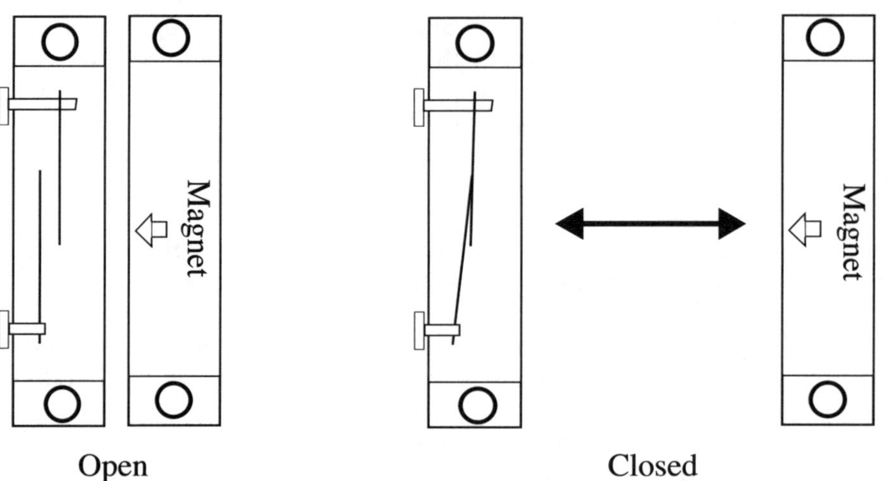

Although either switch can be used with an X-10 system, there are advantages to a normally closed circuit. If an intruder notices your security system and cuts the wires of a normally open circuit, it will be disabled. With a normally closed system, however, cutting the wires will open the circuit, and the alarm will sound. Normally closed magnetic contact switches are the standard switches used for home security and are included with most X-10 components.

By using a magnet to open or close the switch, you can place both halves of the circuit on one side of a window or door. The wires can be attached to the door or window frame, and the magnet can be attached to the door or window itself. This eliminates the need for long wires that allow for the opening and closing of the door or window. These switches also tend to be quite reliable and can stand up to the constant opening and closing without noticeable wear.

Other Switches

Using a magnetic contact switch to monitor the status (open or closed) of a door or window is the most common application in home security. Many other devices are available that can open or close a circuit and set off an alarm or other signal.

Pressure mats are large, flat switches that sense pressure or weight. They are used often under a rug or carpet to detect someone walking into a room. These switches are usually the normally open type.

Mercury switches are small, glass tubes with two exposed contacts and a drop of mercury that is capable of carrying electricity. Depending on the angle of the glass tube, the drop of mercury can be away from the contacts (circuit open) or against them (circuit closed). The mercury drop can carry electricity and complete the circuit. You could attach a mercury switch to a stereo component, for example. If someone lifts the component and the liquid mercury moves away from the contacts, the circuit will open and an alarm will sound.

Moisture sensors usually complete a normally open circuit. They can be used to detect water leakage or flooding.

Glass-breakage detectors contain a vibration sensor that can open a closed circuit using the vibration from a window being shattered.

Foil tape can form a vulnerable part of a normally closed circuit that will be broken (opened) when glass it's attached to breaks.

Once you understand the basic concepts of normally open and normally closed circuits, you'll be able to use a variety of different switches with the Powerflash Burglar Alarm Interface and the Supervised Home Security System. In the examples that follow, you'll learn how to implement magnetic contact switches. Consider using these other types of switches to enhance your system.

Powerflash Burglar Alarm Interface

Although the Powerflash Burglar Alarm Interface looks somewhat like a Lamp or Appliance Module, it's actually a special form of controller. Remember that a controller *sends* commands to modules, and a module *receives* the commands and acts on them. The Powerflash Burglar Alarm Interface sends X-10 commands when it senses a connection between its two electrical contacts.

Any of the switch types described in the previous sections can be used between the electrical contacts of the Powerflash Interface to detect an intruder. When the normally open switch closes, the circuit is completed and the Powerflash Interface sends the appropriate X-10 command. A MODE slide switch gives three different options for the commands that are sent.

The Powerflash Interface also can be used to connect an existing burglar alarm system with the X-10 modules to add more features to the overall system.

Many alarm systems use a low-voltage signal to trip warning devices. Using the INPUT slide switch, the Powerflash Interface also can detect these low-voltage signals (six to 18 volts) and send X-10 commands. For example, by connecting the Powerflash Interface to your present alarm system, you could have all of the lights in your home flash on and off, in addition to the alarm's normal signal. Individual alarms vary greatly, so consult your installer or the manual that came with your alarm system. We'll describe how to use the Powerflash Interface as a separate system to detect closure in a normally open circuit.

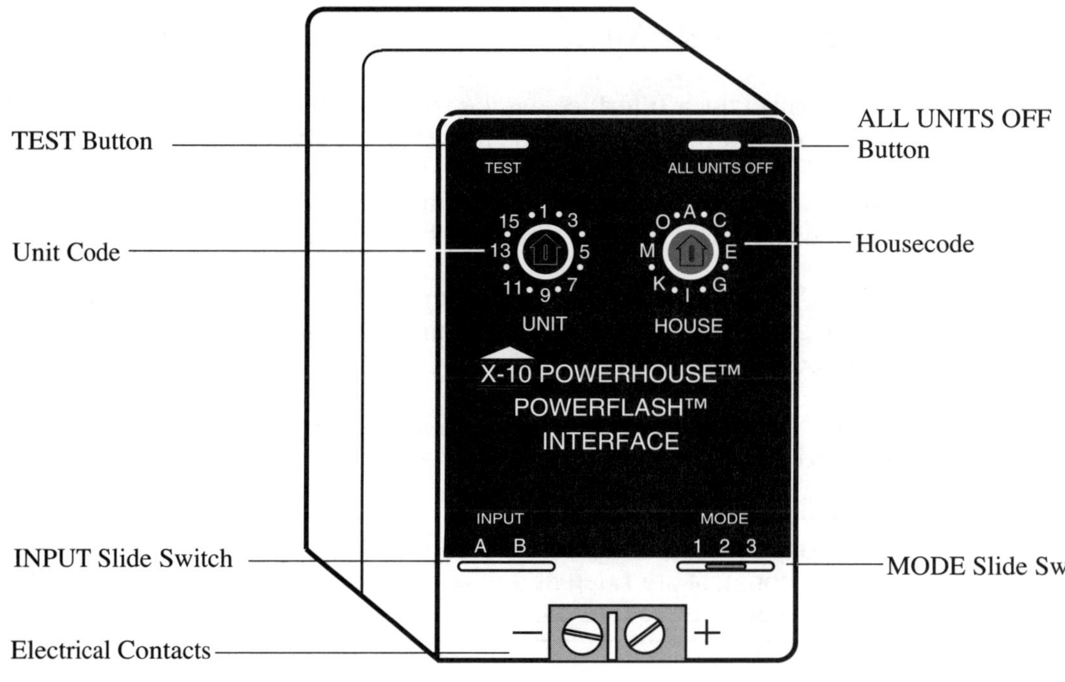

The Powerflash Interface's different modes send different commands through the electrical wiring of your home to activate X-10 modules. The modes have the following functions:

Mode 1 When the Powerflash Interface detects a break in the circuit, it sends the ALL LIGHTS ON command to all Lamp Modules and Wall Switch Modules that have the same Housecode as the interface. It also sends an ON command to all Appliance Modules with the same Housecode and Unit Codes as the interface. When the alarm condition is deactivated, all Lamp and Wall Switch

Modules are left on, but modules with the same Unit Code as the Powerflash Interface will be turned off.

Mode 2 This mode makes the Powerflash flash all lights connected to Lamp or Wall Switch Modules. When the alarm is deactivated, all Lamp and Wall Switch Modules will be left on, but Appliance Modules will be left off.

Mode 3 This setting makes the Powerflash turn on all Lamp and Wall Switch Modules that are set to the same Housecode as the Powerflash when the contacts are closed. When the alarm is deactivated and the contacts are open, the modules are turned off.

INPUT Slide Switch

The Powerflash Interface can be triggered by two types of changes in the circuit that connects the two electrical contacts. You'll choose INPUT A or INPUT B on the slide switch, depending on the type of device you are connecting. The simplest application uses INPUT B to sense the closing of a normally open circuit.

INPUT A sets the Powerflash to sense a low-voltage signal, such as the signal sent by many conventional burglar alarm systems, a photocell, and other devices.

INPUT B sets the Powerflash to detect the opening of a normally closed circuit.

Do not connect 120 volts AC directly to the electrical contacts. These contacts are rated at a maximum of 18 volts. If you connect higher voltages, severe damage and injury could result.

Now that you know the different options, you're ready to set up the Powerflash Interface.

Set the Housecode dial on the Powerflash to the same letter as the one on the modules you want to control.

When the Powerflash sends commands, your modules will receive them. You can set individual Housecodes for each group of modules as your system gets more sophisticated. For now, just use Housecode A.

Set the INPUT slide switch to B.

This sets the Powerflash to sense a change in a normally open circuit.

Set the MODE slide switch to 1.

This setting makes the Powerflash turn on all Lamp and Wall Switch Modules that are set to the same Housecode as the Powerflash. The lights will remain on after the alarm is reset. Refer to the mode descriptions on the previous page if you'd like a different action to occur. Note that any Lamp Module set to the same Unit Code as the Powerflash Interface will turn off when the circuit closes.

Connect the electrical terminals to a normally open magnetic contact switch (purchased separately), using 18-gauge wire.

The Powerflash is compatible with normally open switches only when the mode is set to B. If you plan to use it to connect to an existing alarm, be sure to match the polarity (+ and -) with the alarm system.

Press the TEST button.

All Lamp and Wall Switch Modules that are set to the same Housecode will go on, as will Appliance Modules that are set to the same Housecode and Unit Code. This test ensures that the Powerflash is working correctly.

Press ALL OFF on the Powerflash Interface to turn off the modules again.

Close the normally open magnetic contact switch by moving the magnet away from it (by opening a door or window, if that is how you connected it).

The results should be the same as if you pushed the TEST button. Experiment with different mode settings to see their effects. Remember, any normally open switch can be connected to the Powerflash.

Powerflash Interface Applications

The Powerflash Interface is very versatile and can be triggered by the low voltages (six to 18 volts AC or DC) that are commonly produced by photocells, microphones, or virtually anything that sends a low voltage or closes a normally open circuit.

In Mode 1 and Mode 3, the Powerflash can send an ON command to an Appliance Module, which could turn on a stereo when you open a door, for example.

Supervised Home Security System

After exploring the options of the Powerflash Interface, you might consider buying a number of them to monitor your whole house. As your system expands, a few limitations become apparent. If you have only one door attached to the system and the alarm goes off, it's pretty clear what happened. If you have eight doors and windows connected, you may not be able to tell whether the problem is in the basement or in the attic. If a Powerflash Interface breaks or a magnetic contact switch goes bad, you wouldn't know without physically checking the system periodically.

Using the existing electrical system in your house is very convenient for controlling lamps and appliances, but it can be inconvenient when you want to protect doors and windows. Using radio frequencies, commands can be sent between controllers and modules without any wires at all. X-10 has an entire product line of door/window sensors, plug-in base units, motion detectors, and sirens that can be combined to make a complete Home Security System.

The X-10 Protector Plus Supervised Home Security System combines a number of sophisticated features in a Base Receiver that monitors sensors and displays their status. It also allows for delays in entering and exiting, and has other powerful features usually found only in more expensive systems.

The system is made up of several types of components: the plug-in Base Receiver, door/window radio transmitters (with magnetic contact switches or other types of switches), and hand-held remote-control systems for arming and disarming the system. You can add other X-10–compatible products and more door/window sensors to protect additional doors and windows. The plug-in Base Receiver can protect up to 16 doors or windows with individual sensors, and more than 16 when multiple doors and windows are attached to single sensors. In the security system, the door/window sensors act as controllers (sending commands). The plug-in Base Receiver initially acts as a module (receiving commands), then transmits a response through the Power Line Carrier system to turn on or flash the lights, sound a siren, or take other action via standard X-10 commands.

The hand-held Remote Control can be used to arm and disarm the system remotely. Up to eight of these Remote Controls can be used by members of your family. The Remote Control also can be used for basic control of X-10–connected lights and appliances.

Base Receiver Placement

The placement of the Base Receiver is very important. Find a centrally located outlet that can't be seen from the main entrance of your home. This prevents an intruder from finding the source of the alarm and disconnecting it. The outlet that you choose should not be connected to a wall switch of any type. If the wall switch is inadvertently turned off, your alarm also will be turned off.

Because the Base Receiver's indicator lights are helpful in finding out which door or window is open and tracking down problems, they should be visible to family members. The Base Receiver also contains the alarm siren, so try to find an outlet from which the siren can be heard outside.

Remember that the Base Receiver should be:

- Hidden from the main entrance
- Connected to an unswitched outlet
- Visible to family members
- Audible outside the house

Setting Up the Base Receiver

Here's a diagram of the Base Receiver:

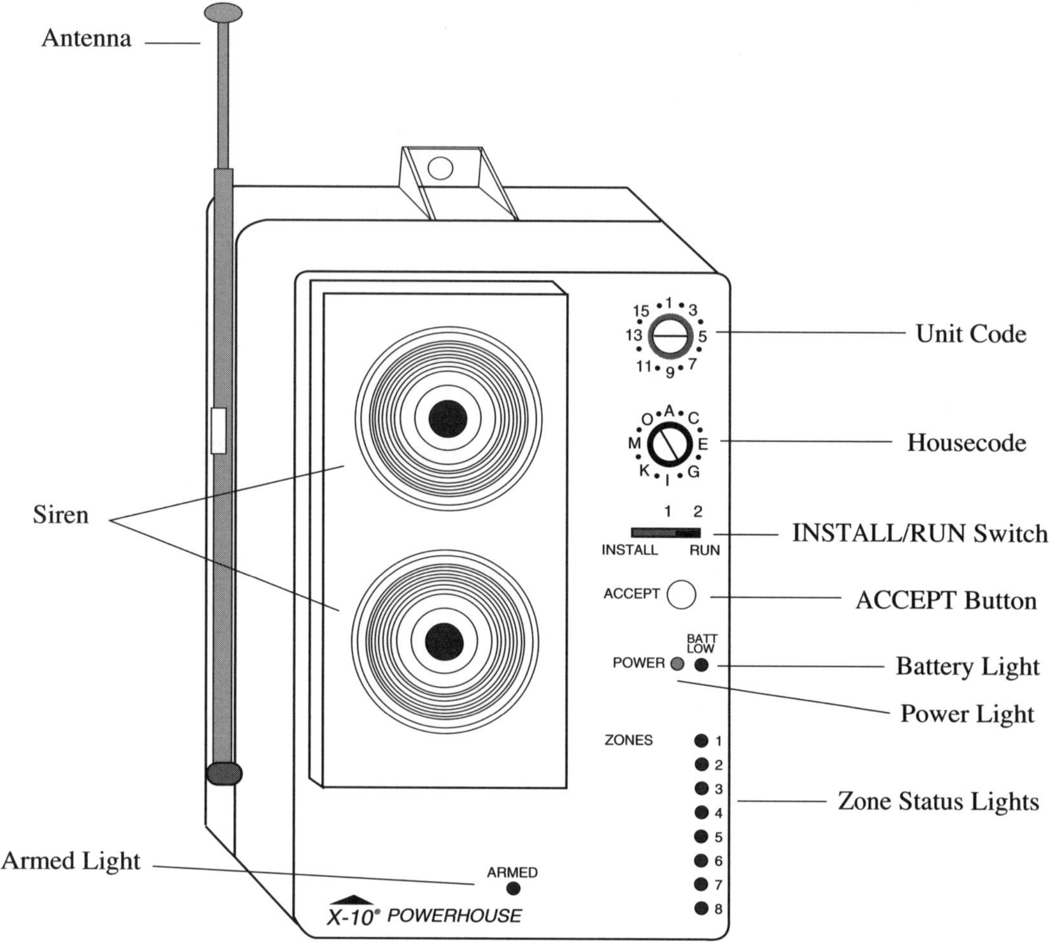

You may not be able to find an outlet that meets all of the requirements, but don't worry; just find the best location based on the criteria. Setting up the Base Receiver is easy. Here's what you'll do:

Set the Housecode on the Base Receiver to the same letter as the ones on the rest of the modules you'd like to include in your security system. If you don't have any other modules, set the Housecode to A.

As indicated in the overview, the Base Receiver can turn lights and appliances on and off to deter intruders. Setting the Housecode to the same letter as other modules allows you to control the modules from the Base Receiver.

Set the Unit Code on the Base Receiver to an unused code (1 through 16). Set the INSTALL/RUN switch to INSTALL.

All switches are now set for the initial installation.

Slide the battery cover off the top-right corner of the Base Receiver and install a nine-volt alkaline battery. Replace the cover.

The battery maintains all of the information in case there's a power outage or someone accidentally unplugs the Base Receiver. The system does not work while the power is out.

Plug the Base Receiver into the unswitched AC outlet that you've chosen and extend the antenna.

The Base Receiver is ready to receive information from the Remote Controls and the door/window sensors.

Setting Up the Remote Control

Here's a diagram of the Remote Control:

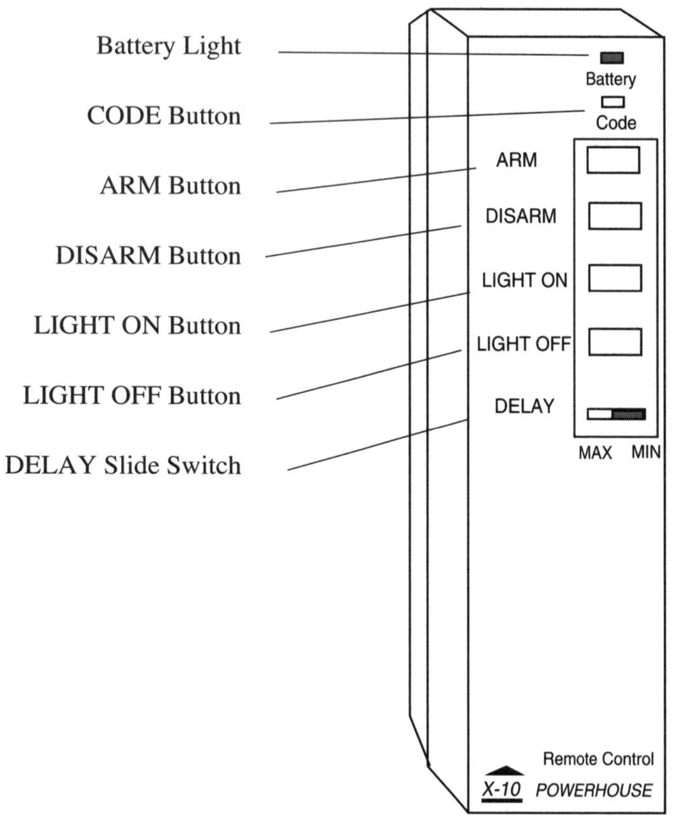

The full-size Remote Control can be hand-held or wall-mounted in an out-of-the-way, yet handy place. The Remote Control uses radio frequency signals to communicate with the Base Receiver. Radio frequencies allow you to control the system from inside your house, through walls, and even from outside a short distance away.

Slide the back cover off the Remote Control and snap in a nine-volt alkaline battery. Replace the cover.

Always use alkaline batteries in your Home Security System to ensure adequate voltage and long life. The Home Security System doesn't use code dials as other X-10 modules do; it sets its own addresses with an internal random code generator.

Make sure that the Base Receiver's RUN/INSTALL slide switch is set to INSTALL.

Press the Remote Control's CODE button with the point of a pencil.

The CODE button is located just below the battery light near the top of the Remote Control.

Press ARM on the Remote Control.

A tone will sound. The Base Receiver has identified the Remote Control and assigned it a unique code. Repeat these steps for any additional Remote Controls you may have, up to a maximum of eight per Base Receiver.

Installation of the Remote Control is complete.

Setting Up the Miniature Remote Control

The Miniature Remote Control provides most of the functions of the full-size Remote Control in a much smaller package. It is very convenient to keep on a key chain or in a purse. Installation is nearly identical to that of the full-size Remote Control.

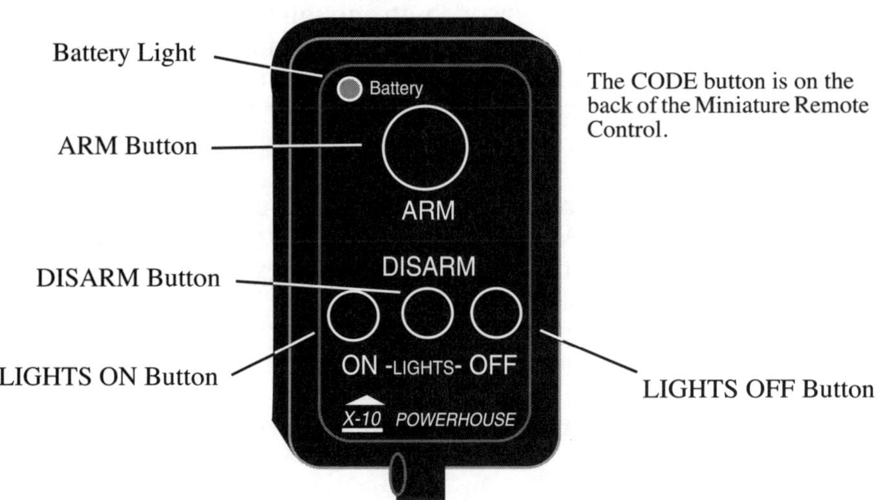

Make sure that the Base Receiver's RUN/INSTALL slide switch is set to INSTALL.

Press the Remote Control's CODE button with the point of a pencil.

The CODE button is located on the back of the Miniature Remote Control. The Base Receiver assigns a unique code to the Miniature Remote Control, and it's ready to use.

Press ARM on the Remote Control.

Installation of the Miniature Remote Control is now complete.

Placement of the Door/Window Sensors

It's impractical to have a Door/Window Sensor on every door in your house. Who would want to break into your closets, anyway? Do place sensors on outside windows that are away from the street and hidden from view. Sliding glass doors and back doors are also a tempting target for intruders, as are garage doors. Walk around your house and think like a burglar. With the flexibility of the Door/Window Sensors and no need to run wires, you have a wide range of options.

You can mount Door/Window Sensors near the opening edge of any door or window. If you have pets or children, you might want to position the sensors high enough to be out of reach. You also can use 18-gauge wire to extend the distance between the magnetic contact switch and the Door/Window Sensor, if you'd like it out of sight. You can replace the existing wire by disconnecting it from the two screws located in the battery compartment.

Use the double-sided tape provided to temporarily mount and test the Door/Window Sensor. When you're satisfied with the location and operation, be sure to use screws to make the installation more reliable.

For permanent installation:

Remove the battery cover from the back of the Door/Window Sensor.

Use the provided screws to attach the battery cover plate to the wall.

Don't screw on the cover too tightly or it may break. If the cover is too tight against the wall, it will be difficult to slide the Door/Window Sensor onto the mounted cover.

Slide the Door/Window Sensor down onto the mounted cover plate.

The magnetic contact switch should be mounted on the frame near the opening edge of the door or window. If you mount the switch on a metal door frame, make sure that the magnetic contact switch and the magnet (the half without screw terminals) are no more than 3/16 inch apart. On wood surfaces, they can be 3/8 inch apart.

Be sure to install the magnet half of the switch (the one with no screw terminals) on the moving portion of the door or window, and the actual switch (with screw terminals) on the stationary portion.

Magnetic contact switches and magnets have arrows on them. Always make sure the two arrows are facing each other.

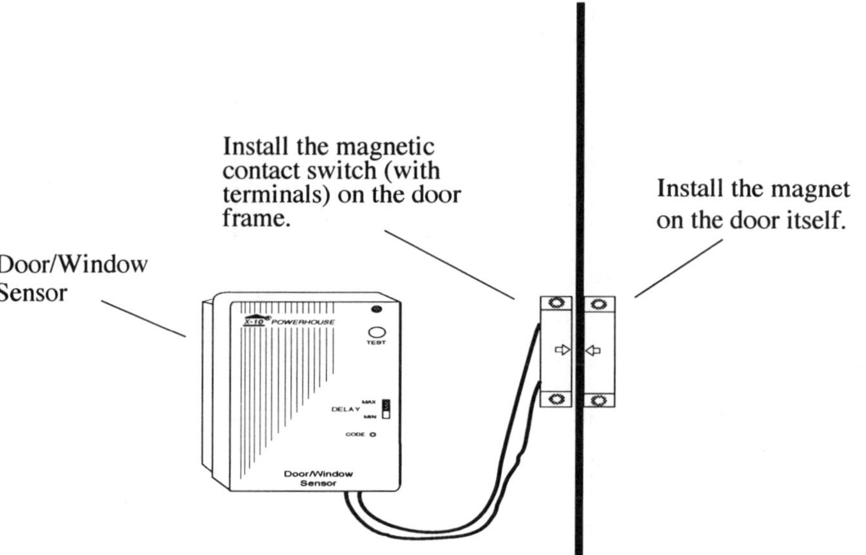

Mount the magnetic contact switch (with screw terminals) on the window or door frame (the stationary portion), and mount the magnet on the door or window itself.

Mounting the Door/Window Sensor near the top of the door will keep it from being kicked.

Connect the wires from the Door/Window Sensor to the screw terminals on the magnetic contact switch.

There is no order for connecting the wires; just ensure two good connections.

Check to make sure that the two halves of the switch are well-aligned. As you open and close the door or window, the light on the Door/Window Sensor should turn on.

Setting Up the Door/Window Sensor

You've already determined the best location for the Door/Window Sensor and temporarily mounted it. Here's a diagram of the sensor:

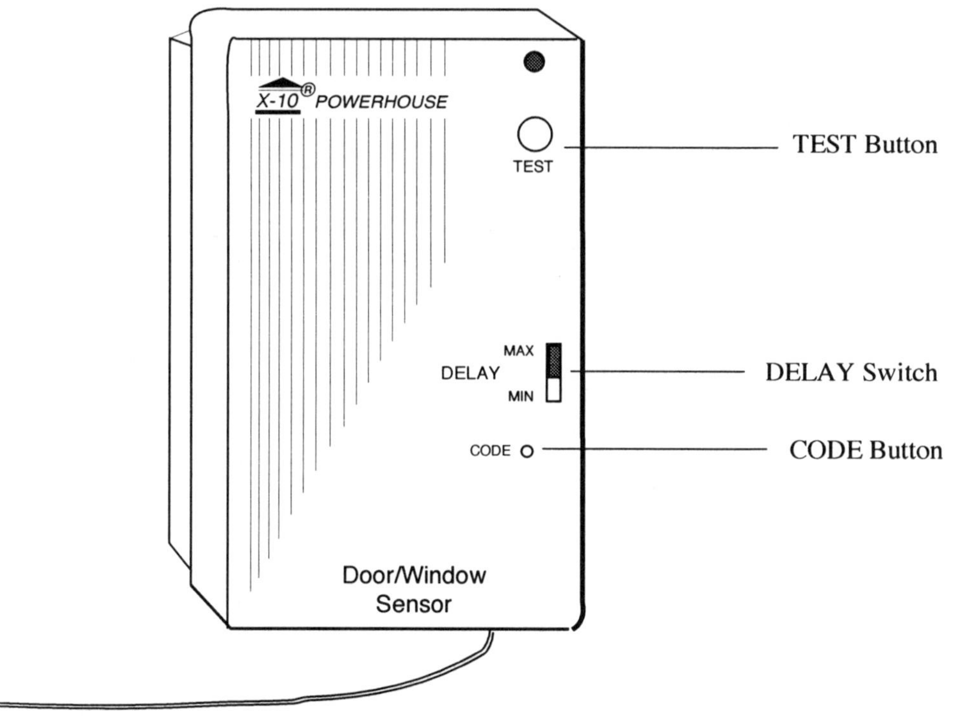

To set up the sensor:

Set the Base Receiver's RUN/INSTALL slide switch to INSTALL.

The Base Receiver is now ready to identify the Door/Window Sensors.

If you're using the Door/Window Sensor on a door:

Set the DELAY slide switch to MAX.

This setting will make the Door/Window Sensor send a command to the Base Receiver, telling it to give a pre-alarm beep and turn on the lamps and modules set to the same Housecode and Unit Code as the Base Receiver. Thirty seconds later, if the system is armed in MAX mode, the alarm will sound and all lights connected to Lamps and Wall Switch Modules set to that Housecode will flash on and off.

If you're using the Door/Window Sensor on a window or door that should never be opened while the system is armed:

Set the DELAY slide switch to MIN.

When the door or window is opened, the alarm will trip instantly (even if the system is armed for delayed entry via the Remote Control—more on this in the Remote Control section).

Door/Window Sensors can operate with most types of normally open or normally closed switches. They come from the factory with a normally closed magnetic contact switch and are factory-set to normally closed. If you want to purchase your own sensor and it is normally open, there's a small slide switch in the battery compartment that changes the sensor to operate with a normally open switch. If you're using the supplied contact switch, leave it alone.

Press the CODE button on the Door/Window Sensor. It's located just below the DELAY slide switch on the front of the sensor.

Press the TEST button near the top-right corner of the sensor.

The Base Receiver will emit a tone to indicate that it has accepted the sensor. The next unused zone indicator light will come on to indicate to which zone the Door/Window Sensor was assigned.

Place the appropriate number sticker on the sensor to show its zone number.

It's important to keep track of which Door/Window Sensors are assigned to which zones. When an alarm goes off or there is a problem, the zone number will tell you which door or window is open.

Set the RUN/INSTALL slide switch on the Base Receiver back to RUN. The system is ready to arm.

First we'll discuss different security options and then you'll finish arming the system.

Home Security Options

X-10 (USA) and other manufacturers have created a number of compatible additions to the basic Home Security System. Here are brief descriptions of a few of them.

Powerhorn

The Base Receiver has an 85-dB (**decibel**) built-in siren that will attract a great deal of attention, but may not be loud enough to truly deter a would-be burglar—especially in a large house. The Powerhorn is controlled by X-10 commands, so all you need is an electrical outlet. The Powerhorn is extremely loud—a piercing 110-dB. In fact, prolonged exposure to the Powerhorn siren could cause permanent ear damage.

The Powerhorn is very easy to set up and use.

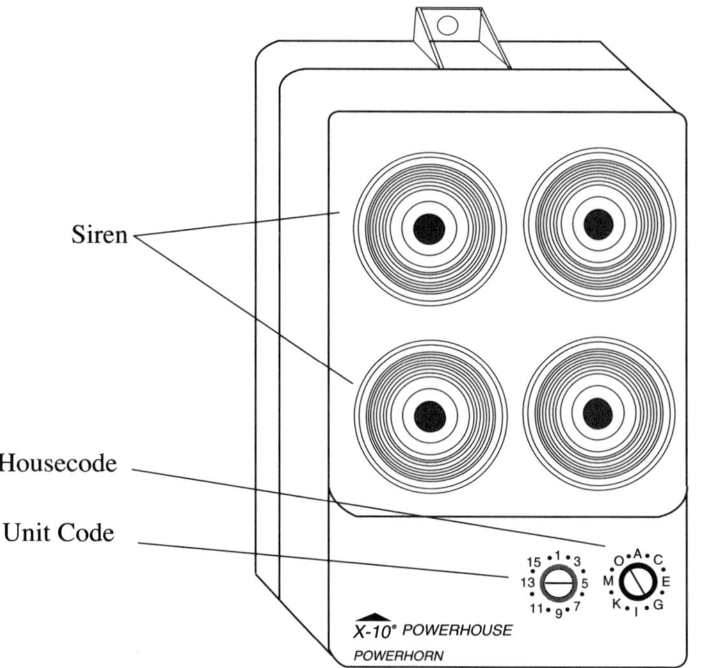

Set the Housecode and Unit Code on the Powerhorn to the same letter and number as for the security system's Base Receiver.

When the built-in siren on the Base Receiver sounds, the Powerhorn also will respond.

Find a nonswitched outlet (no wall switch control) away from the Base Receiver and plug the Powerhorn into the outlet.

The Powerhorn will receive commands from the Base Receiver and sound its piercing siren when the alarm is tripped. Next we'll test the Powerhorn.

Stand away from the Powerhorn and trip the security system.

Lights connected to Lamp and Wall Switch Modules will flash on and off four or five times, and then the Powerhorn will sound. It will turn off a few seconds after the alarm resets or is disarmed.

If you want to activate the Powerhorn from the Powerflash Burglar Alarm Interface, simply set the Powerflash Interface to Mode 2 and set the Housecodes and the Unit Codes to the same positions on each device. By using a Powerflash Interface and a Powerhorn, you can add a siren to your existing alarm with no special wiring.

Protector Plus Wireless Motion Detector

The Protector Plus Wireless Motion Detector is a specialized controller, that sends X-10 commands to a Base Receiver, which then can sound alarms or activate other X-10–controlled lights and appliances. The Wireless Motion Detector is—surprise—wireless and operates from a nine-volt battery. It can be set to trip immediately after detecting any motion or, to help prevent false alarms, it can be set to trip only if two movements or a continuous movement are detected within a specified period of time.

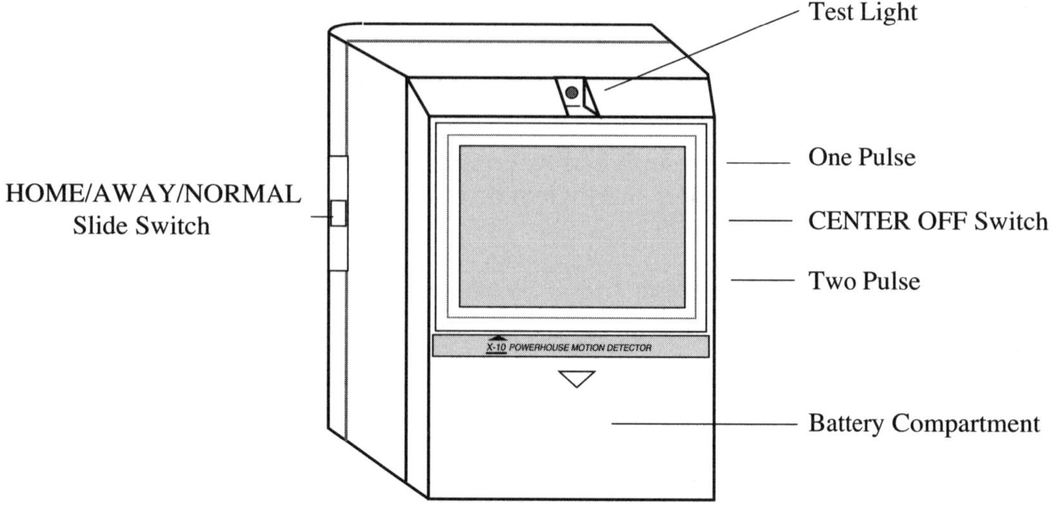

Placing the Wireless Motion Detector

Motion Detectors are most useful in centrally located areas and points of heavy traffic. A single Motion Detector can provide coverage for most of a house if it is placed correctly. Find a main hallway or central entrance point for a group of rooms so that you can protect all of them with one sensor.

Motion Detectors sense a change in temperature, including changes caused by cats, dogs, and air from heat ducts or air conditioners. If you have pets, the best way to avoid false alarms is to place the Motion Detector in a hallway that can be closed off to pets. As soon as any door to the hallway is opened, the alarm will trip.

You can make horizontal and vertical adjustments to the Wireless Motion Detector with the bracket that's included. You may be able to aim it high enough to avoid pets, but still detect an intruder. This will take some experimenting. The Wireless Motion Detector has a red test LED (light-emitting diode) that lights when motion is detected.

Use this LED to adjust the height and coverage area.

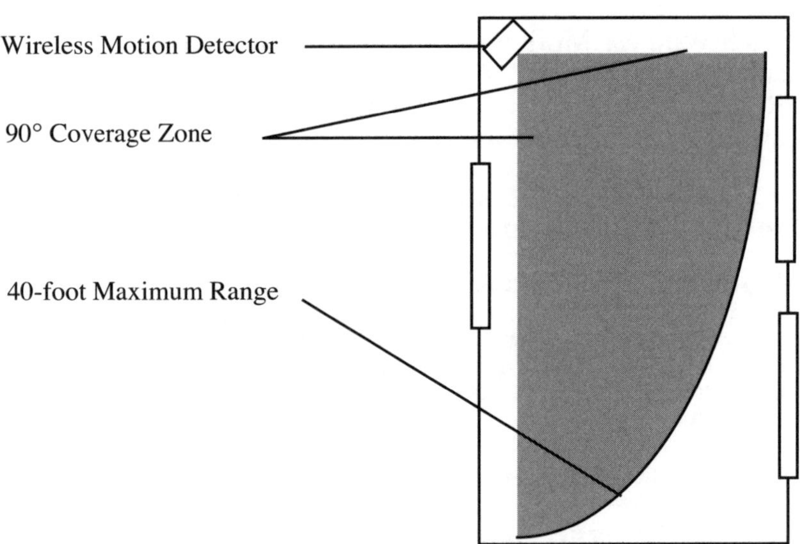

Installing the Wireless Motion Detector

Install a nine-volt alkaline battery in the battery compartment in the front panel of the Motion Detector.

Always use alkaline batteries in Home Security System units. They'll give much better performance and require less frequent replacement. Some nonalkaline batteries may not work even when they are new.

Set the Base Receiver's INSTALL/RUN switch to INSTALL.

Now the Base Receiver will be ready to identify the Wireless Motion Detector.

Press the CODE button on the back of the Motion Detector with the point of a pencil.

The unique code for the Motion Detector will be established.

Press the TEST button on the back of the Motion Detector.

The Base Receiver will chime. The next available Zone Indicator LED will light up to indicate which zone number that the Wireless Motion Detector is watching.

Each Wireless Motion Detector has its own zone, and the zone's status is indicated by an individual zone indicator light on the Base Receiver. Write down the zone number for each Motion Detector and keep the list near the Base Receiver.

If you don't hear a chime, press the CODE button, then press the TEST button again.

If you plan to use a Remote Control with the Home/Away feature to disarm your security system before you enter your home, you'll probably want to set the Motion Detector to the Home/Away position. If you want to use a Remote Control without Home/Away, set the Motion Detector to Normal.

To set the Motion Detector to trip the alarm if it detects any motion:

Set the CENTER OFF switch to 1 (a single movement).

To make the Motion Detector trip the alarm after it detects two movements or continuous movement:

Set the CENTER OFF switch to 2 (two movements).

If you don't want the Motion Detector to trip the alarm at all, set the CENTER OFF switch to the Normal position, in the center. The red test LED still will light when motion is detected. This is a good setting to use to test the system without setting off the ear-splitting siren.

Using the Supervised Security System

By now you should have placed and installed the Base Receiver and installed one or more Door/Window Sensors. You may have installed a Wireless Motion Detector or a Powerhorn as well, but these are not required.

To test the system:

Set the INSTALL/RUN slide switch on the Base Receiver to RUN 2.

In Run 2 mode, the Base Receiver will chime when each door or window is opened, instead of sounding the alarm—much less annoying when you're testing the system.

Open each door or window in turn.

When each door or window is opened, the Base Receiver will chime and the appropriate zone indicator light will turn on. When the door closes, the zone indicator light will turn off.

Arming the System in Instant Mode

Everything should be ready to go. Let's give it a try. (Don't do this late at night—the neighbors won't appreciate it.)

Set the INSTALL/RUN slide switch on the Base Receiver to Run 2.

Set the DELAY switch on the Remote Control to MIN.

The Miniature Remote Control will always be set to MIN.

Press ARM on the Remote Control.

The Base Receiver will beep twice to acknowledge receiving the command.

Press TEST on the Door/Window Sensor.

This instantly will set off the alarm. The siren in the Base Receiver (and the Powerhorn, if installed) will sound, and any lights connected to Lamp and Wall Switch Modules set to the same Housecode as the Base Receiver will flash on and off.

To stop the alarm:

Press DISARM.

The siren will stop, and the lights will stop flashing but remain on.

Test each of the Door/Window Sensors in this manner.

Arming the System in Delay Mode

The Delay mode will give you about one minute to leave the house before the system arms itself and about 30 seconds to disarm the system when you enter through an armed door (DELAY slide switch set to MAX).

Set the DELAY switch on the Remote Control to MAX.

Press ARM on the Remote Control.

Lamps connected to modules set to the same Housecode and Unit Code as the Base Receiver will turn on. An entry light or a hall light is usually a good choice.

The Base Receiver will chime for about one minute while you leave the house. A beep will signify that the system is now armed, and Lamp or Wall Switch Modules with the same Housecode and Unit Code will shut off.

Wait for at least a minute and open a door (DELAY slide switch set to MAX).

A pre-alarm beep will sound from the Base Receiver, and lights connected to Lamp and Wall Switch Modules with the same Housecode and Unit Code as the Base Receiver will turn on. After 30 seconds, if the system is not disarmed, the alarm will sound and all lights connected to Lamp and Wall Switch Modules with the same Housecode will flash.

If you open a window (DELAY slide switch set to MIN), the alarm will trip instantly.

Press DISARM on the Remote Control.

The siren will shut off and the lights will remain on.

Pressing any two adjacent buttons (LIGHT OFF and LIGHT ON or ARM and DISARM) simultaneously will sound the alarm instantly.

Using the Miniature Remote Control

The Miniature Remote Control will perform the same functions as the Remote Control, but always will activate the system in Instant mode. There is no entry or exit delay. It also has a Panic Alarm that you can set off by pressing ARM and DISARM at the same time.

The Miniature Remote Control also will perform LIGHT ON and LIGHT OFF functions for any module that is set to the Base Receiver's Housecode and Unit Code.

Trouble Alarm

If you try to arm the system and hear a continuous two-tone sound, there is a problem and the system will not arm. You can either correct the problem or ignore it by bypassing the sensor that is causing the problem.

To correct the problem:

Press DISARM and check the sensor located in the zone with the flashing indicator light.

To ignore the problem:

Press the ACCEPT button on the Base Receiver.

Press ARM on the Remote Control again.

The problem zone indicator will flash rapidly. The system will arm, but the problem zone will be bypassed and thus not protected.

Compatible Products

Interactive Technologies, Inc. (ITI)

2266 N. Second St.
North St. Paul, MN 55109
Fax: (612) 779-4890

CareTaker Plus
CareTaker Plus is a security system that combines 32 zones of security (hard-wired or wireless) with lighting control, energy management, and, soon, home banking. CareTaker Plus can send wireless powerline carrier signals to X-10 lamp modules, enabling the system to provide enhanced functionality, such as the ability to have a path automatically lit to the telephone or security system touchpad, so that the homeowner easily can find and disarm the system.

Price: contact manufacturer.

Radio Shack Plug 'n Power

700 One Tandy Center
Fort Worth, TX 76102
Phone: (817) 878-4852
Fax: (817) 878-6508

Plug 'n Power Supervised Security System
Plug 'n Power Supervised Security System modules are X-10-compatible. Radio Shack makes a complete line of X-10—compatible products. In many cases, the functionality of the Radio Shack products is identical to that of the X-10 products.

Price: varies by product

6 Windows

Overview

Assuming that you haven't skipped right to this chapter, you've already learned a lot about home automation. In fact, you already know enough to build a very functional system that will control lights, appliances, and even a security system.

In this chapter, you'll learn how to control a reasonably complex home-automation system with an X-10 Home Automation Interface and an IBM personal computer or compatible computer running the Microsoft Windows 3.1 or Windows 95 operating system.

Using the interface with an IBM PC gives you several advantages over systems that use the other controllers described in this book:

- You can control modules set with any Housecode and any Unit Code; this means that you can control up to 16 x 16 = 256 devices!
- You can create up to 128 timed events.
- You can program each module to go on and off at specific times, on specific days of the week.
- You can program Lamp Modules to dim or brighten to a certain intensity at a given time. This might be done, for example, to add a technical touch to an otherwise very romantic moment.

As you go through this chapter, you'll first learn how to attach the Home Automation Interface to your computer. Then you'll learn how to set up the Home Automation software and use it to enter information about the modules you've installed. Next you'll learn how to erase module information and control modules either immediately or with timed events. Finally you'll learn how to save timed events in a file, to print lists of timed events, and to exit from the program.

When you've finished reading this chapter, you should be able to use your computer to turn devices on and off both immediately and with timed events. You'll also know how to save groups of events in a file that you can read into the computer and load into the interface.

This chapter assumes that you're familiar with the operation of your computer. If you aren't, review the owner's guide before continuing.

Setup

Before you try to use the interface with your computer, you'll need to ensure that the interface is functioning properly. Here's how to do that:

- Set the address of a Lamp Module to A1, attach the module to a lamp, and plug the module into an electrical outlet.
- Next plug the interface into a different electrical outlet. (Although you can use any electrical outlet in the house, choose one in the same room so that you don't have to run around.)
- Press the top of the rocker button labeled "1" on the interface to turn the lamp on. Once the lamp is on, press the bottom of the same button to turn off the lamp.

If you experience any problems, be sure that you've set the Lamp Module correctly. If you still have problems, call X-10 (USA) Inc.'s Customer Service Department for help (the telephone number is given in the "Compatible Products" section of the "Controllers" chapter, beginning on page 54).

One last thing you should do before connecting the interface to your computer is to install a nine-volt battery in the compartment on the back of the interface. The battery will provide backup power to the interface when it is not plugged into an outlet or when the electricity is off. Without the battery, you'll have to reprogram every timed event whenever the interface is unplugged or the power goes off.

Connecting the Interface to Your Computer

The interface works with IBM PC (including PS/2) computers and IBM-compatible computers that have a serial (RS-232) card installed in them, or come with a built-in serial port.

Before you do anything else, you'll need to connect the interface to your computer.

Connect the interface to the RS-232 serial port on your computer using the cable that comes with the interface.

If you are not sure how to do this, consult the manual that came with your computer. If you have an IBM PC XT, PC AT, or IBM-compatible, you may need an additional 9-pin to 25-pin converter cable.

Next you'll copy the Lighthouse software to your hard disk.

Preparing the Software

Installing the software is very straightforward.

Turn on the computer. When you see the Windows desktop, insert the Lighthouse diskette. Then choose Run... from the File menu in Program Manager.

You will be prompted for the name of the program you want to run.

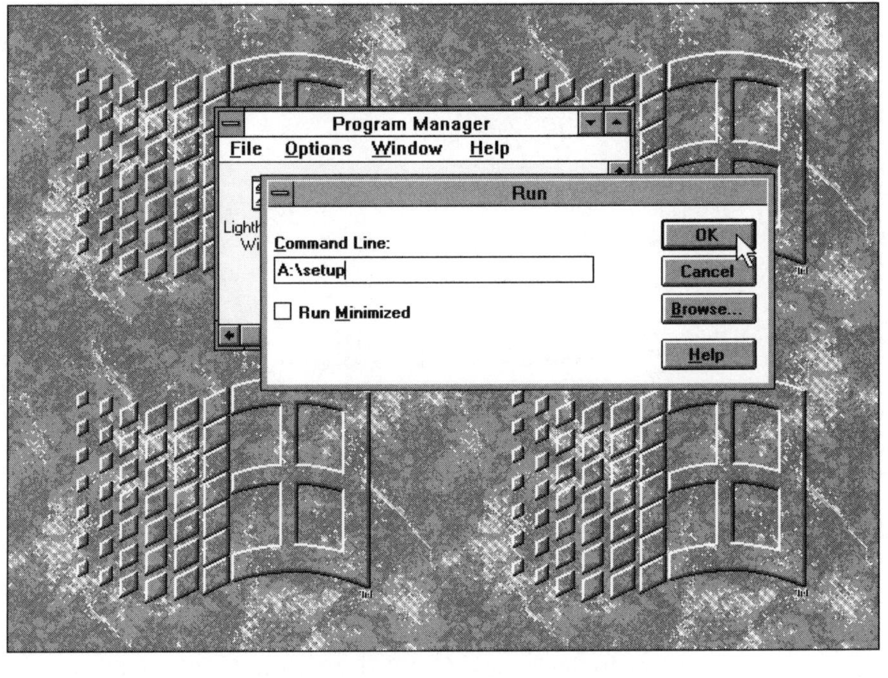

Type "A:\setup" and click OK.

The Installer will place the software in a subdirectory called "lighthou" on your internal hard disk. It also will install an Icon for the software in the Windows 3.1 Program manager.

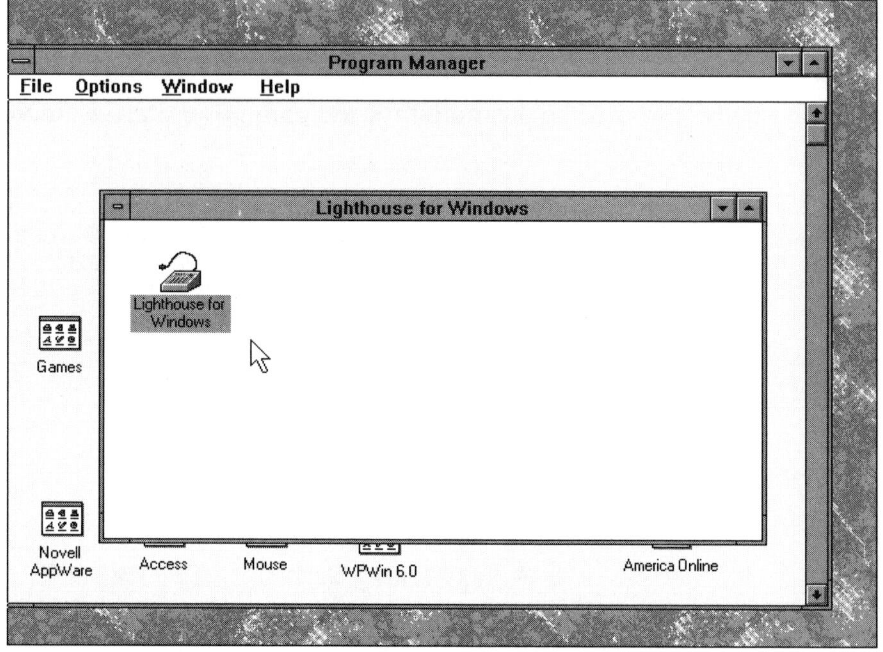

How It Works

To help you learn about the Home Control software, the following sections will lead you through a series of exercises. You'll create a sample Unit List, a sample scene, and a sample schedule.

The first thing you'll need to do is start the software.

Double-click the Lighthouse for Windows software icon to start the application.

The first time that you run the application after installing the software, the help system will open automatically (see screen below).

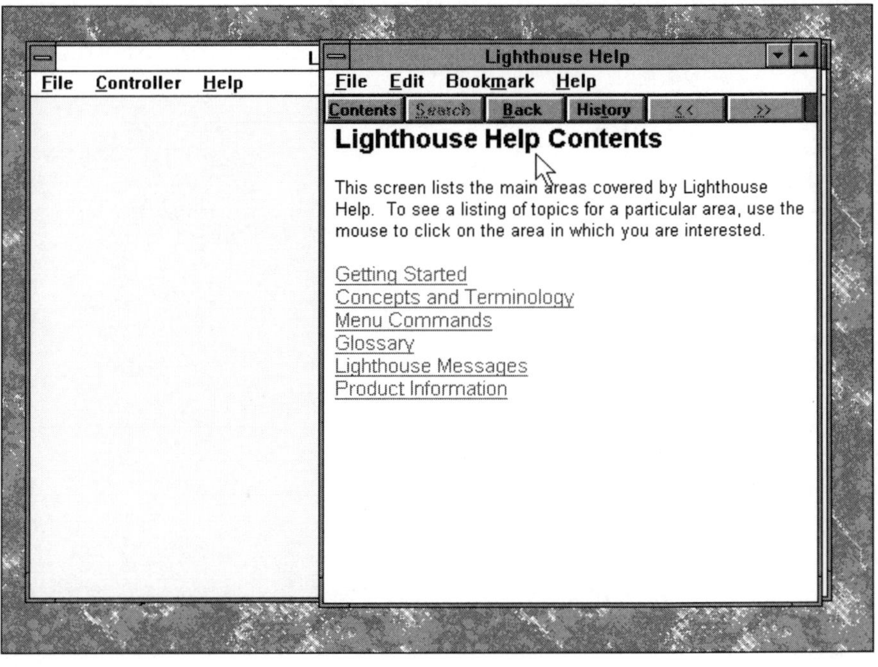

We'll cover Help later in the chapter. So for now, you'll put away the Help system.

Choose Exit from the File menu.

Now you should see the screen shown below. Note that the very first time you run the software, the help system will open automatically. There are three menus: File, Controller, and Help. First you'll check the status of the Controller. That way, you can ensure that the internal clock in the controller is set correctly. If you don't do that, all of the timed events that you create will happen at the wrong time, which would be unpleasant—if not worse.

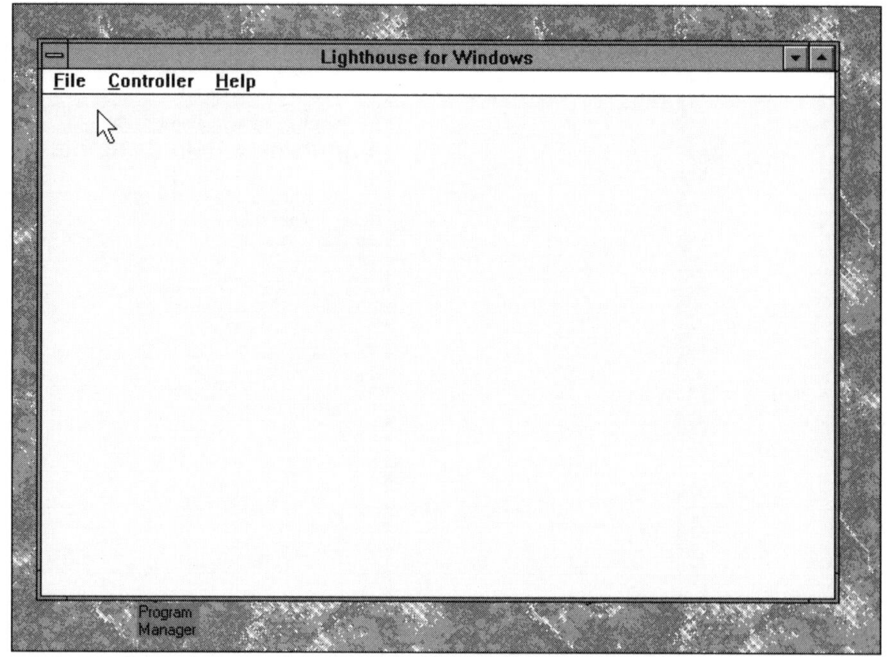

Choose Get status from the Controller menu.

You'll see a screen like the one shown below. Because you've never used the interface before, its status will be "cold," and the time shown probably will be wrong.

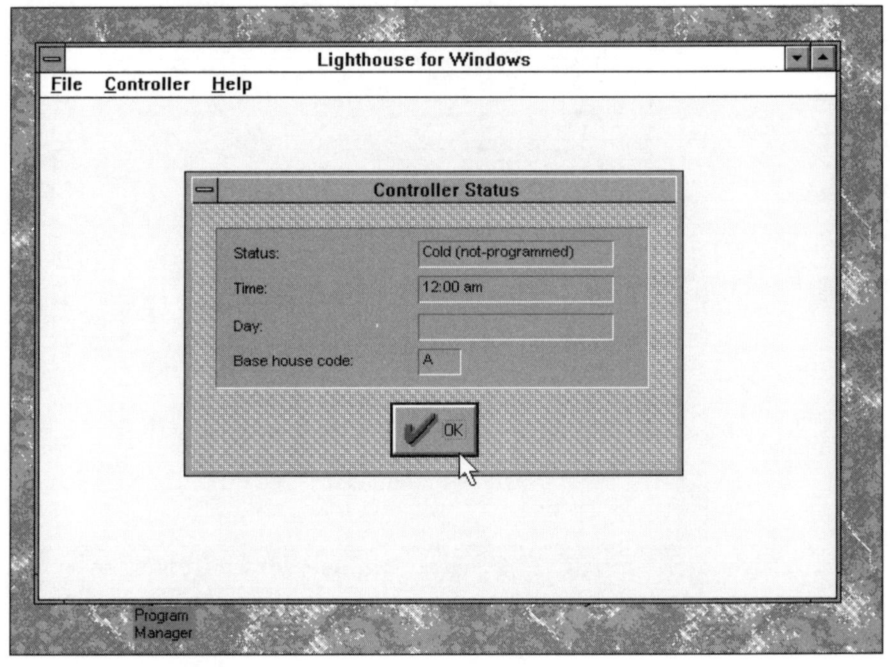

The first thing you'll need to do is set the time correctly for the interface's internal clock.

Click OK. Then choose Set clock... from the Controller menu.

You'll see a screen like the one shown below.

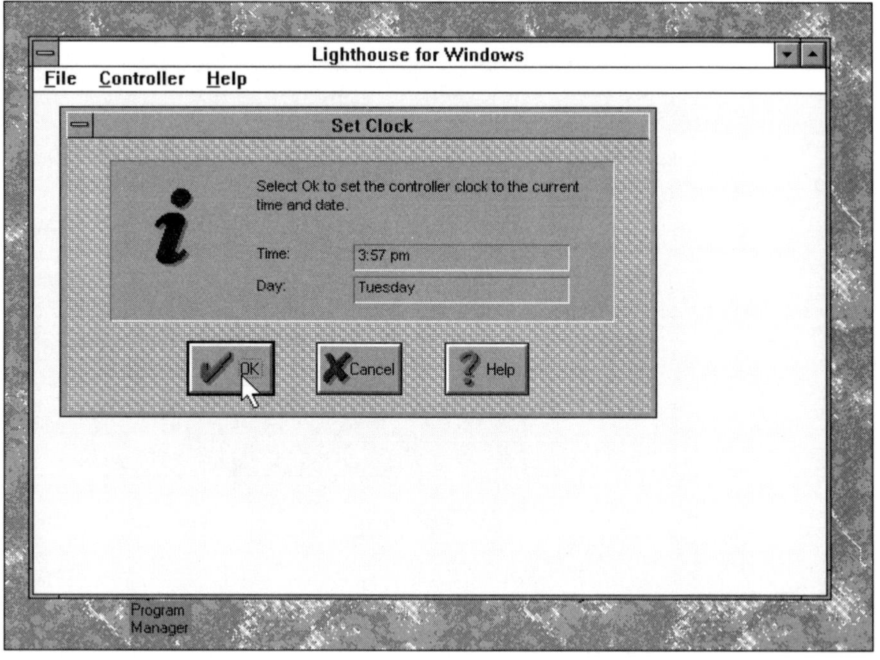

Check to make sure that the time and day shown are correct. Then click OK.

Note that if the time and day shown are wrong, you'll need to change them in the Date/Time control panel before going on.

Overview of the Lighthouse Software

Now you're ready to set up the interface to control devices in your home. But first, you'll need to open the datafile.

Choose Open from the File menu.

Three new menus will be added to the application: Lists, Reports, and Window. You'll use commands in the Lists menu to tell the interface what kind of devices you have in your home, and to define events to control these devices. The Reports menu has commands for generating documentation on your home-automation system, and the Windows menu allows you to navigate among various windows that you may have open at one time.

There are four steps to programming the interface with the Lighthouse software. First, you'll create a unit list, which is an inventory of all X-10 devices in your home.

Next you'll create a scene list. A scene describes some combination of units in your home that are on, off, or (for lamps) dimmed at the same time. For example, a scene called "morning" might specify that lights in the bedroom, dining room, and hallway are on, but that the front porch light is off.

After you've defined a list of scenes, you'll create a schedule, which defines when various scenes should be in effect. For example, you might specify that the morning scene should start at 8:00 AM, the day scene at 10:00 AM, and the evening scene at 6:00 PM.

This will provide you with a great deal of flexibility and control. You can group several devices together and create timed events to control them, then quickly and easily modify the timed events for all devices in the scene.

Here's an example: You have a scene that consists of 10 lamps all being turned on and dimmed to 50%. You create a schedule that says this scene will occur every day at 6:00 PM. Then, later in the year, you decide that you'd rather have the lights turn on at 5:00 PM. Instead of setting timed events for all 10 lamps, you can just change the time that the scene occurs to 5:00 PM. Easy!

Creating a Unit List

Remember, the first step in programming the interface is to create a unit list. This will define all of the X-10 modules that you have in your home-automation system.

Choose Unit list from the Lists menu.

You'll see a window like the one shown below.

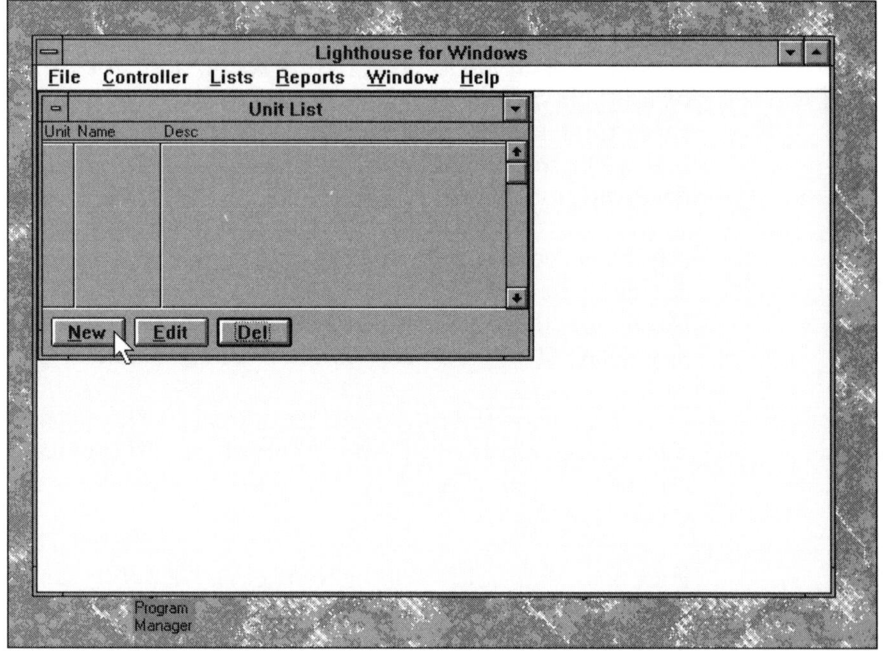

Click New.

A dialog will appear, letting you enter information for the new unit.

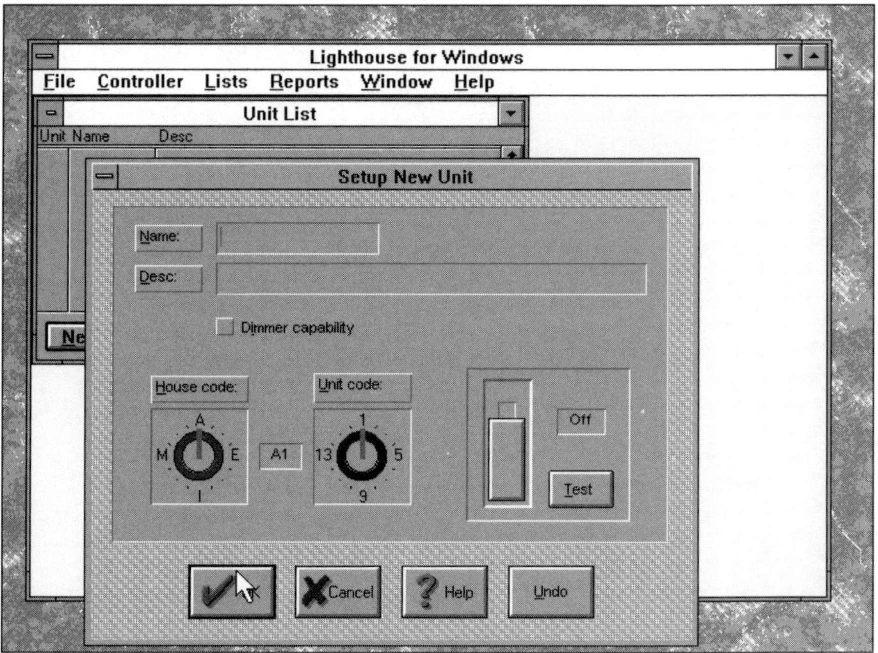

Here's what you'll do to set up the unit:

- Enter a name and a description for the unit.
- Select the checkbox labeled "Dimmer capability" if the unit that you're controlling is connected to a Lamp Module or a switch that can dim incandescent lights.
- Select a Housecode and a Unit Code by clicking the appropriate locations on the dials.
- (Optional) Test the unit by selecting a dimmer level and clicking Test. The interface then will send a command to the unit to turn on and dim to that level.

If you are confused at any point while using the application, click the Help button for explanations or hints that might help you get "unstuck."

Using the instructions outlined above, set the Housecode and Unit Code for the new unit to "A" and "5," respectively, to match those that you gave to the test module described at the beginning of the chapter. When you are finished, click OK.

At this point, you normally would add similar information about all devices that are part of your home-automation system. For the purpose of the example, though, we are going to assume that you've entered information about three other modules and that your screen looks like the one shown below.

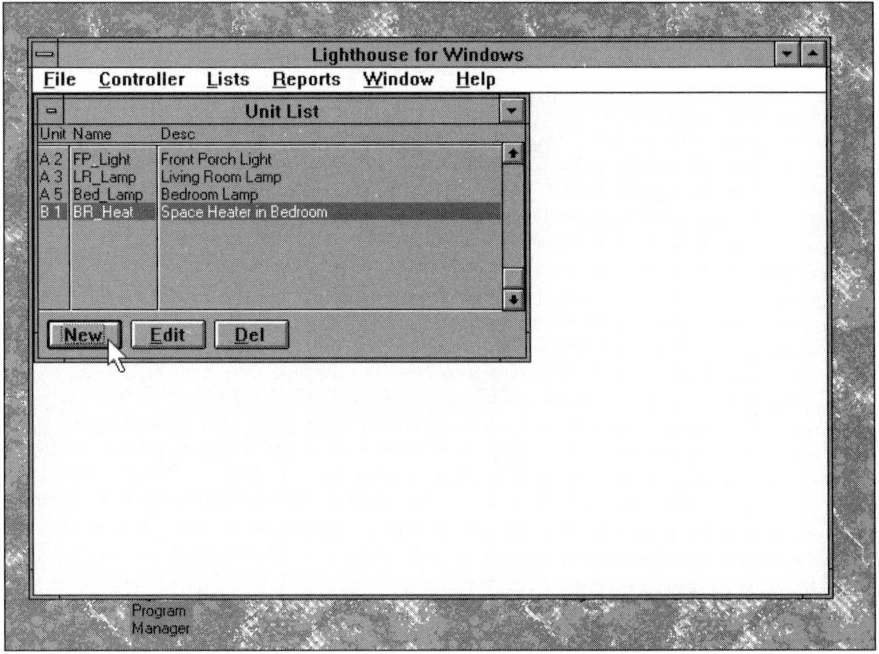

Defining Scenes

Once you've created a unit list defining all of the X-10 devices in your home, you'll need to arrange these units into **scenes**. The steps that follow will show you how you'll create a simple scene using the unit list you created above. This is a scene you might want in place when you get home from work: The front porch light, the living room light, and the space heater in the bedroom are all on. The first thing you'll need to do is open the scene list.

Choose Scene list from the Lists menu.

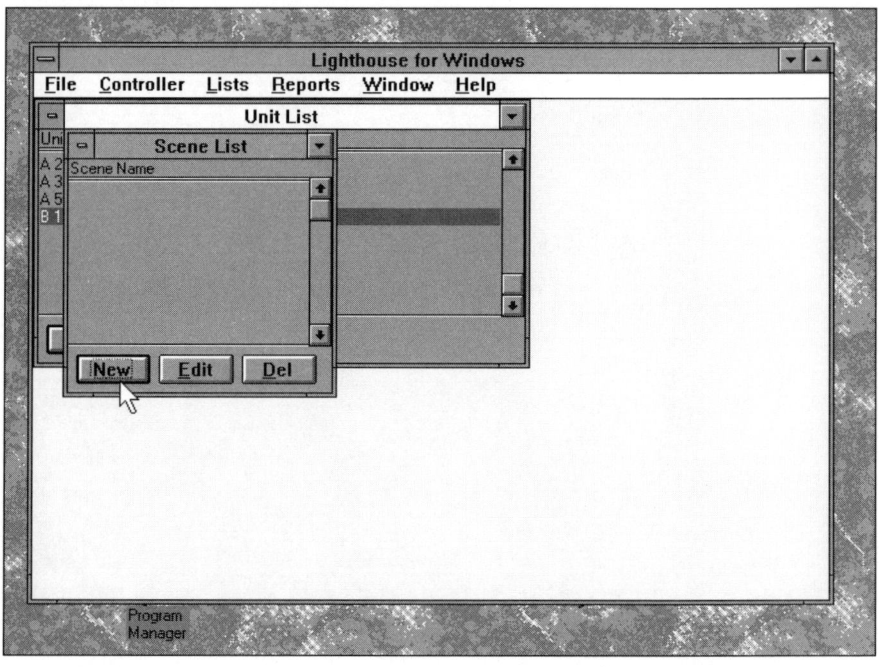

The scene list will be empty because you haven't defined a scene yet.

Click New to create a new scene.

A dialog will appear, allowing you to define a new scene. First you'll type a name for the scene. Later you'll create **schedules** that determine when various scenes are in effect. You therefore should choose a name that will be meaningful when you are defining schedules and determining when various scenes should be active. In general, a scene might describe a time of day, such as "night" or "dawn," or an event, such as "party" or "romantic dinner." In this case, you'll be defining how you'd like your home to behave around dusk, so "Early Evening" is a good name for the scene.

Type "Early Evening" to name the scene.

Next you'll specify which devices should be on, off, or dimmed for the scene. You'll set the front porch light first.

Click on the button labeled "FP_Light," right below the scene name.

A sliding scale will appear, letting you specify whether the lamp should be on, off, or dimmed to a certain intensity. In this case, you'll want the lamp to be dimmed to 63%.

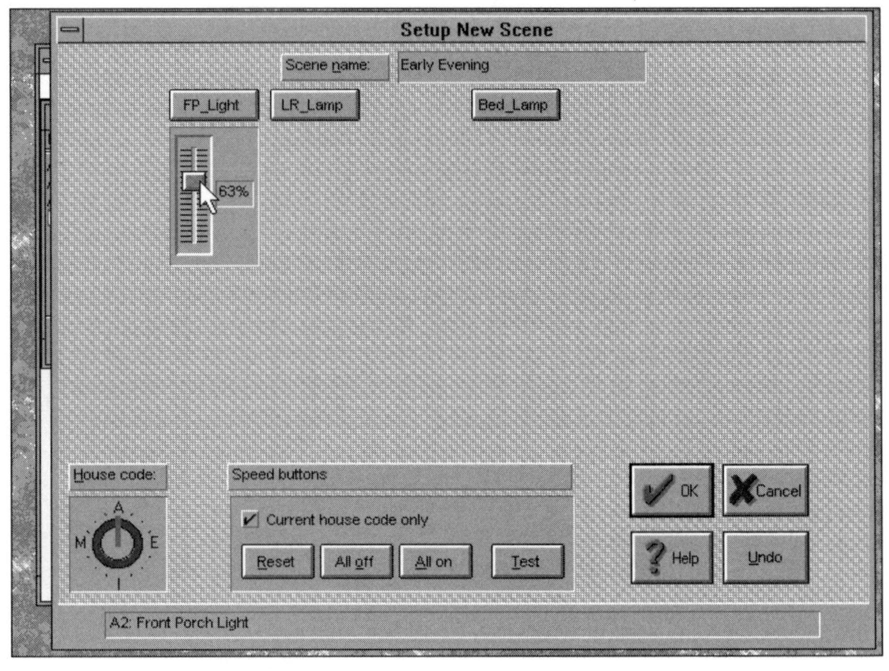

Click and drag the sliding scale to set the intensity of the lamp at 63%. Then use the same technique to set the intensity of the living room lamp to 81%.

Your window now should look like this:

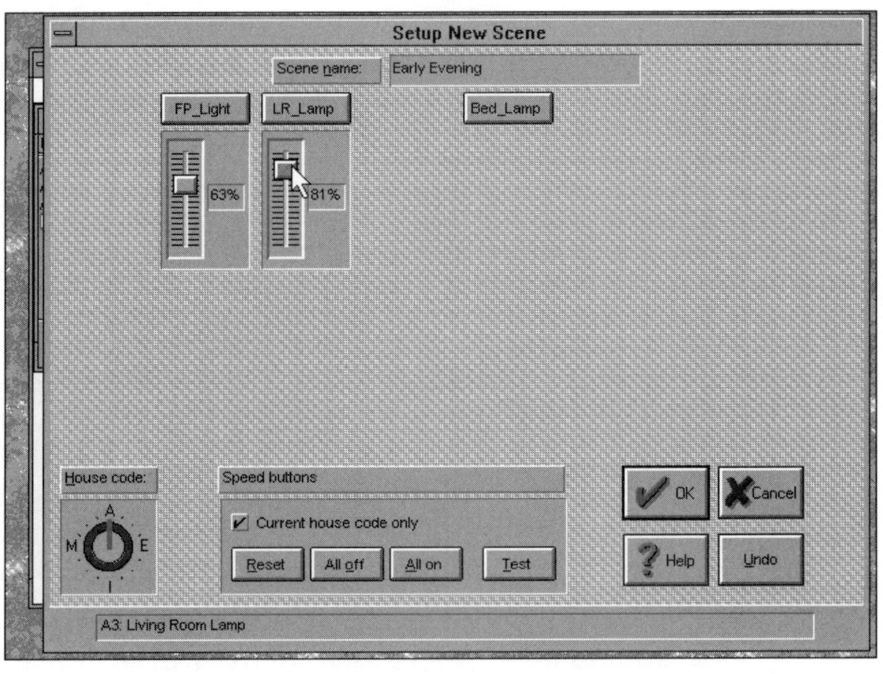

The last thing you'll do to complete the scene is to specify that the space heater should be on. But there's no button for BR_Heater. Where is it?

Look at the lower-left corner of the screen, where you'll see a dial set to Housecode A. Remember that when we created the unit list, we put the space heater on Housecode B to separate it from the lights in the house. To specify that the heater should be on for your scene, you'll need to change Housecodes.

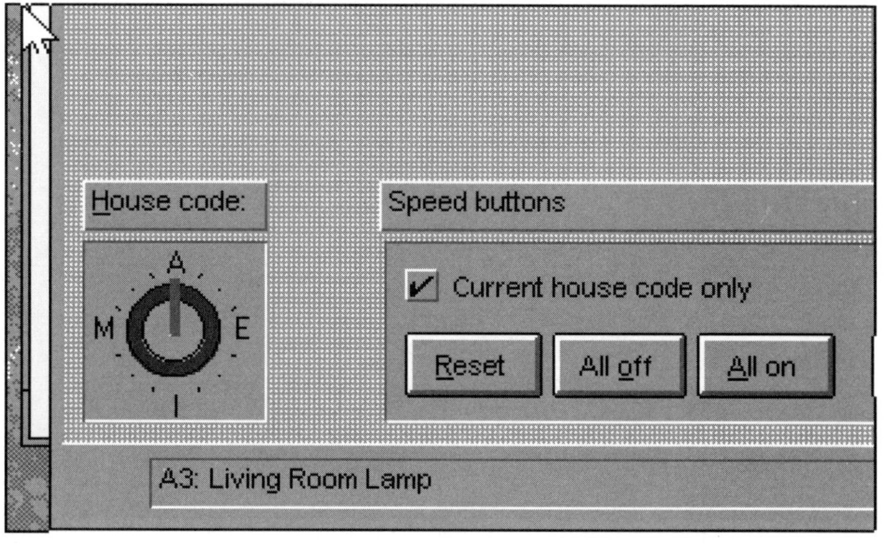

Click the appropriate spot on the dial to change to Housecode B.

Your screen now should look like the one shown below.

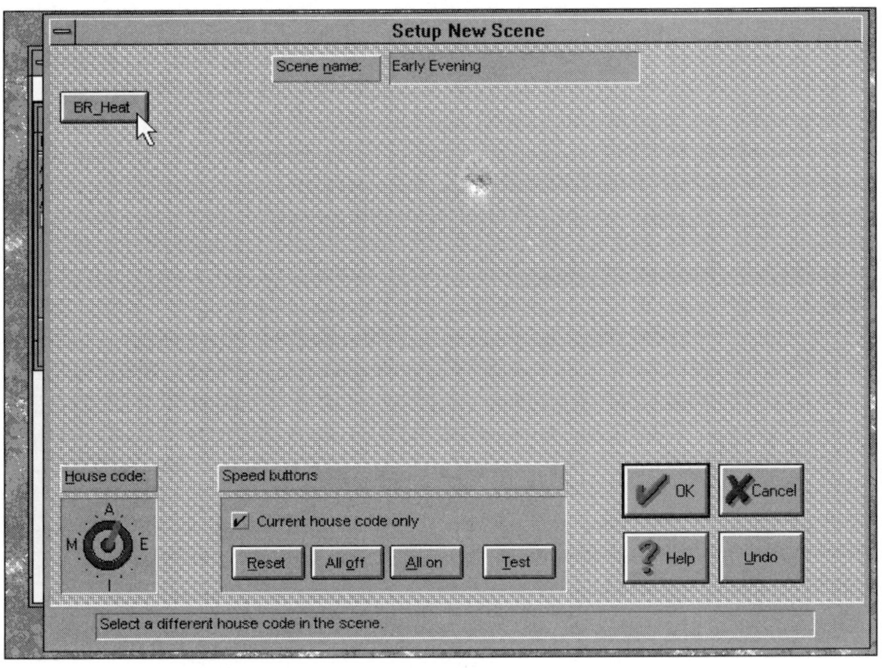

Now you'll specify that the heater should be on when the scene is active.

Click the button labeled "BR_Heat." When the control appears, click and drag it up until the word "on" appears to the right. Then release the mouse button.

Now the space heater will come on whenever the scene is active.

Before closing the dialog box, you should take a quick look at the Speed Buttons at the bottom of the screen. You can use these to make scene editing more efficient. Here's what the buttons do:

Reset. Use this button to cancel any edits that you've made to the scene already.

All off and All on. These buttons set all devices to off or on.

Test. Use this button to test the scene to ensure that it works the way you want it to. This is particularly useful for ensuring that lights are dimmed to the appropriate level.

Note that you can restrict the speed buttons to work only on the devices currently shown on the screen by checking the box labeled "Current house code only."

You've now finished creating and editing your first scene. Congratulations!

Click OK.

Creating Schedules

At this point, you've defined all of the modules you use in your system and created a scene that specifies how these units should be grouped together and controlled to create a particular effect. The last thing to do before programming the interface is to create a schedule that specifies when this scene (and any others) should be active. To make the schedule more realistic, we are going to assume that you have followed the directions in the previous section to create three more scenes: one for early morning, one for day, and one for night. Assuming you've done this, your screen should look like the one shown below.

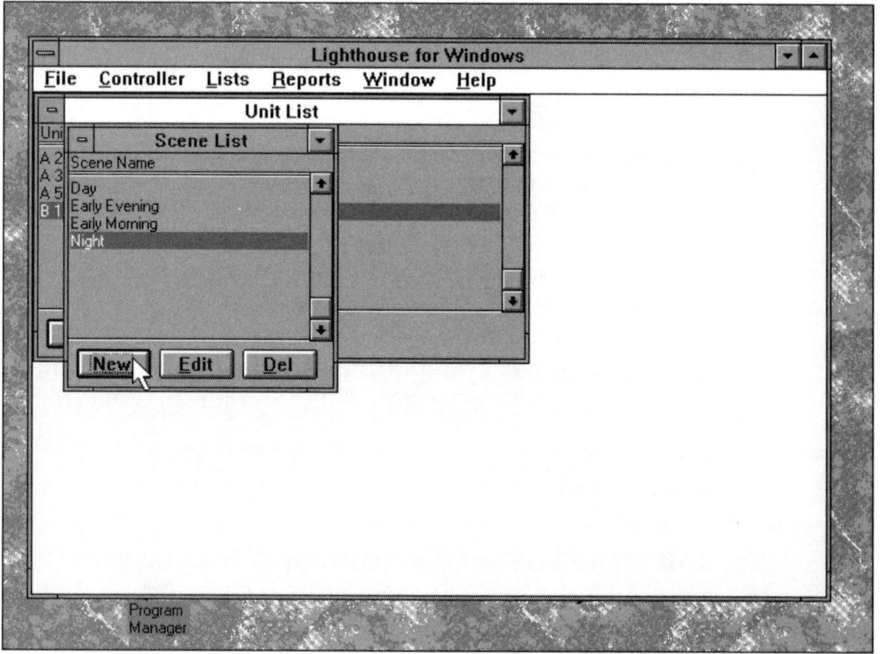

Now you're ready to create a schedule.

Choose Schedule list from the Lists menu.

The schedule list will appear on the screen. There are no schedules listed because you have not created any. You'll fix that now.

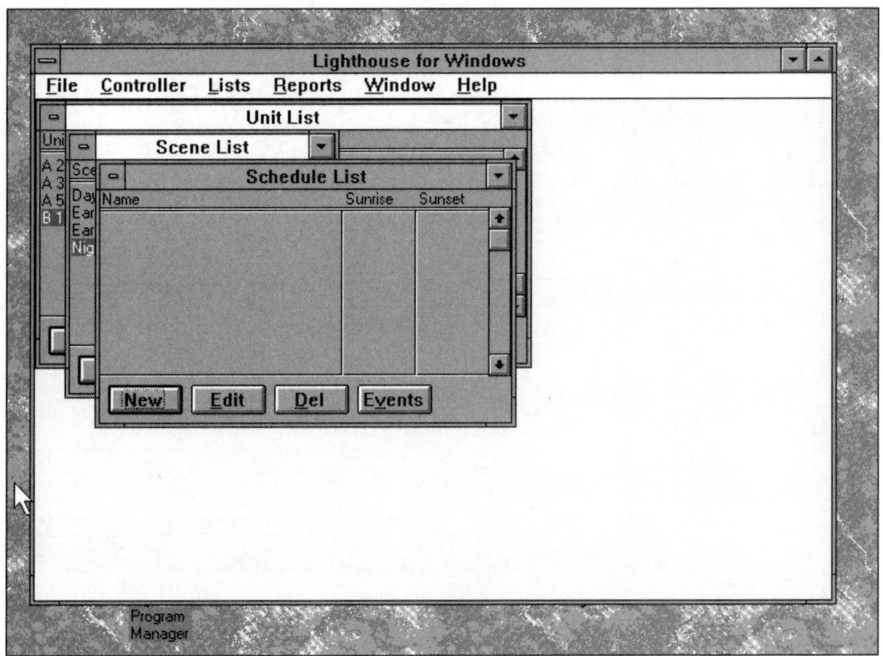

Click New to create a new schedule.

A dialog box will appear, asking you to name the new schedule and

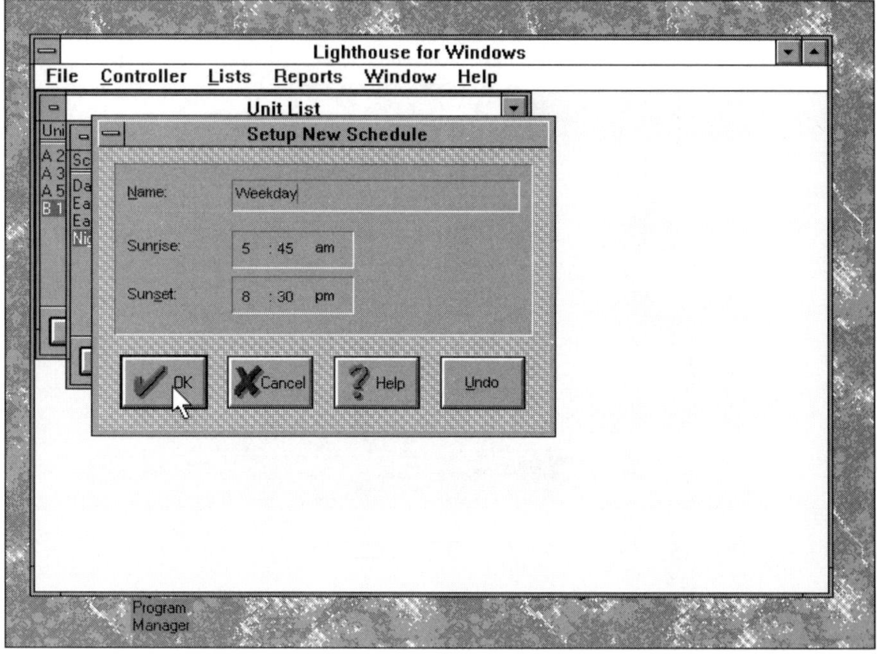

to specify the times for sunrise and sunset. You'll specify sunrise and sunset here so that later you can define timed events that happen at a certain time before or after sunset. That way, as the seasons change, you can just change the time for sunrise and sunset here, and all of your scenes will still appear at the right time (so the Early Evening scene can come on at 4:00 PM in the winter, and 7:30 PM in the summer, for example). We won't change the sunrise or sunset for this example.

Type "Weekday" for the name. Then click OK.

You're probably thinking, "Why did we name it Weekday?" Or at least you should be. We choose that name so that we could create another schedule later called Weekend. Still puzzled? We'll explain in a few pages.

Now your screen should look like the one shown below.

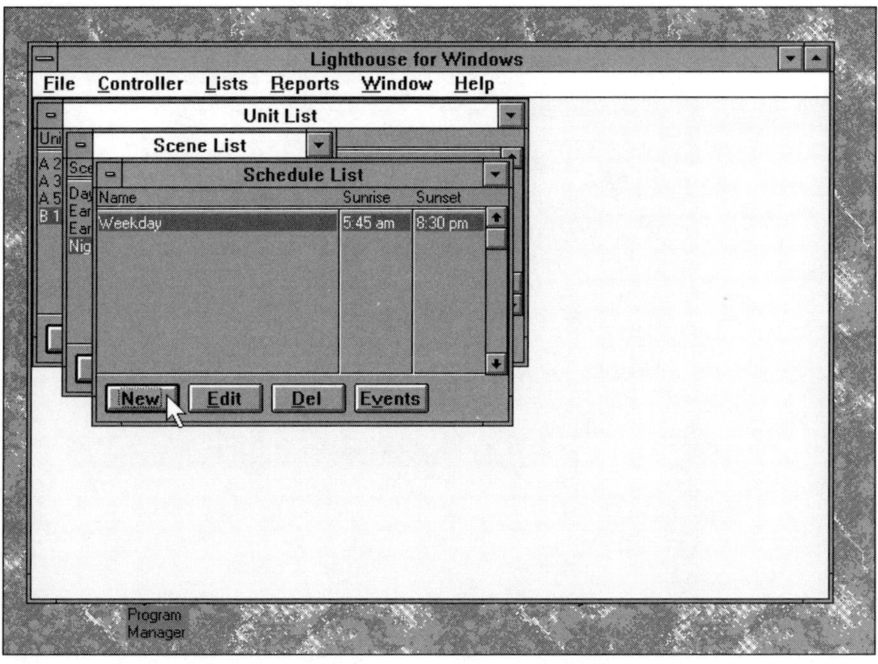

You'll need to tell the schedule when the various scenes should be active. You'll do that now by defining Events for the schedule.

Click Events.

You'll be presented with the event list for the schedule, which is

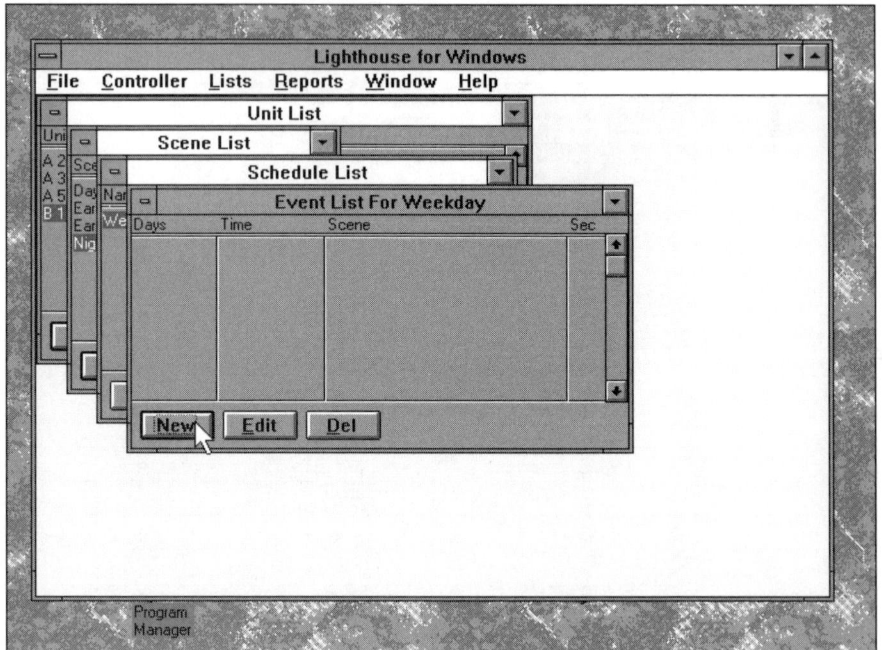

empty because you haven't defined any events yet. You'll fix that next.

Click New.

A dialog will appear allowing you to define the event. There are three things that you'll need to do to define the event: Specify what scene should be active, choose the time when the event should occur, and select the days of the week on which the event should execute. You'll define an event now that will activate the Early Evening scene every weekday half an hour after sunset.

First you'll select the scene.

Choose Early Evening from the pop-up list at the top of the screen.

Next you'll specify a time of day for the event. You have three choices. You can specify an exact time, such as 5:00 PM or 12:00 noon. Alternatively, you can specify that the event take place at a certain time relative to sunset or sunrise. In this case, you'll want the Early Evening scene to activate half an hour after sunset.

Click the diamond labeled "After sunset by," Then type "30" in the box.

Clicking the box labeled "Security Variations" will cause the event to occur at a random time one hour before or after the time you've specified above. This is a useful feature when you want to convince ne'er-do-wells that someone's home, even when the house is empty.

Check the box labeled "Security variations."

At this point, we'll pause to re-examine the schedule name that we chose a little while earlier. Now it should make sense to you why we want separate schedules for Weekday and Weekend. During the week, you might want certain scenes to occur at different times. For example, you might want all of the lights in the house to turn off at 11:00 PM on weeknights, but not until 1:00 AM on the weekends, when you tend to stay out later.

Next you'll specify that this event should happen only on weekdays.

In the space next to "Day of week," click on the diamond labeled "Selected days." Then select every day except Saturday and Sunday.

Your screen now should look like the one shown below.

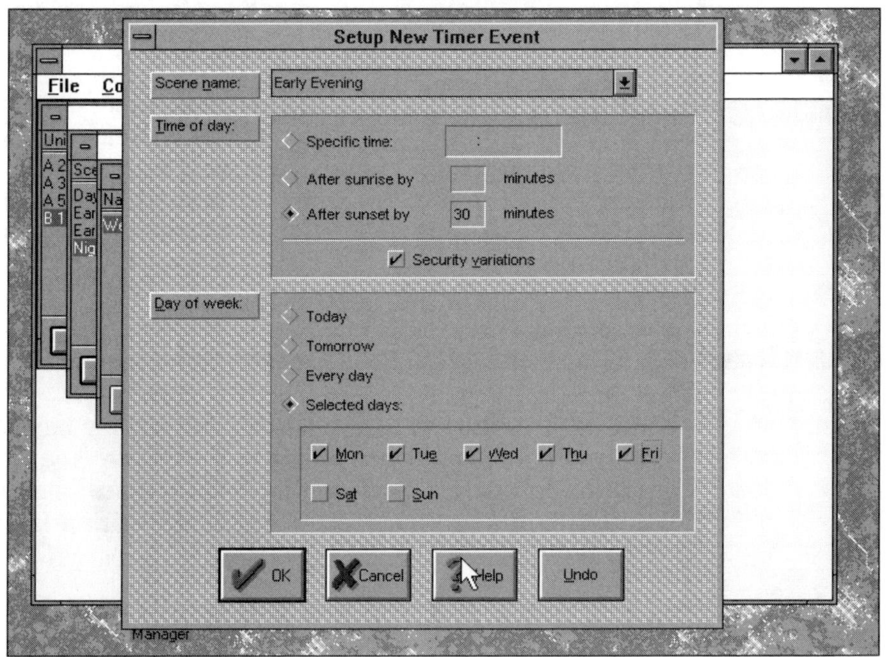

Click OK to finish defining the event.

Once again you'll see the Event List for the schedule Weekday, but this time, your new event will be included.

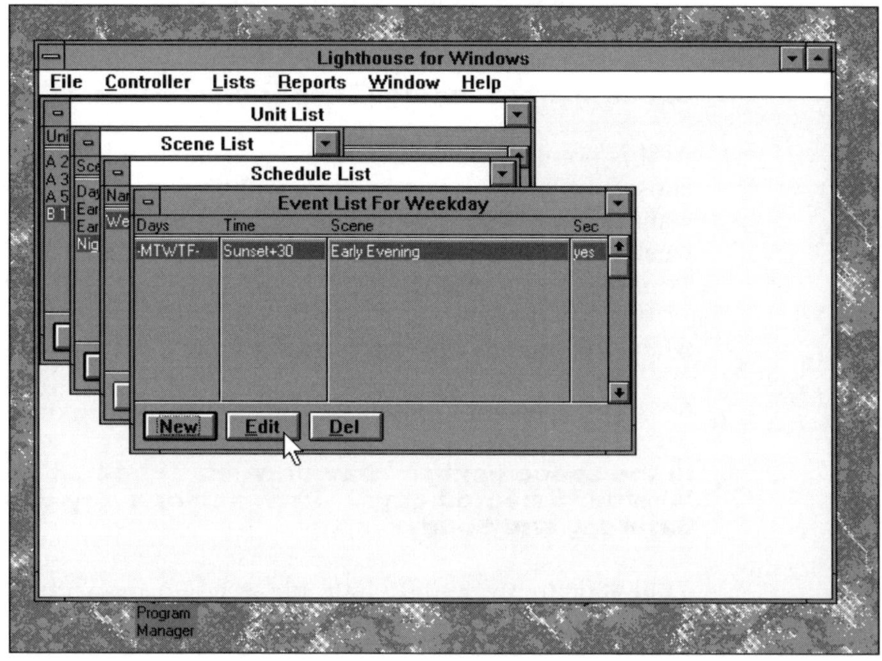

At this point, you normally would define other events to activate other scenes throughout the day and then create a second schedule for the weekend, with associated events to control scenes on Saturday and Sunday. What you've already done is enough for this example, though, and we'll leave further customization for you to do on your own.

Downloading Commands to the Interface

Up until this point, all of the work you've done has been stored in the database files that the Lighthouse software keeps on your computer. In order to activate the system, you'll simply download this information to your X-10 Home Automation Interface. You'll do that now.

Choose Download from the Controller menu.

A dialog will be displayed while the appropriate commands are being downloaded to the controller. Once the commands are downloaded, the controller no longer needs to be attached to the computer. You can move the controller anywhere in the house, and it still will control devices according to the schedule you've created in this example. The only time you'll need to reconnect it to the computer is when you want to change something—for example, when you want to add devices to the system, modify scene layouts, or change scenes and times in schedules.

Creating Reports

Sometimes you'll want to have a log or report to help you plan revisions and updates to your home automation system. The Lighthouse software can produce Unit, Scene, and Schedule reports.

To access any of the Lighthouse reports, you'll choose the appropriate command from the Report menu. The report will be displayed on the screen, where you can review it. You also can print the report to keep a permanent record.

Getting Help

Even though the Lighthouse software is well-written and easy-to-use, you may get stuck from time to time. If that happens, the Lighthouse help system should be able to get you out of trouble. To access the help system, just choose the appropriate command from the Help menu. Here's an overview of your options.

Contents. This is the major source of help information, arranged by subject. To see information about a particular topic, just click on the underlined topic name, and the help system will load the appropriate information automatically.

Using Help. If you're having problems using the Contents portion of the help system, this is the place to go. You'll be presented with step-by-step instructions for navigating the help system.

Product Information. This option provides you with information about controllers and modules available from X-10 (USA), Inc.

About Lighthouse... You'll find information about the developer of Lighthouse software.

Exiting from the Program

When you're satisfied with the work you've done, you'll exit the program as you would any standard Windows application.

Choose Exit from the File menu.

You'll be back at the familiar Windows desktop.

Clearing the Interface

If you ever want to completely clear the interface of all timed events, you'll just remove the battery and unplug the interface for a few seconds. This clears all of the memory.

Moving the Interface

Once you've downloaded commands to the interface, you can move it anywhere and it still will execute your timed events. That is, you don't have to leave it connected to your computer. The only time that you need to connect the interface to your PC is when you want to update the timed events in the interface or to control devices immediately.

Where To Go From Here

Now you should know everything you need to build a complete home-automation system around the X-10 Home Automation Interface. As you add devices to your system, you should have no trouble adding them to your unit list and scene descriptions.

As always, if you have problems, see Appendix B, "Troubleshooting," beginning on page 233.

Home Automation Systems, Inc.

151 Kalmus Drive, Suite L-4
Costa Mesa, CA 92626
Phone: (800) SMART-HOME
(714) 708-0610
Fax: (714) 708-0614

PLATO for Windows
PLATO for Windows TW

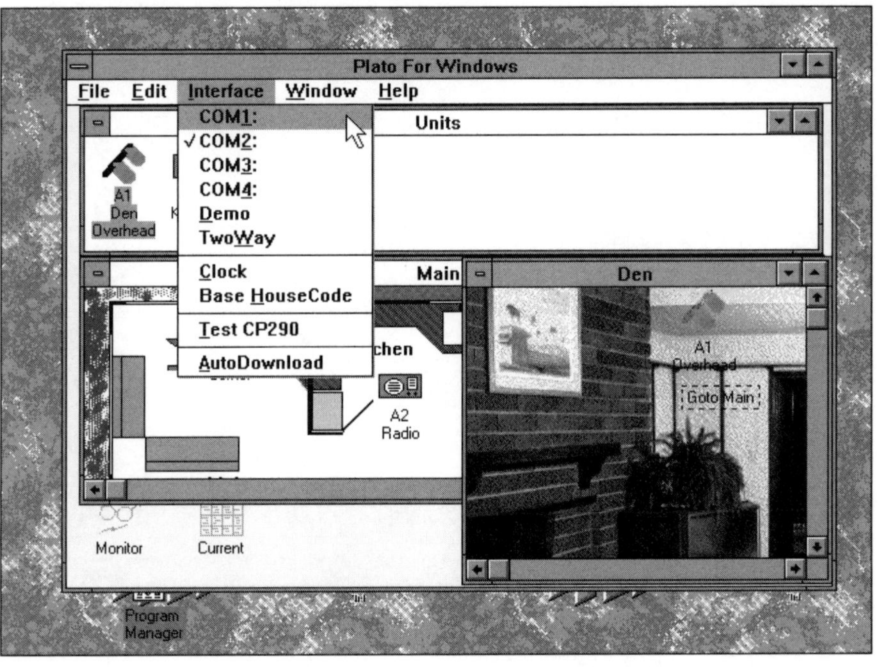

PLATO for Windows is a graphical interface for programming and controlling X-10 devices using the CP-290 Home Automation Interface. It provides advanced event scheduling features and allows you to use floor plans or scanned photographs to represent rooms in the home. Icons that represent X-10 devices can be overlaid on these images. A slider bar on the icons allows you to adjust the brightness of lamps. PLATO for Windows TW adds the ability to receive X-10 signals and execute macros. Voice recognition and infrared control options are available.

A demonstration video and information packet are available for $29 from Home Automation Systems. Ask for part number HAS-1400.

Price: Contact Home Automation Systems

7 *Apple Macintosh*

Overview

Assuming that you haven't skipped right to this chapter, you've already learned a lot about home automation. In fact, you already know enough to build a very functional system that will control lights, appliances, and even a security system.

In this chapter, you'll learn how to control a reasonably complex home-automation system with a Home Automation Interface and an Apple Macintosh computer.

Using the interface with a Macintosh computer gives you several advantages over systems that use the other controllers described in this book:

- You can see icons representing each module on the computer screen, so it's easy to remember what modules control which devices.
- You can control modules set with *any* Housecode and *any* Unit Code; this means that you can control up to 16 x 16 = 256 devices!
- You can program up to 128 different timed events.
- You can program each module to go on and off at specific times, on certain days of the week.
- You can program Lamp Modules to dim or brighten to certain intensities at certain times.

As you go through this chapter, you'll first learn how to attach the Home Automation Interface to your Macintosh. Then you'll learn how to create **module icons** and how to use them to control devices both immediately and with timed events. Finally you'll learn some advanced commands for displaying different floor plans on the screen and managing the interface.

When you've finished reading this chapter, you should be able to use your Macintosh to turn devices on and off both immediately and by using timed events. You'll also know how to create a customized floor plan for the Home Automation software, so you can more easily identify modules in your home.

This chapter assumes that you're familiar with the operation of the Macintosh computer: using menus, dragging, double-clicking, and so on. If these terms are not familiar, review the owner's guide before continuing.

Setup

Before you try to use the interface with your computer, you'll need to ensure that the interface is functioning properly. Here's how to do that:

- Set the address of a Lamp Module to A1, attach the module to a lamp, and plug the module into an electrical outlet.
- Next plug the interface into a different electrical outlet. (Although you can use any electrical outlet in the house, choose one in the same room so that you don't have to run around a lot.)
- Press the top of the rocker button labeled "1" on the interface to turn on the lamp. Once the lamp is on, press the bottom of the same button to turn off the lamp.
- Set the Lamp Module to A2 and repeat the preceding step with rocker button 2.
- Continue as outlined above, testing rocker buttons 3 through 8.

If you experience any problems, be sure that you have set the Lamp Module correctly. If you still have problems, call X-10 (USA) Inc.'s Customer Service Department for help (the telephone number is listed in the "Compatible Products" section of the "Controllers" chapter, beginning on page 54).

One last thing you should do before connecting the interface to your computer is to install a nine-volt battery in the compartment on the back of the interface. The battery will provide backup power to the interface when it is not plugged into an outlet or when the electricity is off. Without the battery, you'll have to reprogram every timed event whenever the interface is unplugged or the power goes off.

Connecting the Interface to Your Computer

Setting up the interface is simple. First you'll attach it to your Macintosh computer, using the serial cable included with the interface.

Locate the serial cable included with the interface. Then plug it into the back of the interface.

Once you've examined the connectors on both ends of the serial cable, it should be obvious which end goes into the interface.

Next you'll connect the serial cable to the modem port of the Macintosh. To locate the modem port, look at the group of connectors, or **ports,** on the back of your Macintosh. Each port is designated by a different icon embossed on the plastic just above or below it. The modem port has an icon of a telephone next to it. Now you're ready to connect the cable to the Macintosh.

Plug the other end of the serial cable into the modem port on the Macintosh.

Next you'll copy the X-10 software onto your hard disk.

Make a folder on your hard disk and name it "Home Automation," or something similar. When you've finished, insert the X-10 disk into your Macintosh computer's disk drive and copy all of the files on the disk into the new folder.

If you open the Home Automation folder you've just created, here's what you should see:

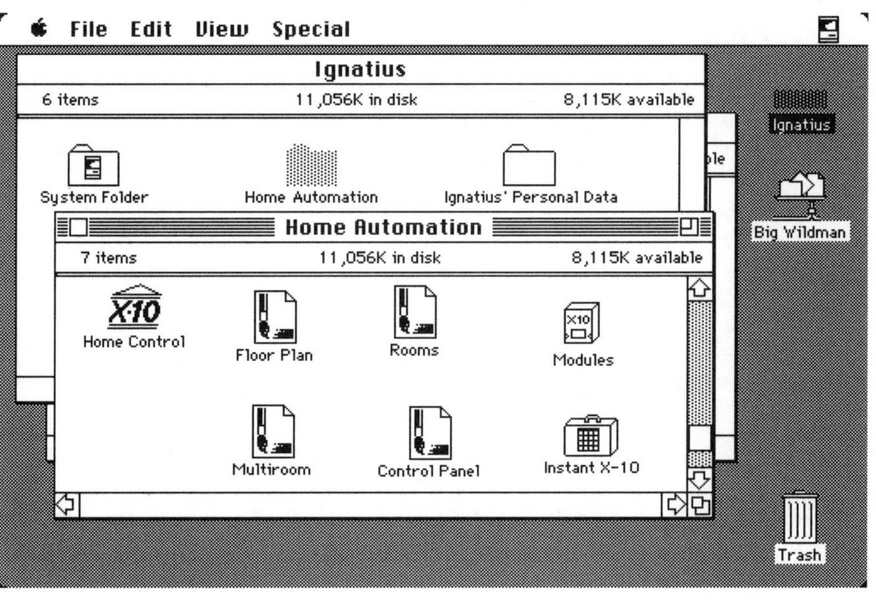

Now you should be ready to go.

Getting Started

The first thing you'll do is start the application.

Double-click the Home Control application to open it.

Because this is the first time you're using the interface, it contains no data, and you'll see the dialog box shown below:

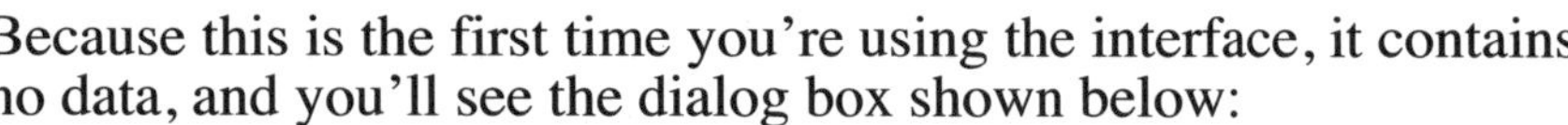

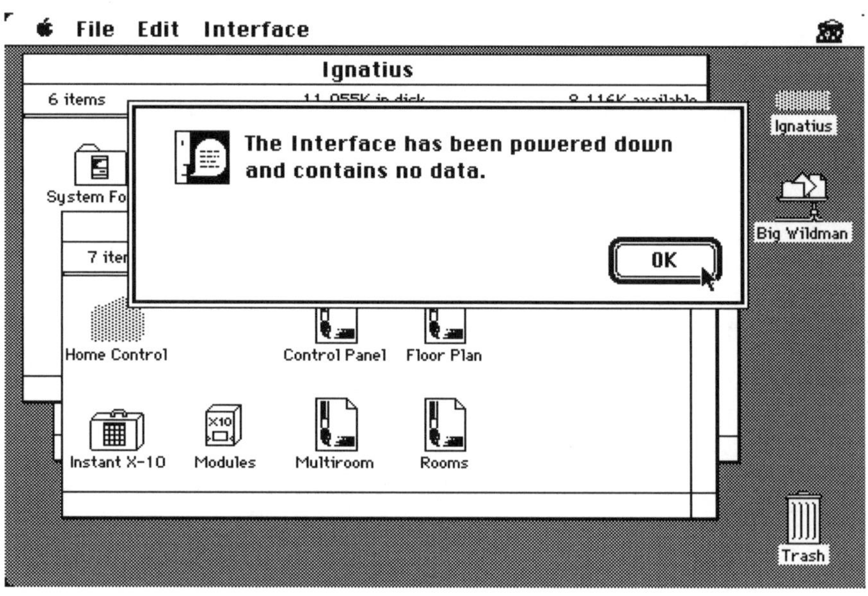

This, of course, is not a life-threatening matter. It just means that you'll have to send information to the interface before you can use it to control things.

Click OK.

You can use the interface for timed events, just as you can with the Mini Timer described in Chapter 2. The interface has a clock that it uses to support timed events, and the first piece of information you need to give the interface is the time and the day of the week. Because your Macintosh knows this information, the X-10 software offers to set the interface clock to the same time as the Macintosh clock.

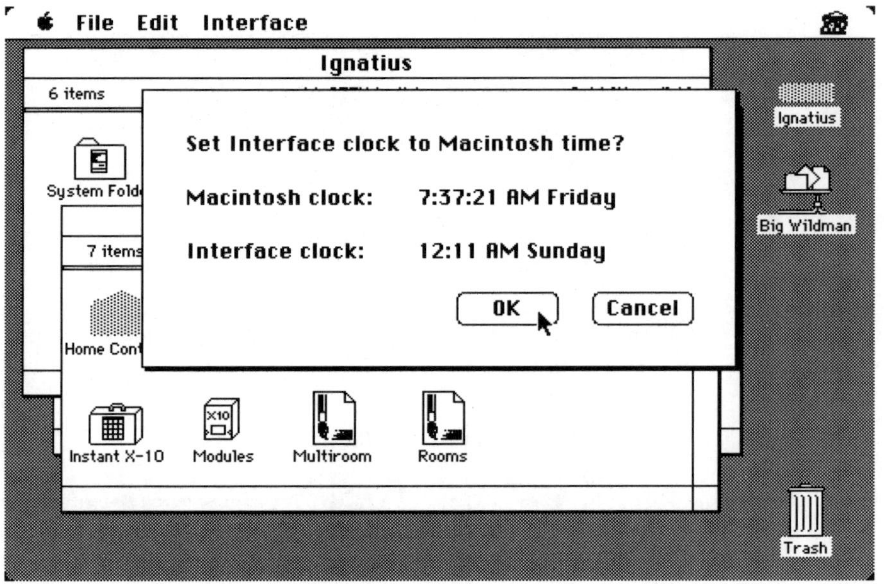

Click OK to set the interface clock.

Note that if the clock in your Macintosh is not set correctly, then the clock in the interface will not be set correctly either. If necessary, refer to the section called "Setting the Interface Clock" later in this chapter.

Now you should be face to face with the main screen of the X-10 Home Automation software. The screen is divided into two areas:

the **Control Area** and the **Module Map.** The Control Area will be on the left. An overview of the controls is shown below.

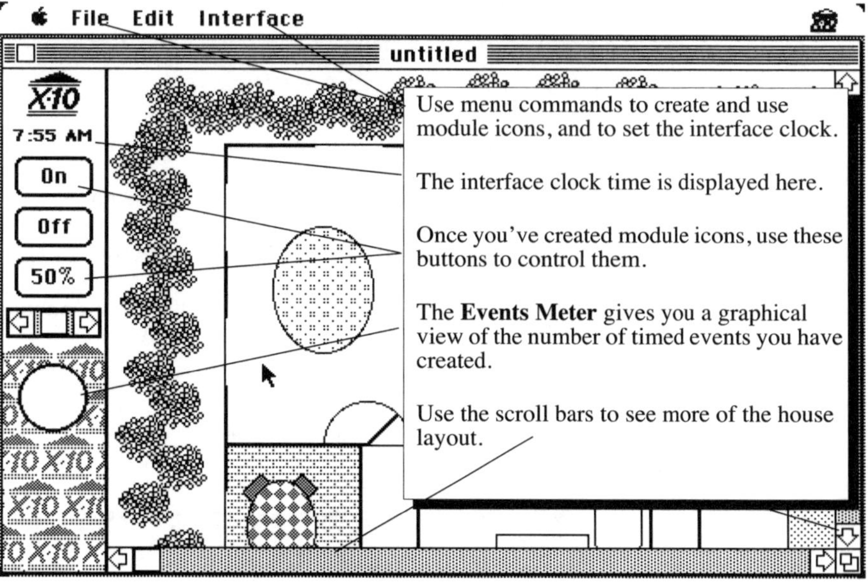

The Module Map is on the right. It consists of a MacPaint-style diagram, called the background, and a group of module icons. The default MacPaint background (the one you see now) represents the floor plan of a sample home. If you're like us, the floor plan doesn't look at all like your house. Don't worry—you can change it later.

You'll also create the other part of the Module Map—the module icons—later. Then you'll use the icons to control a lamp that you'll set up where you are working. Later you can use what you've learned to control other devices: appliances, sprinklers, outdoor lighting, and so on. Before you start creating module icons, though, it's a good idea to test the interface to make sure that it's functioning properly. You'll learn how to test the interface now.

Testing the Interface

The interface software includes a self-test that you can run to ensure that it's operating correctly. Unfortunately, when you run the self-test, you'll erase all of the information in the interface. Therefore, it's a good idea to run the self-test now, before you've created any timed events or stored any module information.

Choose Self Test... from the Interface menu.

A dialog box will appear, asking if you're sure you want to run the self-test and warning you that doing so will erase all data in the interface.

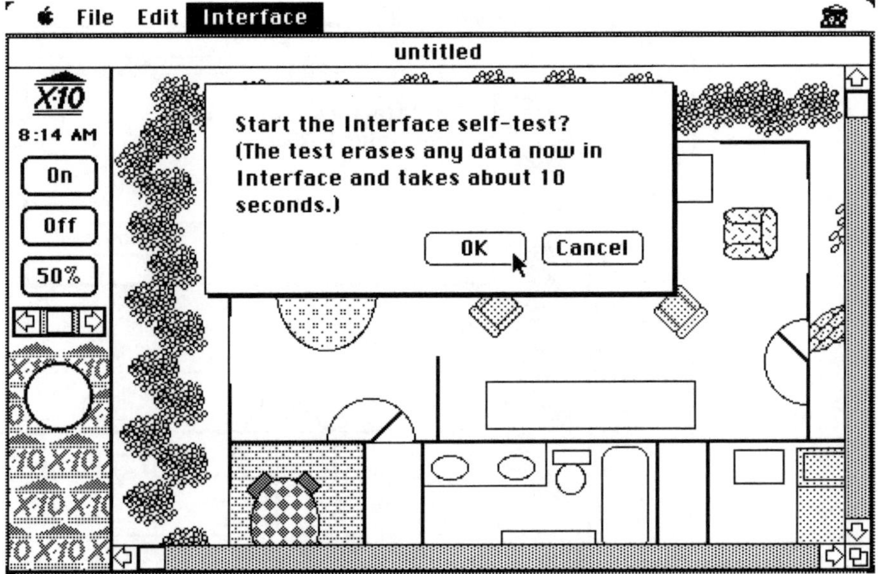

Click OK.

Next a dialog box will tell you that the test is running. If your interface has no problems, you'll see the dialog box shown below when the test is finished.

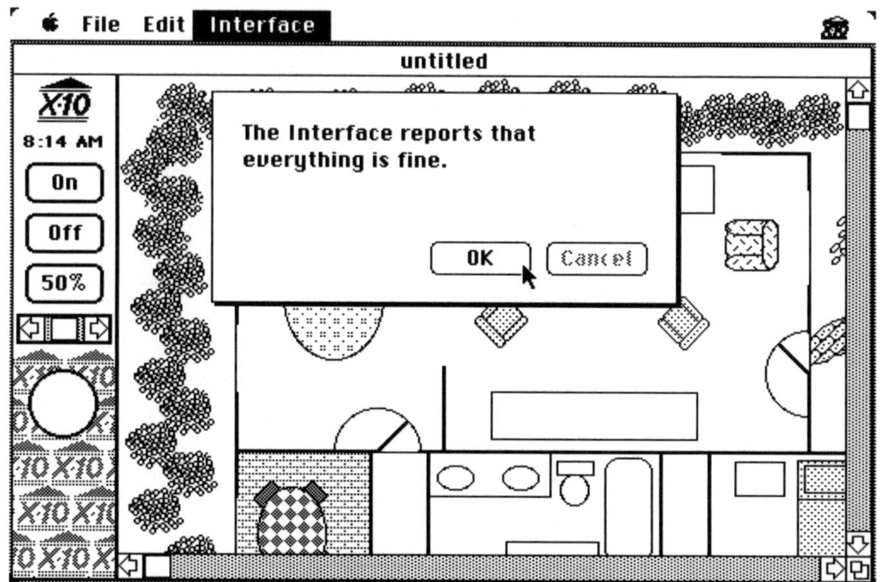

Click OK.

If you see a dialog box telling you that the interface is having problems, you should return the interface and exchange it for a new one.

Now you're ready to begin creating module icons and controlling devices.

Creating and Using a Module Icon

Like most Macintosh applications, the Home Automation application has a graphical user interface. To control devices, you create an **icon** to represent the device and then choose menu commands to set up and control the device.

You'll create a module icon now. For this simple example, you should first set a Lamp Module to Housecode C and Unit Code 5, attach it to a lamp, and plug the module into an electrical outlet in the same room as your Macintosh. That way, when you're doing the exercise that follows, you'll be able to verify that everything is working correctly as you go along. Note that if you do not use

Housecode C and Unit Code 5, the instructions that follow will not work for your module.

If you don't want to continue to use Housecode C for the lamps in your system, don't worry. You can reconfigure the Lamp Module once you've finished this exercise.

Now you're ready to create the module icon.

Edit
Undo ⌘Z
Cut Icon ⌘K
Copy ⌘C
Paste ⌘U
Clear
New Event
New Module...
Edit Module Program...
Set Module Info...
Show Module Program...
Edit Icon...

Choose New Module from the Edit menu.

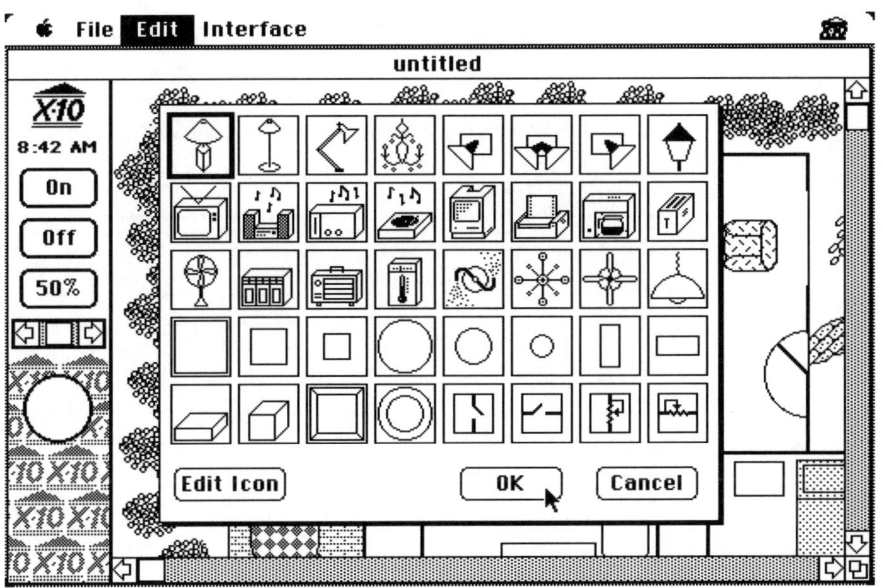

A dialog box will appear, allowing you to choose the type of module icon that you want to create. Each picture represents a different kind of device you can control. The top row contains icons representing various types of lamps. The second row contains appliances, and the third row contains more appliances and lamps. The bottom two rows are for controlling alarm systems and designing your own icons for other uses.

The default, or preselected, icon is the one at the far left of the top row. You can tell that it's selected because it has a heavy black box around it. To select a different icon, you would just click it. In this case, though, you're controlling a lamp, so you'll use the default icon.

Click OK.

The Module Setup dialog box will appear. Here you'll enter a name and set the Housecode and the Unit Code for the module. First you'll enter a name for the module.

Type a name for the module.

You'll choose a unique name that will help you identify the module later, when the screen is full of modules.

Next you'll set the Housecode. To change the Housecode, you'll just click in the box that contains it (see diagram below). This will advance the Housecode by one letter. You'll set the Housecode to C now.

Click the Housecode shown in the dialog box.

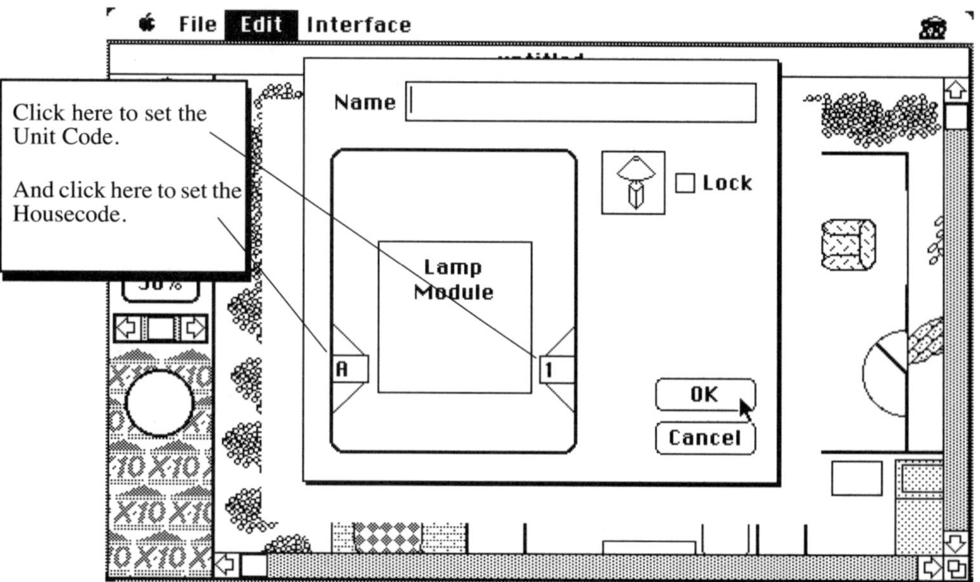

The Housecode will change to B. If it doesn't, you've clicked in the wrong area. You'll look again at the diagram and make sure that you click in the box that contains the A, in the lower-left part of the dialog box. You'll want to set the Housecode to C, so...

Click the Housecode again to change from B to C.

You'll change the Unit Code the same way. You'll change it to 5 now.

Click the Unit Code four times.

Your screen now should look like the one below. If not, review the previous instructions and try again.

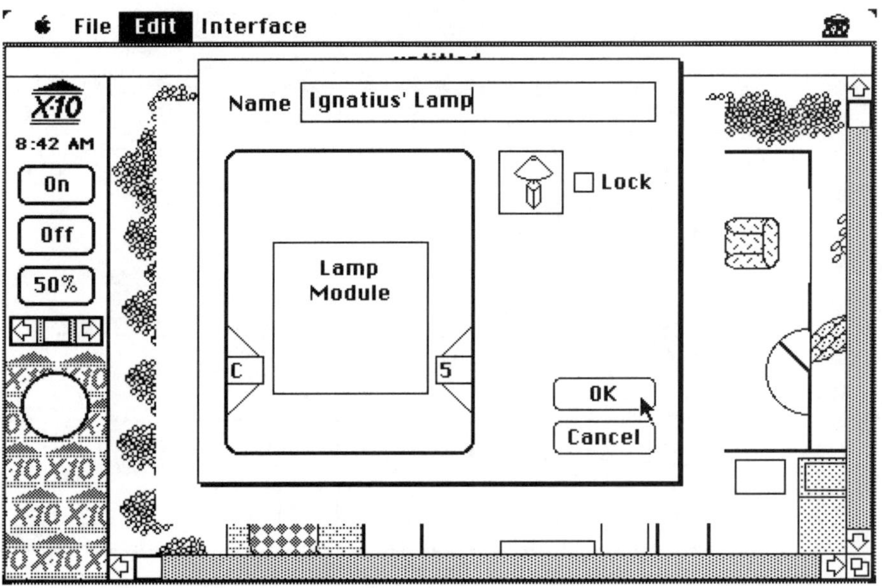

Now that you've set up the module, you're ready to actually do something with it.

Click OK.

The dialog box will close, and you'll see the module icon on your screen. It will be labeled with the name, Housecode, and Unit Code you selected. It also will have landed squarely on a chair in the living room. The first thing you'll do is move the module icon off the chair. If you're familiar with Macintosh, you'll know that to move a module icon, you just drag it.

Drag the module icon you just created a little to the right, between the two chairs shown in the diagram.

Your screen now should look like the one shown below.

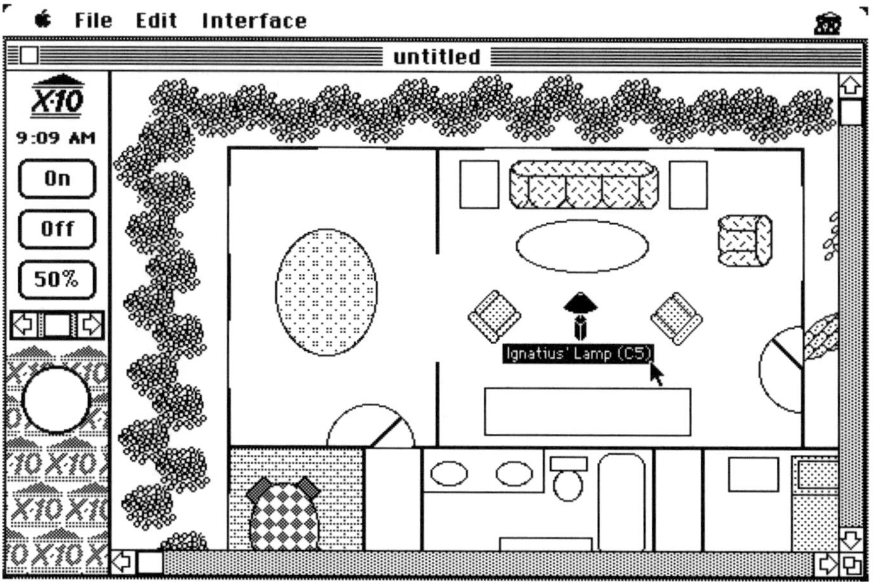

Now you're ready to control the lamp. There's a simple secret you'll need to know to control devices with the Home Automation software:

First you'll select a module icon. Then you'll choose commands to control that module.

You'll control the lamp now. First, though, you'll need to ensure that it's selected. A module icon is selected when it's highlighted (blackened) and its name appears below the icon. Remember that to select a module icon, you click it.

Selected Not selected

First things first: You'll turn on the lamp. To do this, you'll look at the upper left portion of the screen. There are three buttons: On, Off, and 50%. By clicking the first button, you can turn on the selected module.

On **Click On.**

The lamp in your room should turn on. If it doesn't, you'll check the module attached to it to ensure that the Housecode and Unit Code are set correctly (C5). Then you'll make sure that the module icon is selected. Remember that when a module icon is selected, it's highlighted, and the module name, Housecode, and Unit Code appear below it (see diagram above).

Next you'll turn off the lamp.

Off **Click Off.**

The light will go off. Pretty simple, eh? Hang on. Things get a little more complicated, but not much. Next you're going to dim the lamp. To do this, you'll make sure you've attached the lamp to a Lamp Module and not to an Appliance Module. You cannot dim lamps that are attached to an Appliance Module.

50% **Click 50%.**

The lamp will turn on and dim to half its original intensity.

You can control brightness with the sliding control that appears below the 50% button. You'll change the intensity by dragging the white elevator box to the right or the left. Dragging to the right increases brightness; dragging to the left decreases brightness. You also can move the box by clicking the arrows (see diagram below).

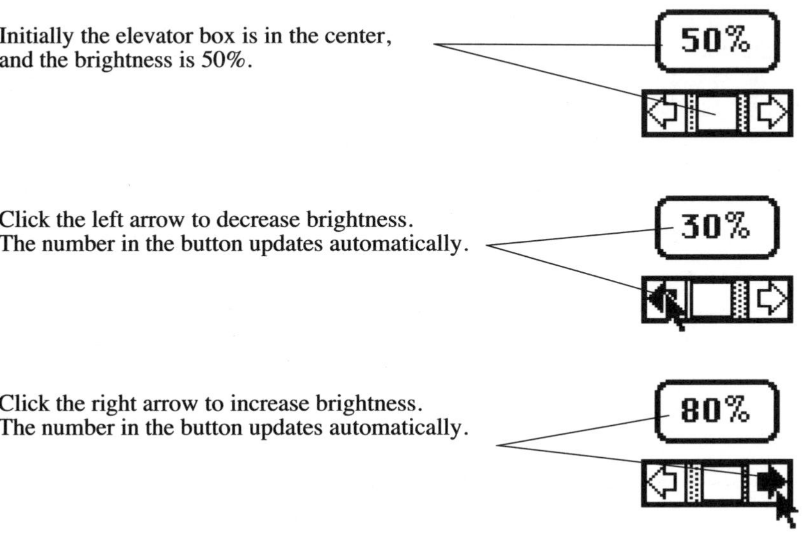

Now you've learned how to create a module icon, how to use it to turn lights and appliances on and off, and how to dim lamps. You also can use module icons to control devices that are attached to a Universal Module. For example, you could use the same procedure to create a module icon to control low-voltage lights or sprinklers.

Setting Up Timed Events

Now that you know how to control devices immediately, you're ready to learn how to create timed events. You do this by programming the module icons that you create. But don't worry—you don't have to be a programmer to figure it out.

You'll program the lamp module icon now.

Choose Edit Module Program from the Edit menu.

A dialog box will appear. The parts of the dialog box are described briefly below.

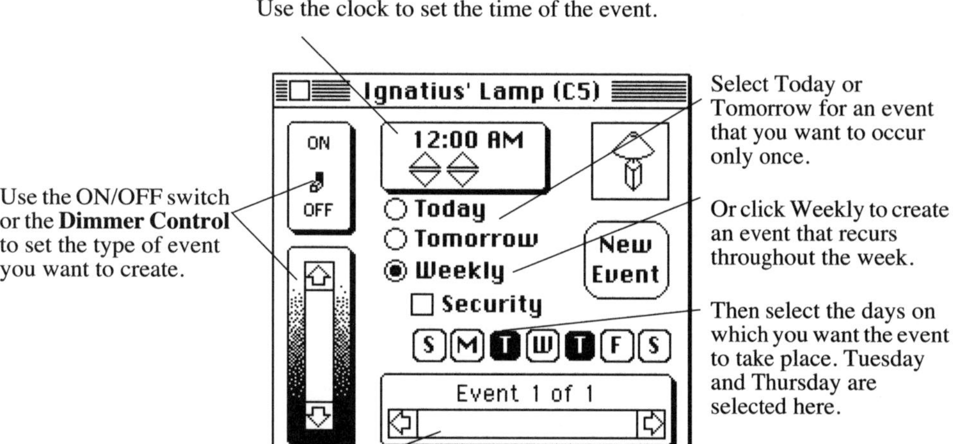

The Edit Program Module dialog box allows you to create timed events. That is, it allows you to turn a device on and off at specific times, and to dim lamps attached to Lamp Modules or Wall Switch Modules at certain times. There are four things you must do to create a timed event:

- Create the event by clicking the New Event button or choosing New Event from the Edit menu.
- Select an event type: On, Off, or Dim.
- Set the time of day for the event.
- Choose a day of the week for the event: Today, Tomorrow, or Weekly (recurring).

You'll go through the steps to create a timed event to turn on the lamp. If you've been following along, the lamp is turned on and dimmed 50%. You should turn it off before creating a timed event to turn it on.

Close the dialog box by clicking its close box. Then select the Lamp Module that you created and click OFF to turn off the lamp. Finally choose Edit Module Program from the Edit menu.

Now you're ready to create your first event.

The first thing that you'll need to do is create a new event.

New Event

Click New Event (or choose New Event from the Edit menu).

Next you'll set the event type: On, Off, or Dim. You'll look at the box in the upper-left corner of the dialog box. The box resembles a light switch and works the same way. That is, you'll create an Off event by setting the switch to OFF and an On event by setting the switch to ON. You'll change the switch setting by clicking the word ON or OFF.

Alternatively, you can create a Dim event by clicking in the Dimmer Control and moving the elevator box up (brighter) or down (dimmer). Note that the elevator box does not appear until you click in the Dimmer Control.

See the diagram below.

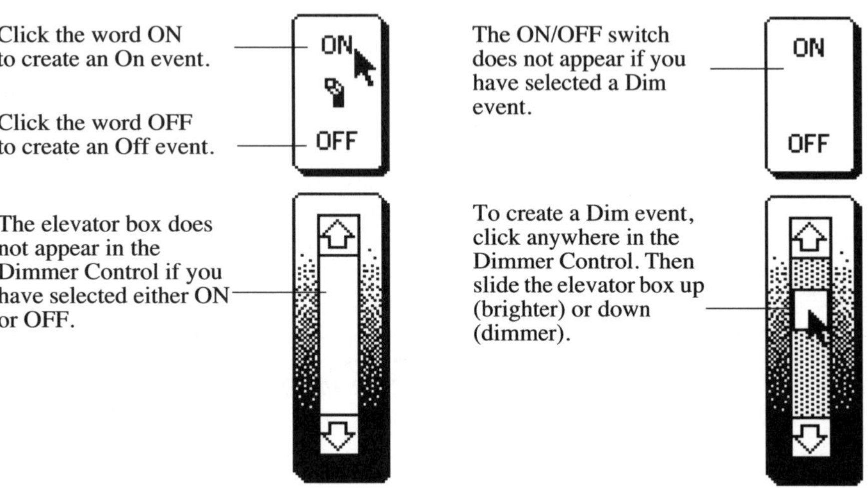

Now you'll create an On event.

Change the event type by clicking ON on the ON/OFF switch.

Next you'll set the day of the week for the event. You'll press one of the three buttons labeled Today, Tomorrow, and Weekly (see diagram below). You'll choose Today or Tomorrow if you want the event to take place only once. If you want the event to recur week after week, you'll choose Weekly.

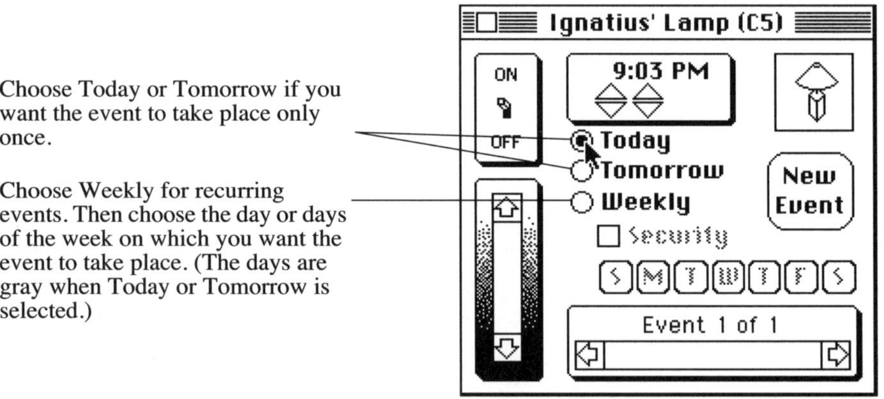

For this exercise, you'll want the light to turn on just today.

Click Today.

Next you'll need to set the event time. You'll use the arrows below the clock in the dialog box.

Because this is your first timed event, you're probably a little skeptical, so you'll want to actually see the lamp go on. To do this, you'll set the event for five minutes from the current time.

Set the clock to five minutes past the time shown in the Control Area by clicking the upper-right arrow shown in the diagram.

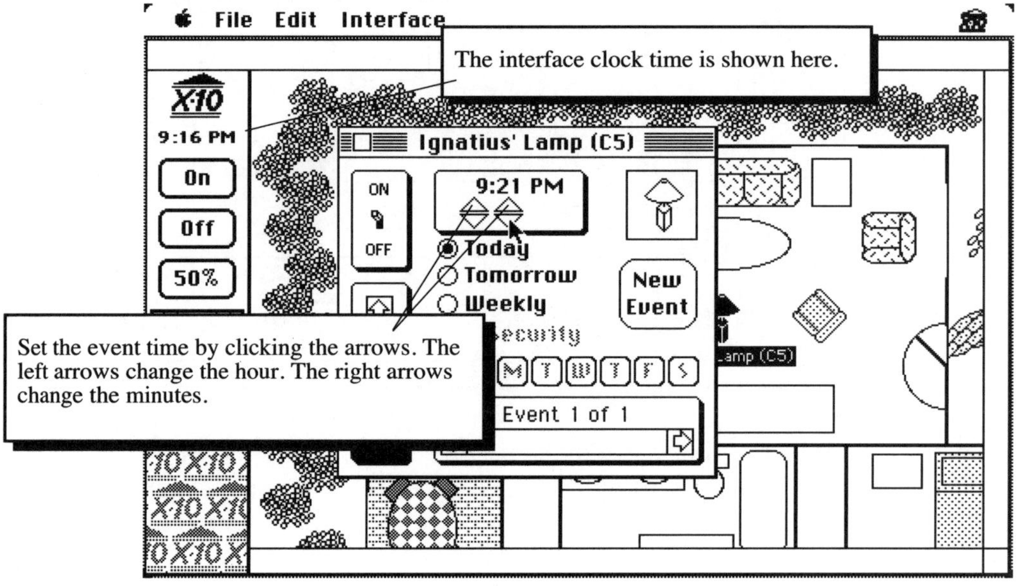

That's it! You'll need to learn more about creating timed events, but that can wait until later.

Now you've created the event, but there's one more thing to do before the light will turn on. So far, you've created the event with the software that runs on your Macintosh. Remember, however, that it's the *interface* that needs to communicate with the module connected to the lamp. Before the events can take place, you'll need to send them to the interface.

You'll do that now, but first you should check to see that the time you've set for the event is later than the current interface time shown in the Control Area. If not, click the arrow to move the clock forward a few minutes.

Choose Send Events to Interface from the Interface menu.

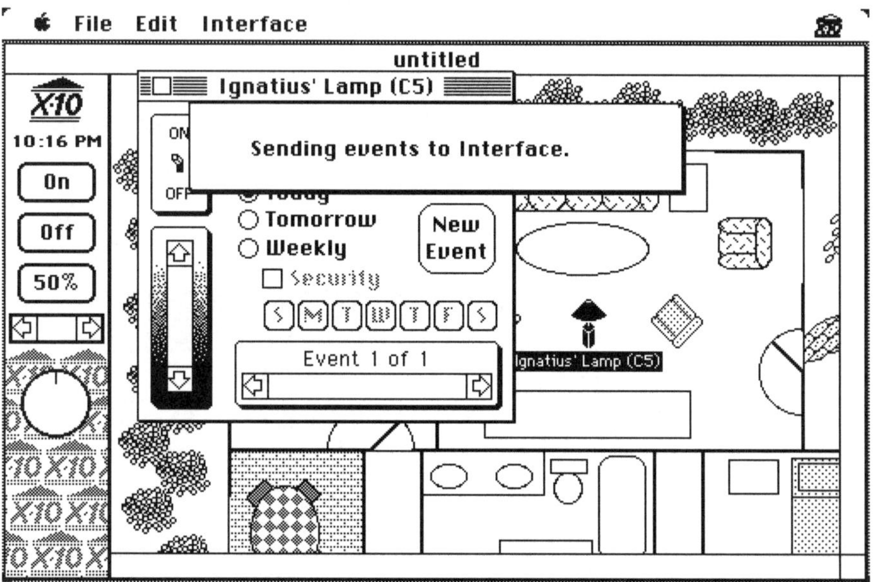

A dialog box will appear briefly, telling you that the Home Automation software is sending the events that you created to the interface. Once the event has been sent, the dialog box will disappear. You'll wait five minutes for the clock in the Control Area to catch up to the time you set for the event. Then the lamp should turn on, and you should be ready to continue.

If the time in the Control Area catches up to the time you set and the light *doesn't* turn on, check to make sure that you've set the Lamp Module correctly. Also you'll check that you've set the time correctly, specifying AM or PM. If you still can't solve the problem, see Appendix B, "Troubleshooting," beginning on page 233.

Now you're ready to create a second event. This time, you'll create a recurring event—that is, one that takes place every week at the same time. As always, the first thing that you'll need to do is create the event.

Click New Event.

You'll notice that the text in the Event List changes to "Event 1 of 2." Now that you've created multiple events for the module icon, you'll need to know which one you currently are viewing. You'll learn how to switch between timed events for a module icon later in this section.

Next you'll need to specify the event type. You'll create an event to turn on the lamp.

Click ON to set the event type.

Now you're ready to select the day of the week. This time, you'll want to create a recurring event.

Select Weekly by clicking the radio button to the left of it.

When you click Weekly, you'll also have to specify on which days of the week you want the event to take place. You'll do this by clicking one or more of the buttons labeled S (for Sunday) through S (for Saturday). Note that if a button is highlighted (blackened), the event will take place on that day. If it isn't highlighted, the event will not take place on that day. If you accidently select a day, you'll click it again to deselect it.

Set the event to take place every Monday, Wednesday, and Friday: Click M, W, and F.

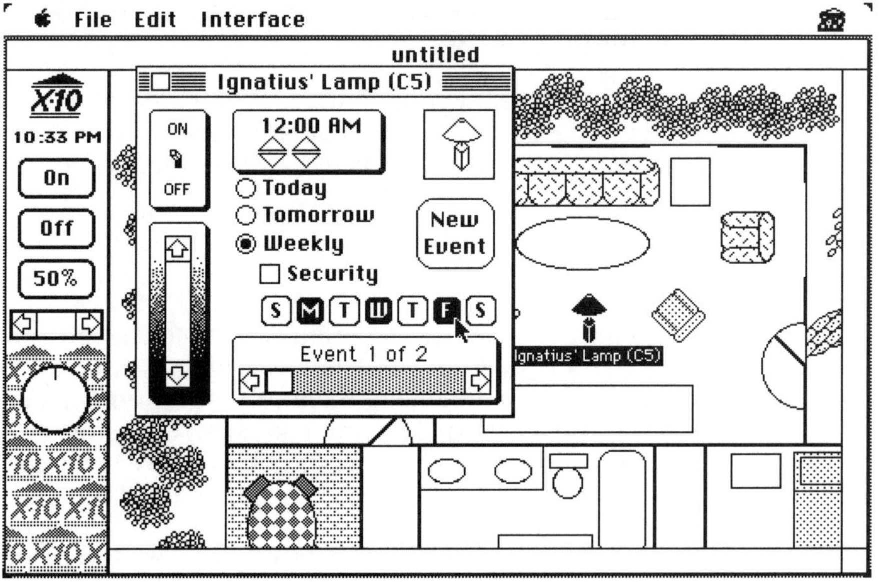

Next you could set the time to any value. For now, you'll leave it at the default: 12:00 AM.

That's it. Now you have two events set for the lamp. You could set more events simply by following the procedures you've just learned.

Remember, once you've created more than one event for a module, you can view and modify the events by dragging the elevator box in the Event List at the bottom of the Edit Module Program dialog box (see diagram below).

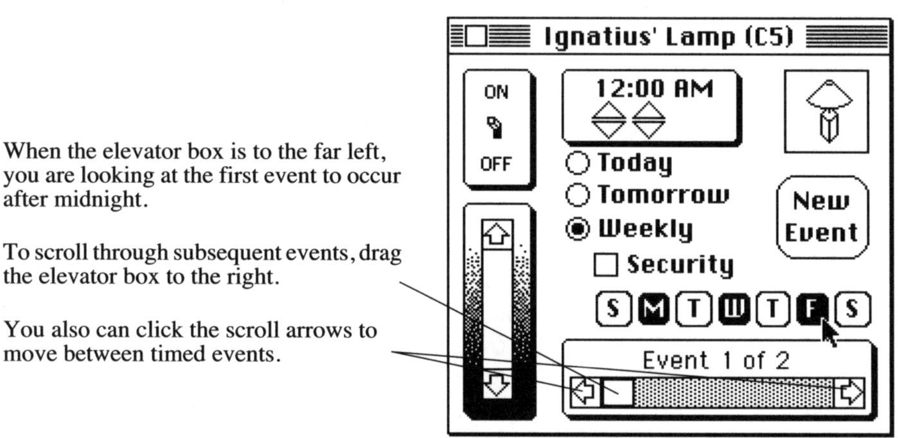

Drag the elevator box in the Event List to the right to display the second event.

You now should see the first event you created, which will turn on the lamp today only. Note that although you created this event first, it appears second in the Event List because it occurs later in the day.

Removing Events

From time to time, you'll certainly want to change the events you've created for a module. For example, you may want to change the time of an event or even delete it entirely. Modifying an event is easy: You'll just scroll to the event and change whatever you want. Removing an event is also easy: As with any Macintosh application, you just cut it out. You'll cut your first event now.

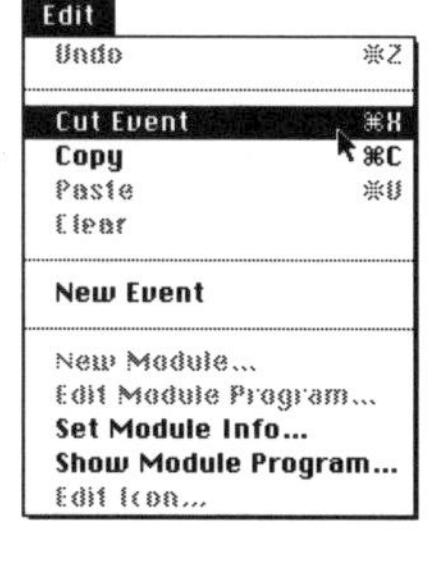

Make sure that the first event you created is displayed. Then choose Cut Event from the Edit menu.

The event will vanish, and you'll be left with only one event, which turns the lamp on at 12:00 AM each Monday, Wednesday, and Friday.

Reviewing Events

If you've created many events, it might be difficult to tell when the device will be on or off just by scrolling through the Event List. Luckily, there's an easier way. You can see a graphical representation of all events for a module by using the Show Module Program command.

Choose Show Module Program from the Edit menu.

A dialog box will appear, showing you the Event List for your lamp.

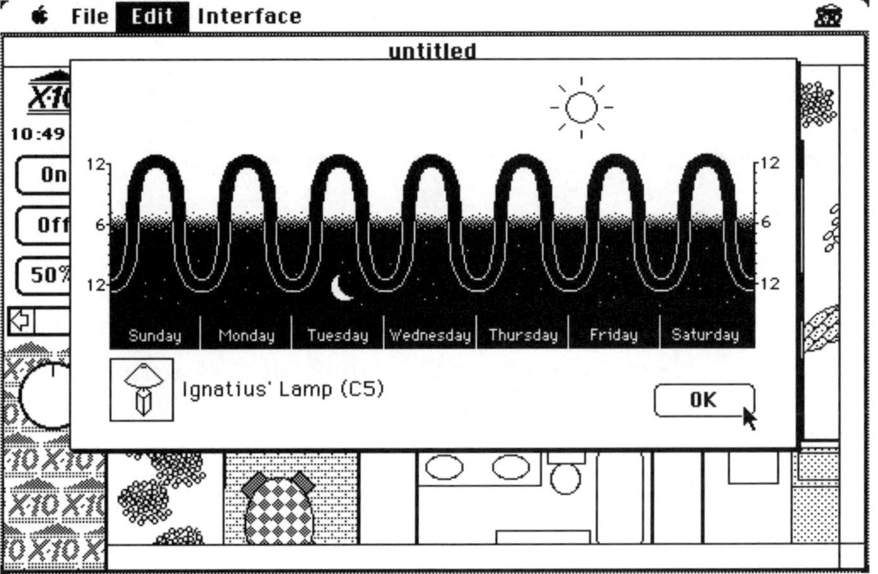

The dark line will show when the module is on. The diagram above will show that the lamp is always on. This may seem strange, but remember that you've created only *one* weekly event, and that event turns on the lamp. Therefore, the lamp is on all week.

Now you'll create an event to turn off the lamp in the morning and see how that affects the module program.

Click OK. Then create a new event to turn off the lamp every Monday, Wednesday, and Friday at 6:00 AM.

If you've forgotten how to do this, review the instructions on page 181.

Now you're ready to review the module program for the week.

Choose Show Module Program from the Edit menu.

Your module program should look like the one below.

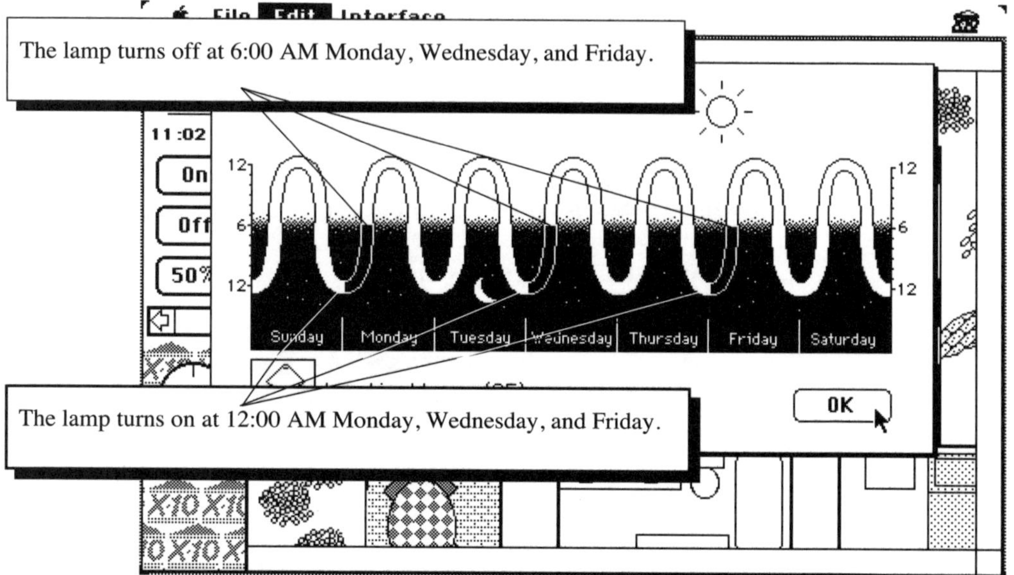

The Show Module Program feature is especially useful when you're reviewing programs for lamps, heaters, sprinkler heads, and so on. Imagine if you created a timed event to turn on the sprinklers, but forgot to create one to turn them off!

When you've finished reviewing the module program, click OK. Then close the Edit Module Program dialog box by clicking the Close box.

Checking the Events Meter

Now you've learned how to create module icons and events and how to send events to the interface. As you already may have guessed, the interface cannot hold an infinite number of events. In fact, it can store only 128 events. Once you've created many module icons and several events for each, it might be difficult to keep track of how many events you've defined and how many more you still can define.

The Home Automation software gives you a visual clue, an **Events Meter,** that always lets you know how much interface storage you have used.

The Events Meter is located in the Control Area (see diagram below).

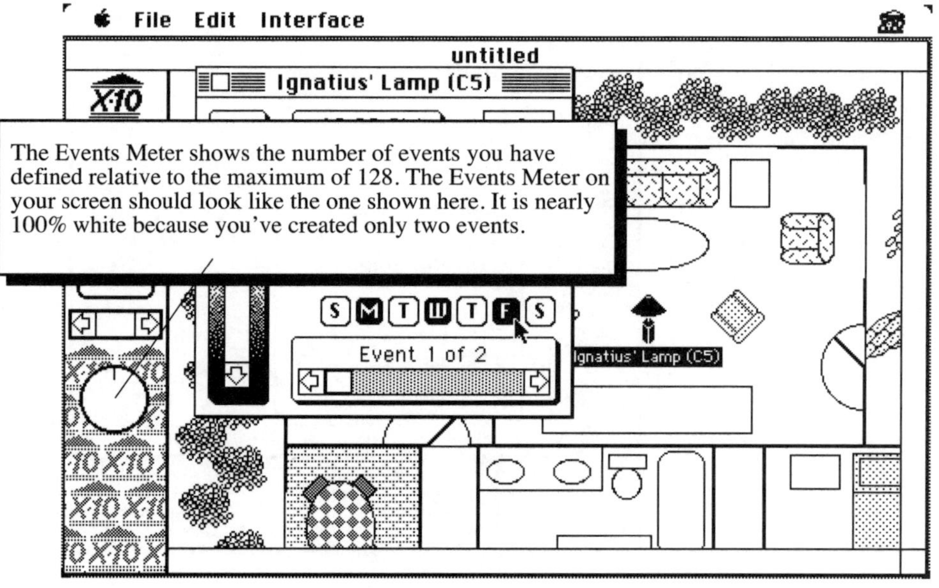

The Events Meter starts out 100% white and becomes increasingly blackened as you create timed events and fill the interface memory.

Changing Module Setup Information

So far, you've learned how to create module icons and timed events, modify events, and how to delete events. But just as you might want to change individual events from time to time or even delete them entirely, you also might want to change module icon information or delete module icons. You'll learn how to do that now.

Let's say that you decide to set all Lamp Modules to Housecode A so that you can turn them off at once with a Mini Controller that also uses Housecode A. You easily can change the module setup with the Set Module Info command. First, though, you'll need to select the module icon for your lamp.

Make sure that the Lamp Module icon that you created is selected (highlighted).

Now you're ready to change the module information.

Edit
Undo ⌘Z
Cut Icon ⌘X
Copy ⌘C
Paste ⌘V
Clear
New Event
New Module...
Edit Module Program...
Set Module Info...
Show Module Program...
Edit Icon...

Choose Set Module Info from the Edit menu.

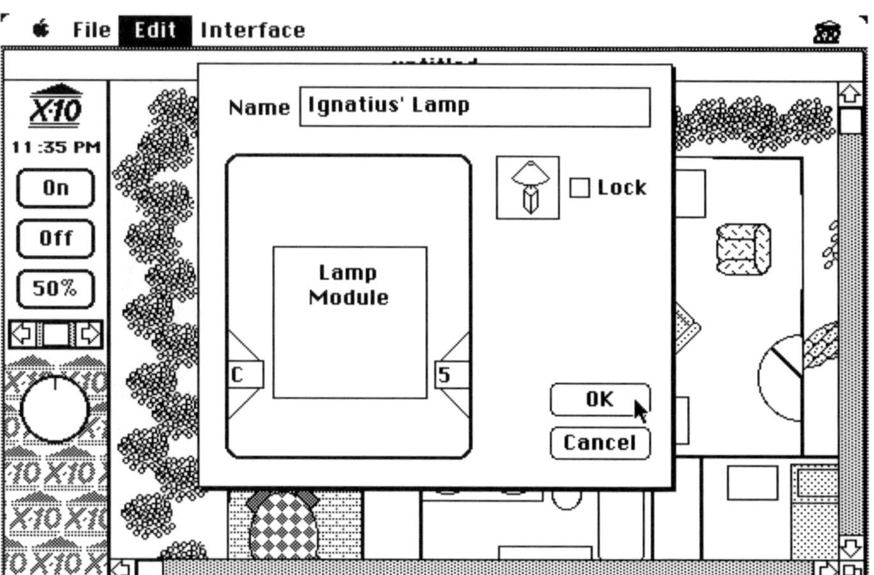

A dialog box will appear, allowing you to modify the Housecode and the Unit Code for the module icon. Remember that to change the Housecode, you'll click the current Housecode to advance it by one. Similarly, you'll click the current Unit Code to advance it by one.

Practice changing the Housecode and the Unit Code. When you've finished, return the settings to their original positions and click OK.

Setting the Base Housecode

Sometimes, when you're in a hurry, you may not want to turn on your Macintosh and run the Home Automation software just to turn on a light or to turn off an appliance. To make life easier, there are eight buttons on the top of the interface that you can use to turn devices with Unit Codes 1 through 8 on or off.

At this point, you should be asking, "OK, Unit Codes 1 through 8, but which Housecode?" You might guess that the interface always uses Housecode A. But you'd be wrong. In fact, the interface can use *any* Housecode. You just have to tell it which one you want to use. You tell the interface to use the rocker buttons with a different Housecode by changing the **Base Housecode.**

Right now, you've got one module icon set to Housecode C. Therefore, it makes good sense to change the Base Housecode of the interface to C. You'll do that now.

Interface
Get Events from Interface
Send Events to Interface
Set Time...
Set Base Housecode...
Self Test...

Choose Set Base Housecode from the Interface menu.

A dialog box will appear, telling you that changing the Base Housecode will erase all events sent to the interface and asking if you want to proceed.

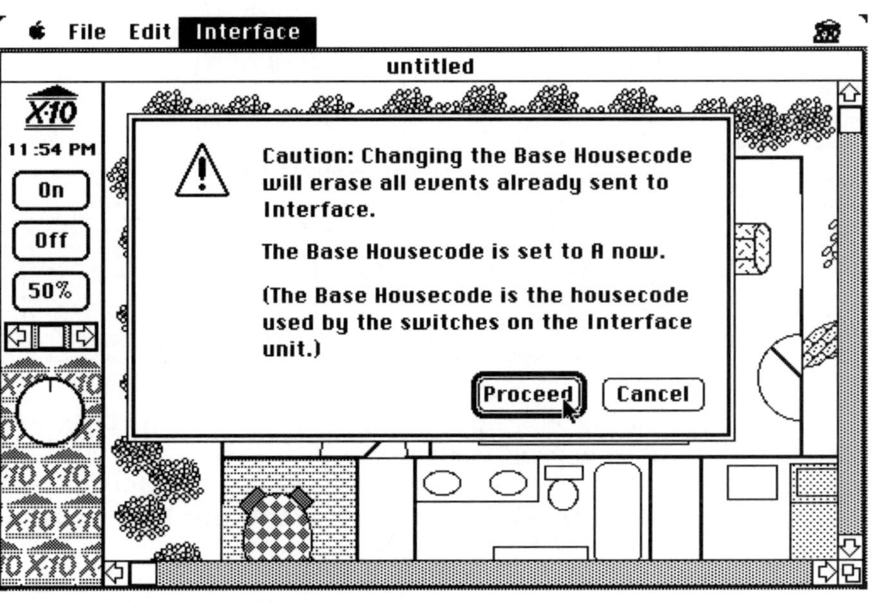

If you'd created many module icons and events, you might be hesitant about changing the Housecode. However, you have only one module icon and two events, so it won't produce a massive trauma.

Click Proceed.

Next you'll see a dialog box that will allow you to change the Base Housecode.

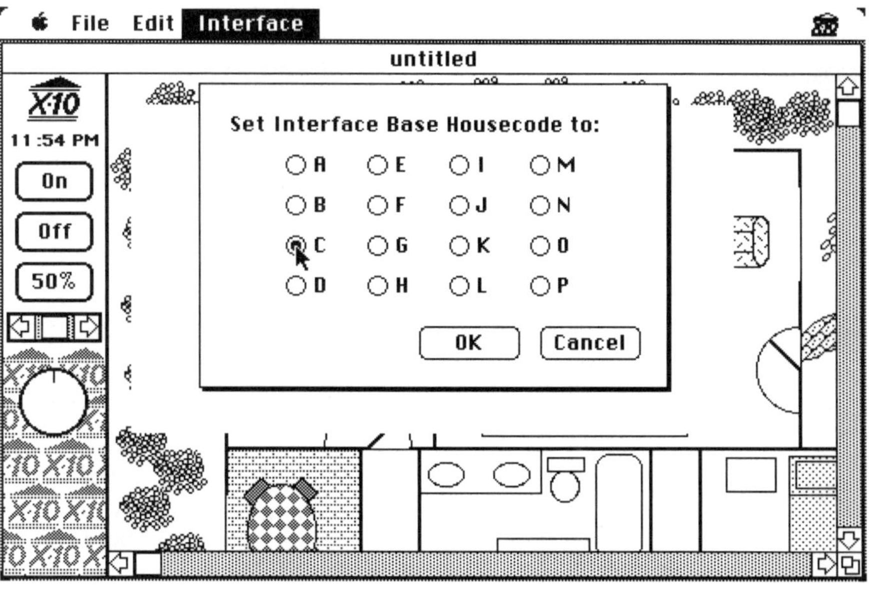

You'll change the Base Housecode by clicking the radio button next to the appropriate letter.

Click the radio button next to the letter "C," as shown above. Then click OK.

Now you can use the rocker buttons on the top of the interface to control the lamp.

Press the bottom of the button labeled "5" on the top of the interface to turn off the lamp.

Pretty nifty.

Deleting Module Icons

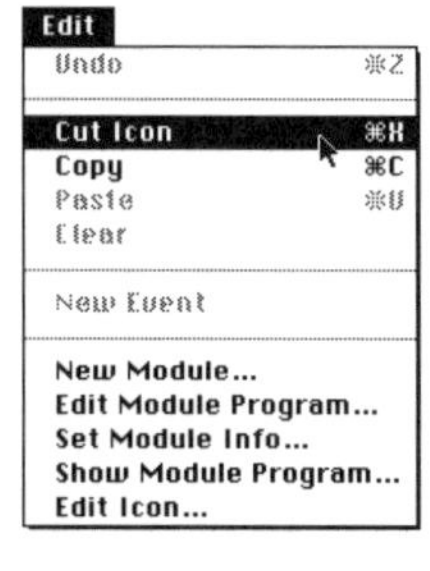

You've learned how to create, modify, and delete events for module icons. But you've learned to create and modify only the module icons themselves. There certainly are going to be times when you want to delete module icons entirely, and it's about time you learned how.

Make sure that the module icon is selected. Then choose Cut Icon from the Edit menu.

The icon will disappear.

Remember, though, that the events you've created won't be erased from the interface until you choose the Send Events to Interface command.

If you decide that you really didn't want to delete the icon, it's easy to get it back.

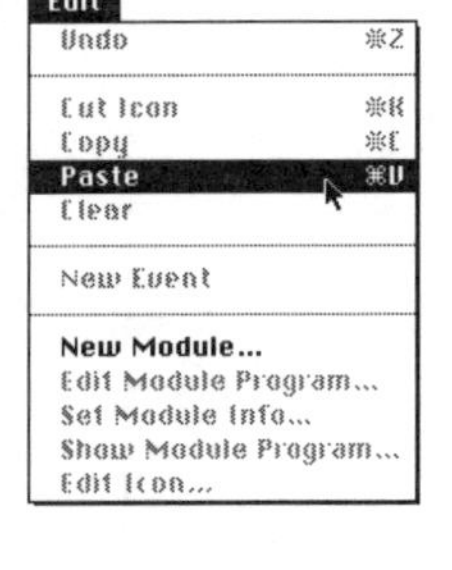

Choose Paste from the Edit menu.

The icon will reappear.

You've learned almost everything about creating module icons and events and controlling the interface with the Home Automation software. The rest of this chapter explains other useful commands and provides some tips and hints that should help you get the most out of your X-10 system.

Configuring and Customizing

Setting the Interface Clock

When you first used the interface, it contained no data, and you set the interface clock to the time of the Macintosh internal clock. In the future, you'll probably want to change the clock time—for example, to adjust for daylight savings time.

Luckily, setting the clock is easy. You'll see how easy now.

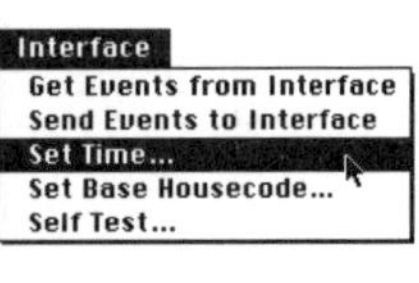

Choose Set Time from the Interface menu.

A dialog box will appear, asking if you want to change the interface clock to Macintosh time. The dialog box will show you the time according to the interface and to the Macintosh clock.

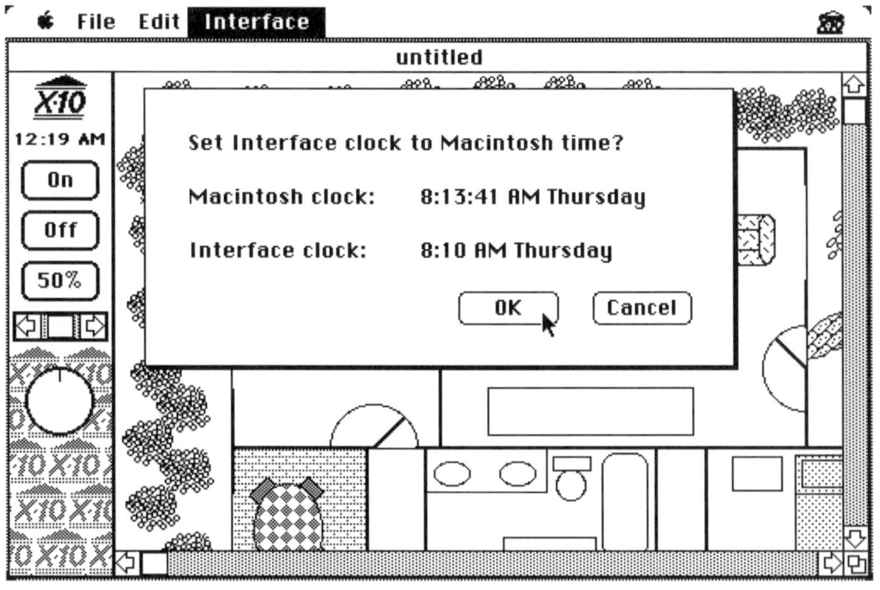

Note that if the Macintosh clock time is not correct, you should *not* set the interface clock until you've changed the Macintosh time in the Control Panel (see your Macintosh owner's manual if you aren't sure how to change the Macintosh time).

If you've completed the preceding sections of this chapter, you've already set the interface clock time, and the two times shown should be about the same.

Click OK.

Changing the Background

Many people open the Home Automation software, look at the background, and immediately say, "My house doesn't look anything like that." Luckily, you can change the background however you want. The background can be any MacPaint document.

Several different backgrounds are included with the Home Automation software. The instructions that follow will show you how to use one of them. But first, you'll need to close the current background.

Choose Close Background from the File menu.

The background will disappear and you'll be left with only your single module icon.

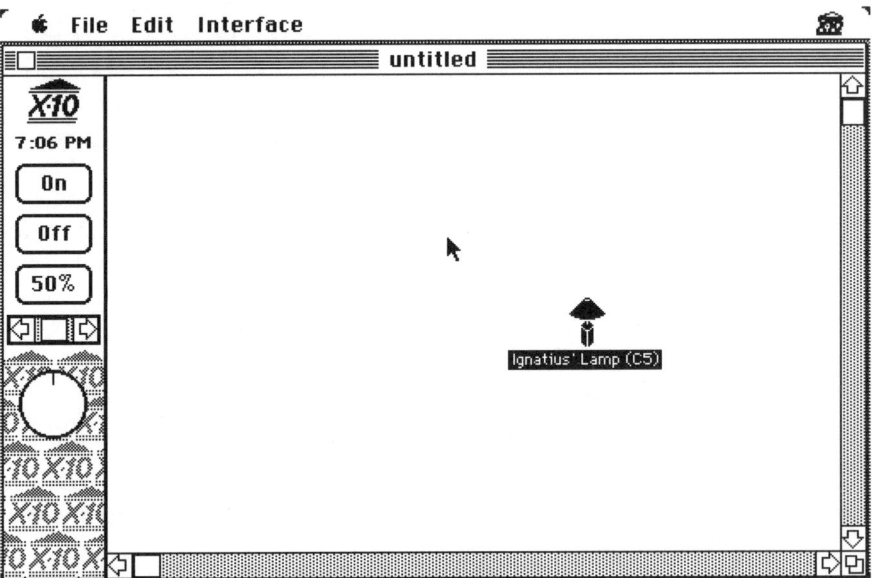

Note that the module icons do not disappear with the background. X-10 (USA), Inc. realized that you might want to change backgrounds without necessarily changing module icon information. Otherwise, you'd have to re-enter all of the module icon information every time you changed backgrounds—a very tedious process.

To give you maximum flexibility, the Home Automation software stores information in three places: backgrounds, the Modules file, and X-10 documents. Each is described below.

Backgrounds are MacPaint documents that give you a reference point for the Module Map. They can help you visualize your home and the location of modules in it. The backgrounds are separate entities, so you can change them without changing either the module icons or the events that you've created.

The Modules file contains information about the modules you've created and the latest background you've chosen for the X-10 software. The Modules file is created by the Home Automation software *automatically*. There is only one Modules file, which you should leave alone unless you want to erase *all* module information. In that case, throw the Modules file into the Trash.

X-10 documents are created by the Home Automation software. They contain information about the timed events that you've created for the modules in your system.

You create X-10 files with the Home Automation software and can have several. Here's why you might want more than one: Generally the modules you install in your home will stay fixed. That is, you install modules for lamps, appliances, sprinklers, and so on, and you don't change them. Events, however, can change for a number of reasons. For example, you might want the lights to go on and off at different times in the winter and the summer. In this case, you could create one X-10 file called Winter and another called Summer. But in both cases, the modules that you've installed would stay the same.

You've just closed the background you were using, but the Modules file and the X-10 file haven't changed, so you are working with the same module icons and the same timed events.

Now you're ready to open a different background.

Choose Open Background from the File menu.

You can choose any MacPaint document to be your current background. Now you'll look at the Rooms background.

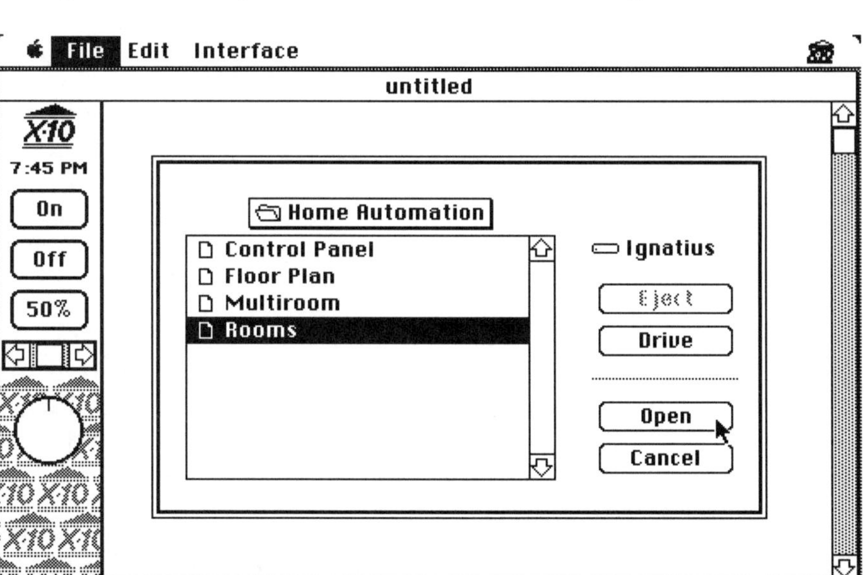

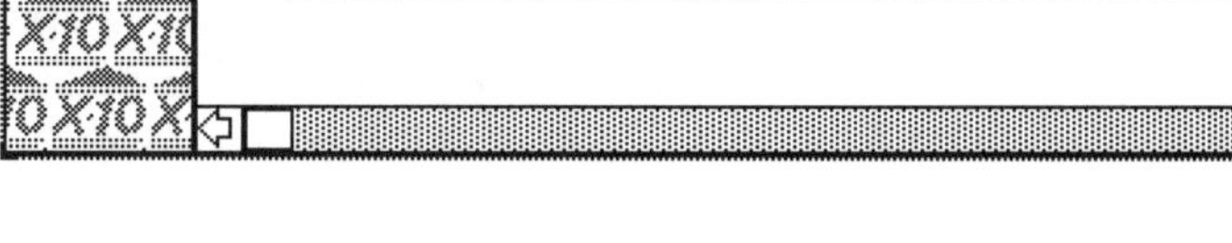

Select Rooms by clicking it. Then click Open.

A new background will appear. Notice that the module icon will be in the same spot, and the Event List will be the same.

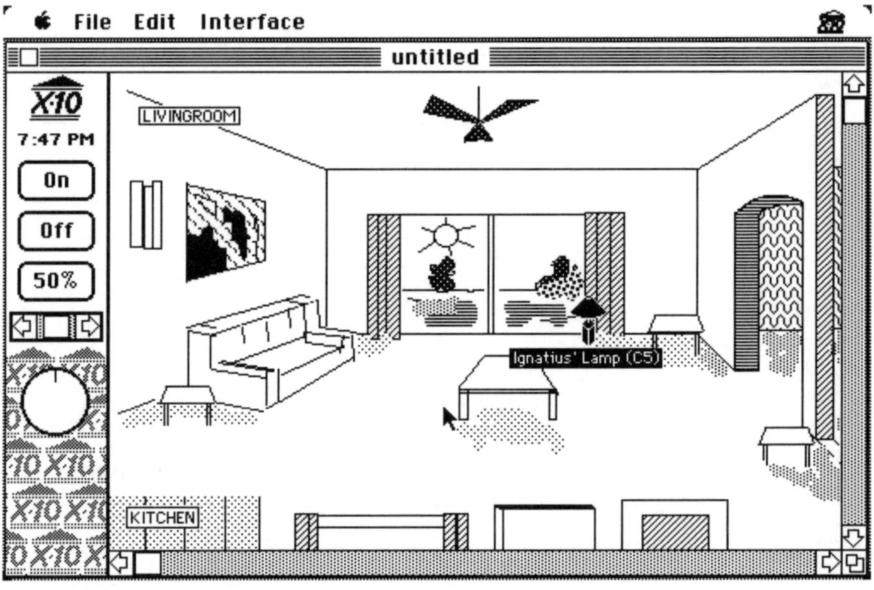

It's important to remember that if you don't like any of the backgrounds that come with the interface, you easily can create your own with a graphics program such as MacPaint. Although the backgrounds supplied with the interface are very attractive, you might be happier with a background that's more like the floor plan of your home. That way, you'll be able to easily identify and work with the icons you create.

Printing

There may be times when you'll want to print a list of the module icons you've created and the timed events you've set for each one. For example, when you're creating a new X-10 file of timed events, you might want to refer to the current interface settings so that you'll know what to change.

Printing a list with the Home Automation software is very easy.

Choose Print from the File menu.

A dialog box, in which you can enter printing options, will appear.

Click OK.

In a few moments, you'll have a printout of information about the module icon that you've created. Your printout should look similar to the one shown below.

Page 1

Ignatius' Lamp (C5)

#	Function	Time	Security	Days		
1	ON	12:00 AM		Mon	Wed	Fri
2	OFF	6:00 AM		Mon	Wed	Fri

Saving Files

Now you're ready to quit the Home Automation software, but first you'll want to save the events you've created in an X-10 file.

Choose Save from the File menu.

A dialog box will appear, asking for a name for the document.

Type a meaningful name for your document, then click Save.

Now you're ready to quit the application.

Choose Quit from the File menu.

You'll be presented with a dialog box asking if you want to send events to the interface before quitting. This reminder will appear because you've modified the Event List of one or more module icons without sending the updates to the interface.

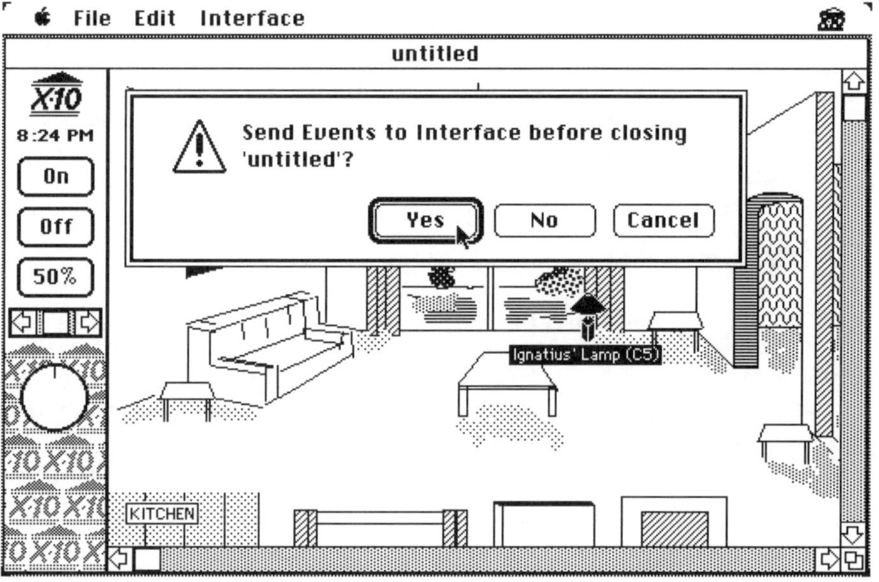

Generally, you'll want to update the interface to include the work you've done. Because this is just an exercise, though, you'll forgo sending events this time.

Click No.

In a few seconds, you'll return to the Macintosh desktop.

Remember that when you changed the Base Housecode of the interface to C, you erased all information in the interface. Now, when you come back to the interface to begin entering real information about your setup, you won't have any "baggage" lying around from the exercise. You'll be starting with a clean slate.

Clearing the Interface

If you ever want to completely clear the interface of all timed events, all you'll need to do is remove the battery and unplug the interface for a few seconds. This will clear the interface memory.

Moving the Interface

Once you've updated the interface with the "Send Events to Interface" command, you can move the interface anywhere and it still will execute your timed events. That is, you don't have to leave it connected to your computer. The only time you'll need to connect the interface to your Macintosh is when you want to update the timed events in the interface or control devices immediately.

Instant X-10

From time to time, you might want to turn a lamp or appliance on or off without running the Home Automation software. For example, if you're working at your desk and your spouse asks you to turn on the heater upstairs, it's a little inconvenient to quit what you're doing, run the X-10 software, find the module icon for the heater, select it, and click ON just to turn on the heater. Fortunately, there's a better way.

With the **Instant X-10 Desk Accessory,** you can turn lights or appliances on or off without leaving the application you're using. You'll just open the desk accessory from within your application and click a few buttons, and you instantly can control lights and appliances in your home.

Installation

Before you can start using Instant X-10, you must install it.

nstall Instant X-10 by dragging its icon from the X-10 disk into your closed System Folder.

The Instant X-10 Desk Accessory is automatically installed in the appropriate location in your System Folder.

Starting Instant X-10

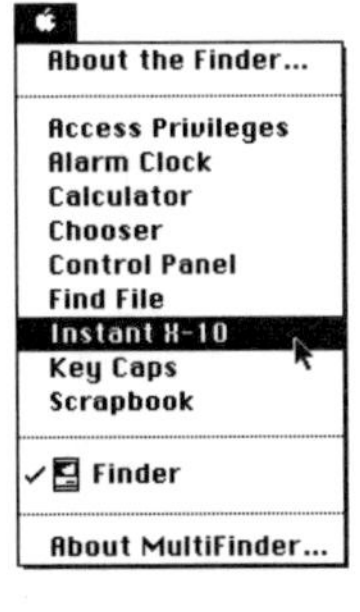

You'll start Instant X-10 the way you start any Macintosh desk accessory—by choosing it from the Apple () menu.

Choose Instant X-10 from the Apple menu.

The X-10 Desk Accessory leaps onto the screen. The major components are described below.

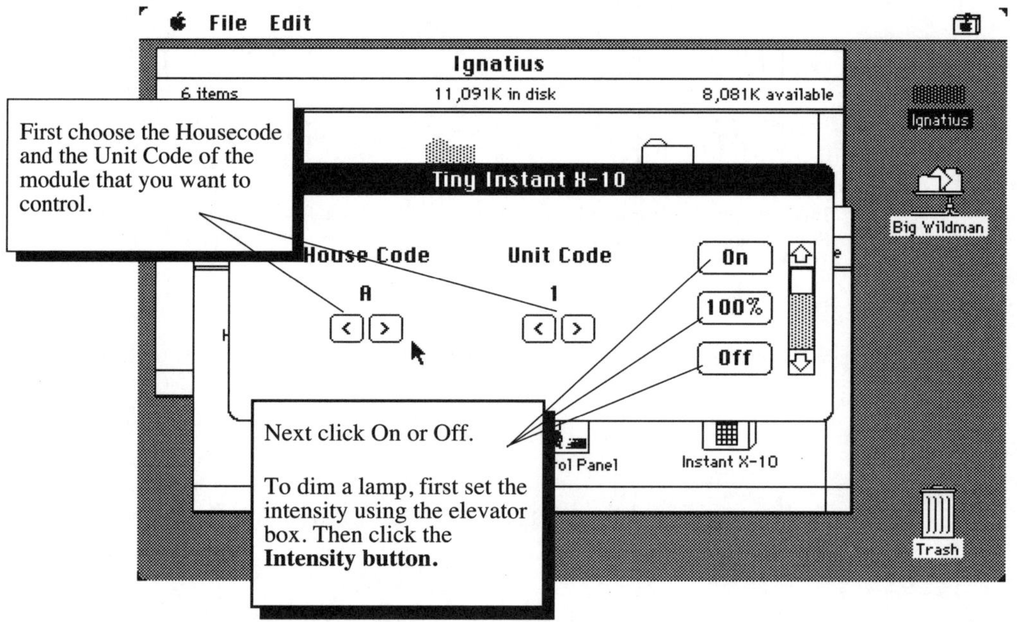

Using Instant X-10 is easy.

Select the Housecode and the Unit Code of the module or modules that you want to control.

You'll select the Housecode and the Unit Code using the < and > buttons, which cycle the Housecode from A through O and the Unit Code from 1 through 16.

Next press On or Off.

To turn on the selected lamp or appliance, you'll just click On or Off. This is not rocket science.

To dim a lamp, you'll first select the intensity you want.

Use the elevator box to set the intensity.

Initially the elevator box will be at the top, and the intensity will be 100%. As you drag the elevator box down, the intensity will decrease. The current intensity always will be shown in the Intensity button.

Once you've set the intensity, click the Intensity button to dim or brighten the lamp.

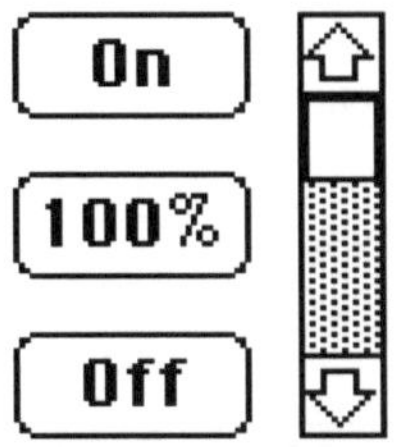

Initially the elevator box is at the top, and the intensity is 100%.

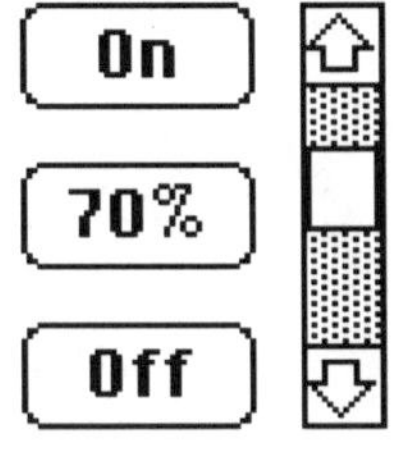

As you drag down the elevator box, the intensity decreases.

Now you've learned everything there is to know about Instant X-10.

Summary

You've finished the chapter. Congratulations. If all's gone well, you've learned to:

- Set up and test the Home Automation Interface.
- Install the Home Automation software.
- Create module icons and use them to control modules.
- Create timed events.
- Review timed events stored in the interface.
- Set the Base Housecode so that you can use the rocker buttons on the top of the interface.
- Change the floor plan by selecting a new background.
- Print information about the module icons and timed events you've created.
- Use the Instant X-10 Desk Accessory to control modules from within any Macintosh application.

8 DOS

Overview

Assuming that you haven't skipped right to this chapter, you've already learned a lot about home automation. In fact, you already know enough to build a very functional system that will control lights, appliances, and even a security system.

In this chapter, you'll learn how to control a reasonably complex home-automation system with an X-10 Home Automation Interface and an IBM personal computer or compatible computer.

Using the interface with an IBM PC gives you several advantages over systems that use the other controllers described in this book:

- You can control modules set with any Housecode and Unit Code; this means that you can control up to 16 x 16 = 256 devices!
- You can create up to 128 timed events.
- You can program each module to go on and off at specific times, on specific days of the week.
- You can program Lamp Modules to dim or brighten to a certain intensity at certain times. This might be done, for example, to add a technical touch to an otherwise very romantic moment.

As you go through this chapter, you'll first learn how to attach the Home Automation Interface to your computer. Then you'll learn how to set up the Home Automation software and use it to enter information about the modules you've installed. Next you'll learn how to erase module information and control modules either immediately or with timed events. Finally you'll learn how to save timed events in a file, print lists of timed events, and exit from the program.

When you're finished reading this chapter, you should be able to use your computer to turn devices on and off both immediately and by using timed events. You'll also know how to save groups of events in a file that you can read into the computer and load into the interface.

This chapter assumes that you're familiar with the operation of your computer. If you aren't, review the owner's guide before continuing.

Setup

Before you try to use the interface with your computer, you'll need to ensure that the interface is functioning properly. Here's how to do that:

- Set the address of a Lamp Module to A1, attach the module to a lamp, and plug the module into an electrical outlet.
- Next plug the interface into a different electrical outlet. (Although you can use any electrical outlet in the house, choose one in the same room so that you don't have to run around.)
- Press the top of the rocker button labeled "1" on the interface to turn on the lamp. Once the lamp has been turned on, press the bottom of the same button to turn off the lamp.
- Set the Lamp Module to A2, and repeat the preceding step with rocker button 2.
- Continue as outlined above, testing rocker buttons 3 through 8.

If you experience any problems, be sure that you've set the Lamp Module correctly. If you still have problems, call X-10 (USA) Inc.'s Customer Service Department for help (the telephone number is given in the "Compatible Products" section of the "Controllers" chapter, beginning on page 54).

One last thing that you should do before connecting the interface to your computer is to install a nine-volt battery in the compartment on the back of the interface. The battery will provide backup power to the interface when it's not plugged into an outlet or when the electricity is off. Without the battery, you'll have to reprogram every timed event whenever the interface is unplugged from an electrical outlet or the power goes off.

Connecting the Interface to Your Computer

The interface works with IBM PC (including PS/2) computers and IBM-compatible computers that have a serial (RS-232) card installed in them or come with a built-in serial port.

Before you do anything else, you'll need to connect the interface to your computer.

Connect the interface to the RS-232 serial port on your computer, using the cable that comes with the interface.

If you're not sure how to do this, consult the owner's manual for your computer. If you have an IBM PC XT, PC AT, or IBM-compatible, you may need an additional nine- to 25-pin converter cable.

Next you'll copy the MS-DOS system files to the X-10 Home Control disk.

Preparing the Software (Without Fixed Disk Drive)

Follow these instructions if your computer does not have a fixed disk drive (also called a hard disk drive). If you do have a fixed disk, skip ahead to the next section.

First you'll need to start the computer.

Insert a DOS system disk in drive A. Then turn on the computer.

You'll wait for the A> prompt before continuing. Before you can use the interface software, you need to prepare it for use as a system disk.

Insert the X-10 Home Control program disk in drive B. Then type "SYS B:". Finally press Enter.

You'll wait again for the A> prompt, which is your signal that the system has finished copying the necessary files to the Home Control disk.

Type "COPY COMMAND.COM B:". Then press Enter.

That's it! Now the disk is ready for use. It's a good idea to make a backup of the prepared disk and store it in a safe place. Once you've done that, you're ready to use the software.

Remove the DOS system disk from drive A. Then remove the X-10 Home Control disk from drive B and place it in drive A.

You don't need to read the next section, which gives installation instructions for users who have a fixed disk drive. Instead skip to "Starting the Program" on page 206.

Preparing the Software (With Fixed Disk Drive)

First you'll create a subdirectory and copy the Home Control software into it.

Turn on the computer. When you see the C> prompt, create a directory named "X10" by typing "MKDIR X10" and pressing Enter.

Next you'll change to the directory you just created.

Type "CD X10" and press Enter. Next place the X-10 Home Control disk in drive A and type "COPY A:*.*".

That's it. The Home Control software is on your fixed disk drive. In the future, when you want to use the X-10 software, follow these steps:

- Turn on the computer and wait for the C> prompt.
- Type "CD X10" and press Enter.

Now you're ready to use the software.

Starting the Program

To help you learn about the Home Control software, the following sections will lead you through a series of exercises. You'll use the interface and the Home Control software to control a single lamp. To do the exercises, you should get a Lamp Module, set its address to "C5," plug a lamp into the module, and then plug the module into an electrical outlet in the room. Once you've done this, you'll be ready to proceed.

Of course, the first thing you'll do is start the software.

Type "X10" and press Enter.

The first thing the program will show you is the time stored in the interface. If the interface has been turned off or if this is the first time you are using it, the time will be wrong.

```
    X-10 INTERFACE
(c) 1986,1987,1988,1989  X-10 (USA) Inc.
The interface contains no data

Enter time(12:00 AM MON) : _
```

Enter the current time and the day of the week.

Be sure to enter the hours, minutes, AM or PM, and the day of the week. The day of the week should be a three-letter abbreviation: SUN, MON, TUE, WED, THU, FRI, or SAT.

Next the software will report the **Base Housecode.** This is the Housecode that will be used when you press the rocker buttons on the front of the interface to operate lights and appliances. You can use any Housecode with the rocker buttons, but you can choose only one. The default, or preselected, value for the Base Housecode is "A." At this point, you'll just use the default value. This isn't a final decision. You'll have a chance to change the Base Housecode every time you start the program.

```
    X-10 INTERFACE
(c) 1986,1987,1988,1989  X-10 (USA) Inc.
INTERFACE UPLOAD TIME is : 12:13 AM gra

Enter time(12:00 AM MON) : 7:15 PM SUN

INTERFACE BASE HOUSECODE is  : A

Want to change it ? (Y/N)
```

Press "N" to respond "no" to the question, "Want to change it?"

Entering Module Information

Now you're ready to enter information about the modules you've installed. Then you can control them either immediately or by creating timed events.

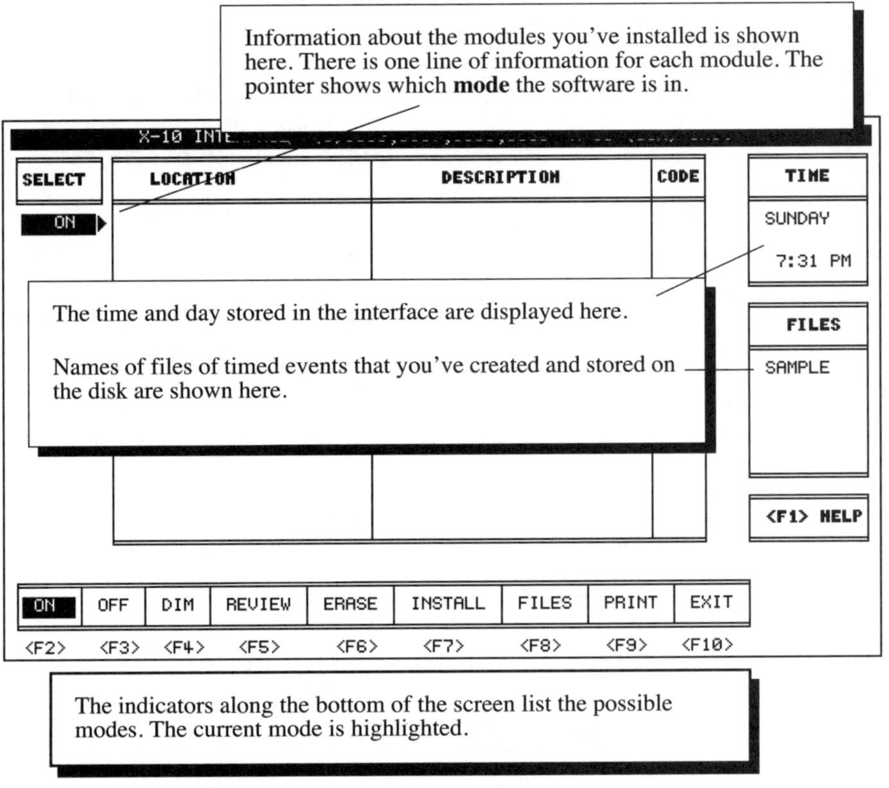

ON

In the center of the screen are three large boxes. They provide information about the modules you have installed. You haven't installed any modules yet, so the boxes are empty. To the left of the three boxes is the **pointer.** It shows you which module you are currently working with.

To the right of the three large boxes are two smaller boxes. The first shows the time and day currently stored in the interface. The second shows the files (collections of timed events) that you've created. Because this is the first time you've used the software, only one file is shown—the sample file that ships with the Home Control software.

At the bottom of the screen will be 10 indicators that show the different software modes you can use. The function key equivalents will be shown beneath the modes. Here's a quick description of the modes:

ON, OFF, DIM	Lets you send X-10 commands to the module selected with the pointer.
REVIEW, ERASE,	Lets you install modules by entering
INSTALL	information about them; also lets you erase and change module information and review the list of timed events.
FILES	Lets you work with files that contain stored information about modules and timed events.
PRINT	Prints a list of all module information that you've created, along with a list of timed events for each module.
EXIT	Allows you to exit from the program.

You'll change the mode by pressing the right (→) and left (←) **arrow keys**.

Press the right arrow key (→) once.

The software will change to Off mode.

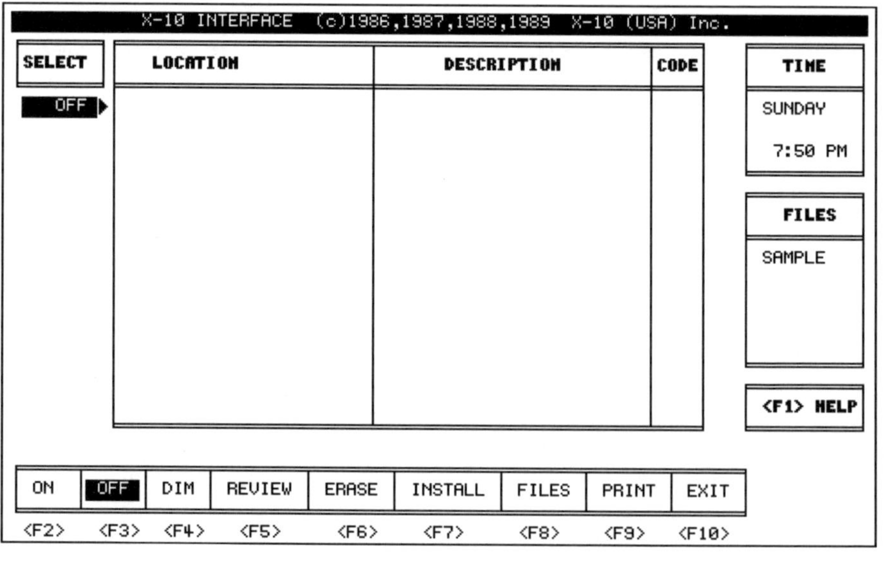

Note that both the indicator at the bottom of the screen and the pointer will change to show that the software is in Off mode.

Install mode allows you to enter information about new modules. Because this is the first time that you've used the interface, you'll need to enter information.

Press the right arrow key four times to select Install mode. Then press Enter.

Note that you also can press the function key labeled "F7" to select Install. If you use F7, you won't need to press Enter.

Above the mode boxes, you'll now see the prompt "Enter the LOCATION." Here you'll enter the location of the module you want to control—for example, Kitchen, Living Room, Front Yard, and so on.

Type "RIGHT HERE" and press Enter.

You'll notice that RIGHT HERE will appear in the Location area, and the pointer box will move to the Description area. The prompt at the bottom of the screen reads "Enter the DESCRIPTION."

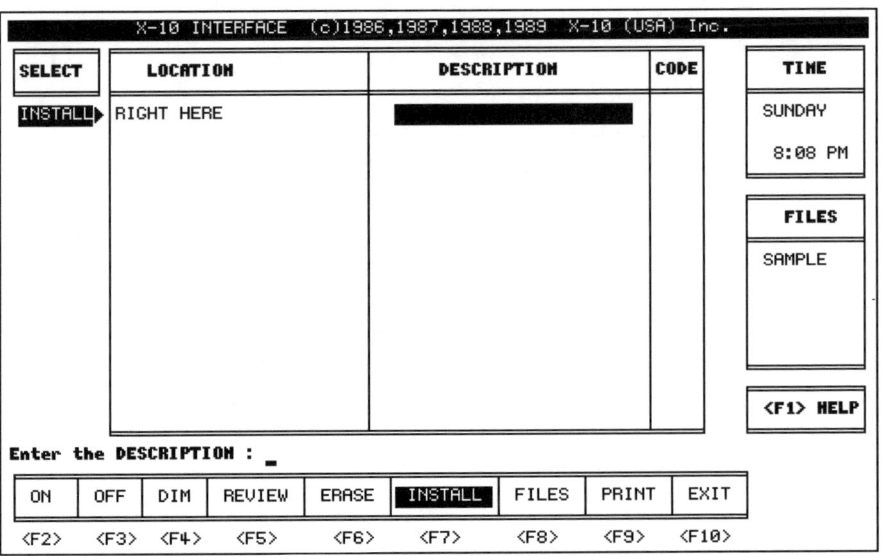

Here you'll type a description of the module you're controlling.

Type a name for the module. Then press Enter.

Your description will be entered into the appropriate box, and the prompt now will read "Enter the code (A 1)." Now you must enter the address (Housecode and Unit Code) of the module you're controlling. The prompt always will show you the address of the next available module—in this case, A1. If you want to accept that address, just press Enter. Now, however, you'll set the address at C5, so that you can control the lamp you set up earlier.

Type "C5". Then press Enter.

Congratulations! If all has gone well, you've just installed your first module. Your screen should look like the one shown below.

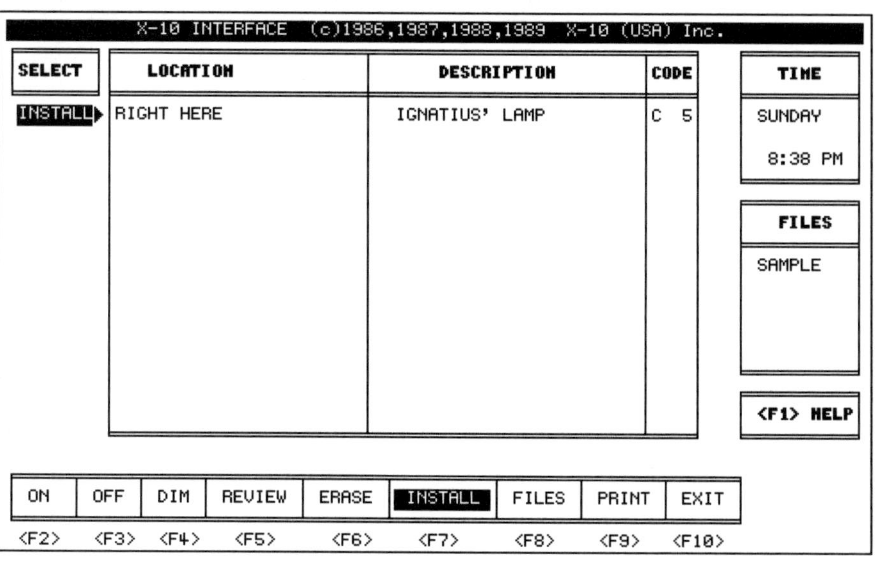

Erasing Module Information

If your screen does not look like the one shown above, then you'll need to erase the line that you just created and start over. Here's how to erase a line.

- Use the left and right arrow keys to select Erase mode (to the left of INSTALL), then press Enter.
- You'll be asked if you really want to erase the line. Type "Y" for yes to confirm that you want to erase it.
- Press the right arrow key once to return to Install mode, then press Enter.
- Follow the instructions above to enter information about the module.

Controlling Modules

Now that you've installed a module, you'll need to know how to do something with it. The first thing you'll do is turn on the lamp. To do this, you'll need to be in On mode.

Press the left arrow key until the software is in On mode. Then press Enter.

The mode indicators will change to time indicators, allowing you to select the time at which you want the event to take place. Your options are described below.

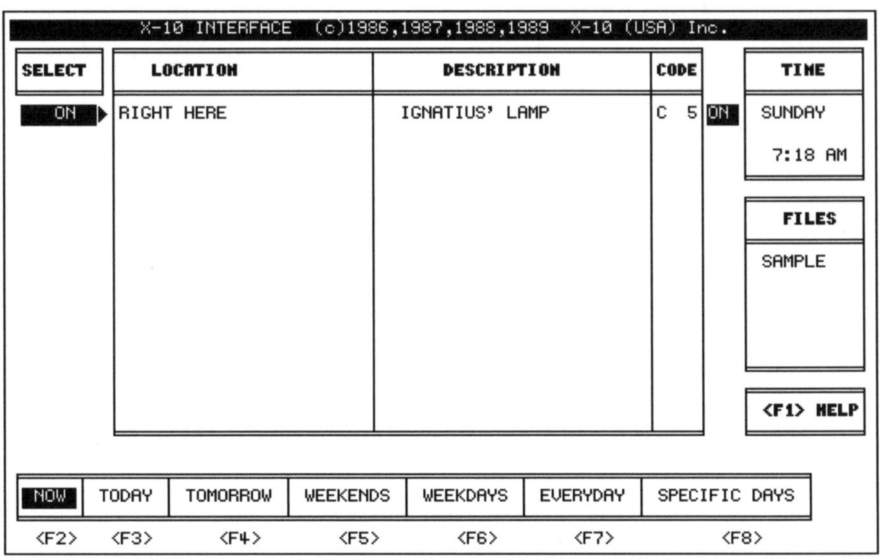

NOW Turns the module on or off immediately.

TODAY Prompts you for a time. The event will take place once within a 24-hour period, beginning at midnight on the day that you create the timed event.

TOMORROW Prompts you for a time. The event will take place once within a 24-hour period, beginning at midnight on the day after you create the timed event.

WEEKENDS Prompts you for a time. The event will take place every Saturday and Sunday of every week, until you erase the event.

WEEKDAYS Prompts you for a time. The event will take place every Monday, Tuesday, Wednesday, Thursday, and Friday of every week, until you erase the event.

EVERYDAY Prompts you for a time. The event will take place every day of every week, until you erase the event.

SPECIFIC DAYS Prompts you for the days of the week on which you want the event to occur. Once you enter the days, you'll be asked for a time. The event will take place every week on the days you specify, until you erase the event.

You'll create a timed event in a little while. First you'll turn on the lamp.

If necessary, use the left and right arrow keys to select NOW. Then press Enter.

A message will be displayed while the interface sends an address command, followed by an ON function command, to the module. Shortly after the message disappears, the lamp should turn on.

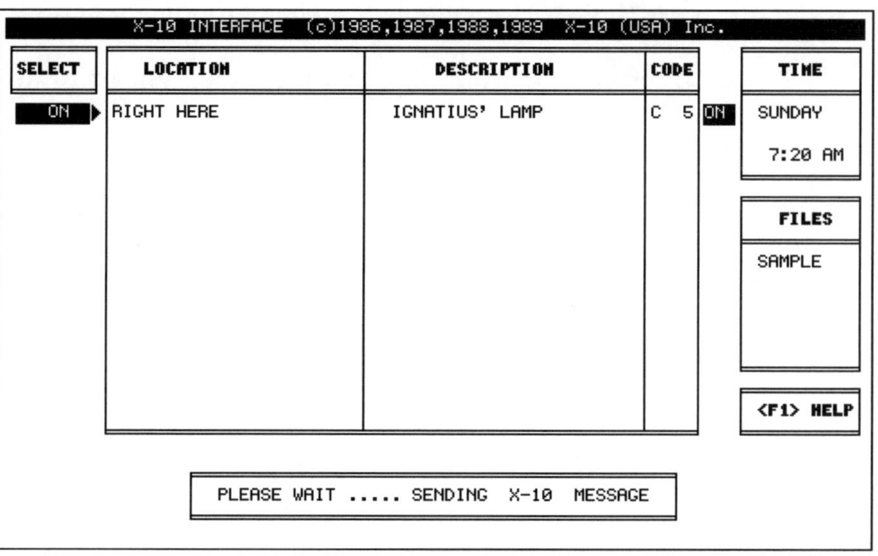

If the lamp doesn't turn on, you'll make sure that the Housecode on the module is C and that the Unit Code is 5.

Using the Function Keys

By now you've probably decided that pressing the left and right arrow keys four or five times to do things is a little annoying. Luckily, there's an easier way: using the function keys.

You'll look at the bottom of your screen.

ON	OFF	DIM	REVIEW	ERASE	INSTALL	FILES	PRINT	EXIT
<F2>	<F3>	<F4>	<F5>	<F6>	<F7>	<F8>	<F9>	<F10>

Below each mode indicator will be a function key designator—<F2>, <F3>, and so on. Each designator will refer to one of the function keys at the top of the keyboard. For example, <F2> will represent function key F2, and so on. To change modes, you can either press the left and right arrow keys to select the mode and then press Enter, or you can press the appropriate function key.

To select DIM, you can either press the right arrow key twice and then press Enter, or you can just press F4.

Press the key labeled "F4" at the top of your keyboard. Do not press Enter.

The mode immediately will change to DIM.

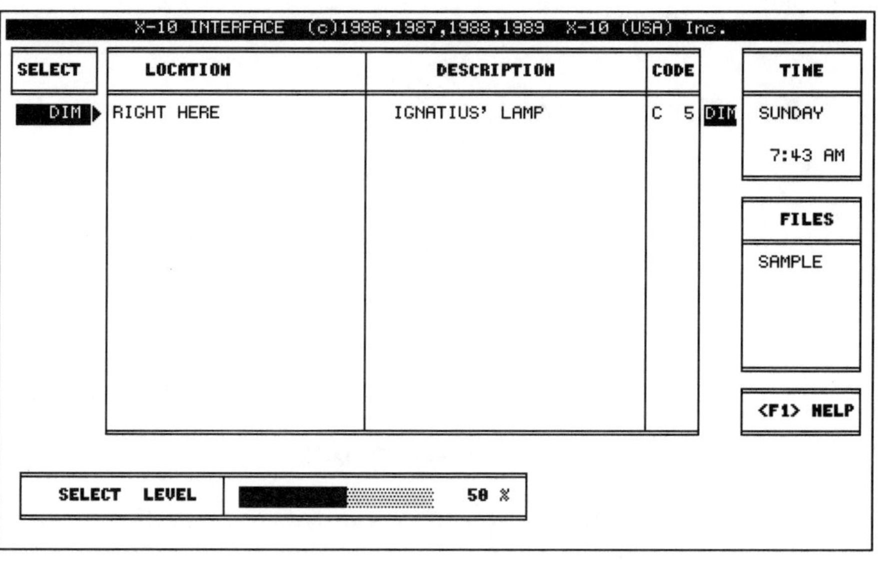

Using the function keys is much faster than selecting modes with the left and right arrow keys. From now on, we'll give instructions using the function keys, but you can use either method.

To dim a lamp, you'll select the level of intensity by adjusting the sliding scale at the bottom of your screen.

You'll adjust the scale using the right and left arrow keys. Pressing the left arrow key once will reduce the intensity by 10%. Pressing the right arrow key once will increase the intensity by 10%.

Press the left and right arrow keys, watching the intensity indicator adjust at the bottom of your screen. When you are finished, move the intensity back to 50%. Then press Enter.

You'll dim the lamp now.

Press F2 to dim the lamp.

The words "Please wait…sending X-10 message" will appear on your screen briefly; then the lamp will dim to 50% of its original intensity.

Setting Timed Events

Now that you've mastered ON and DIM, you'll use the Off mode to turn off the lamp. This time, however, you'll set a timed event. That is, you'll have the lamp turn off at a specific time in the future.

Press F3 to select Off mode.

You'll be presented with the same choice of times that you saw for ON and DIM. This time, you'll choose TODAY instead of NOW.

Press F3 to choose TODAY.

A screen will appear, asking you to enter the time at which you want the lamp to turn off.

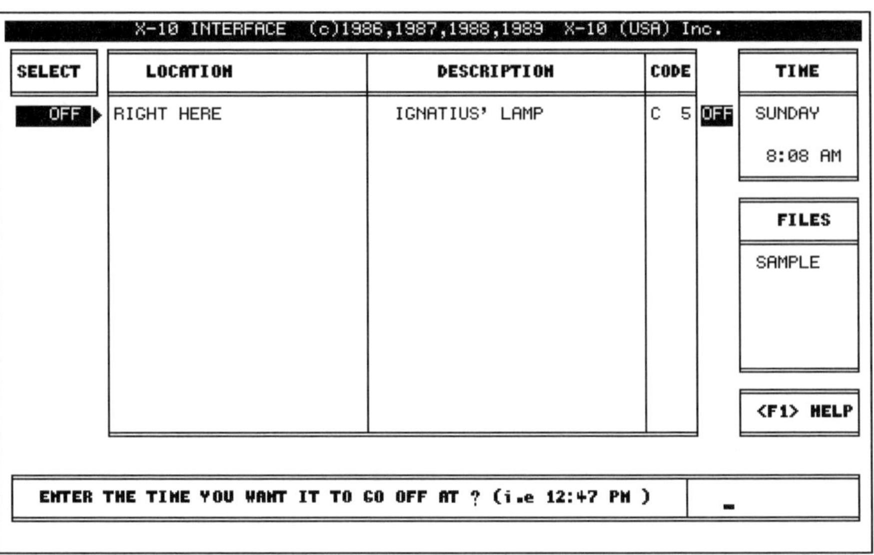

You'll look at the Time box in the upper-right corner of your screen. This will tell you the time stored in the interface. For the screen above, the time is 8:08 AM. The time on your screen will probably be different (unless you happen to be doing this at 8:08 AM!).

You'll set the lamp to go off five minutes from now; that is, five minutes past the time shown in the Time box on *your* screen.

Enter a time five minutes past the time shown on your screen. Then press Enter.

Note that you must enter the time and AM or PM. If you don't, the interface software will not accept your entry and will prompt you to enter another value. Also, be sure to enter a time five minutes past the time shown on your screen, not the time shown in the screen example above. Otherwise you might be waiting a very long time for the light to turn off!

Once you've entered a time in the right format, the software will accept it and ask you if you'd like to program an On time.

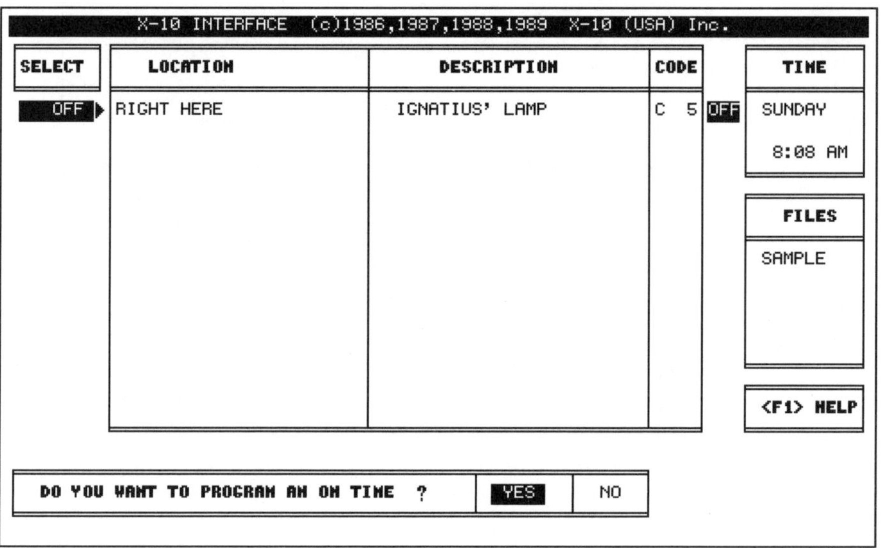

The software designers realize that when you create an event to turn off something, you'll also probably want to turn it on, so they offer you the option to enter the On mode right after you program an Off event. For now you'll concentrate just on getting this first event to work.

Press the right arrow key to select NO. Then press Enter.

You'll return to the main screen, but you'll notice one difference: The name of your module will be in boldface.

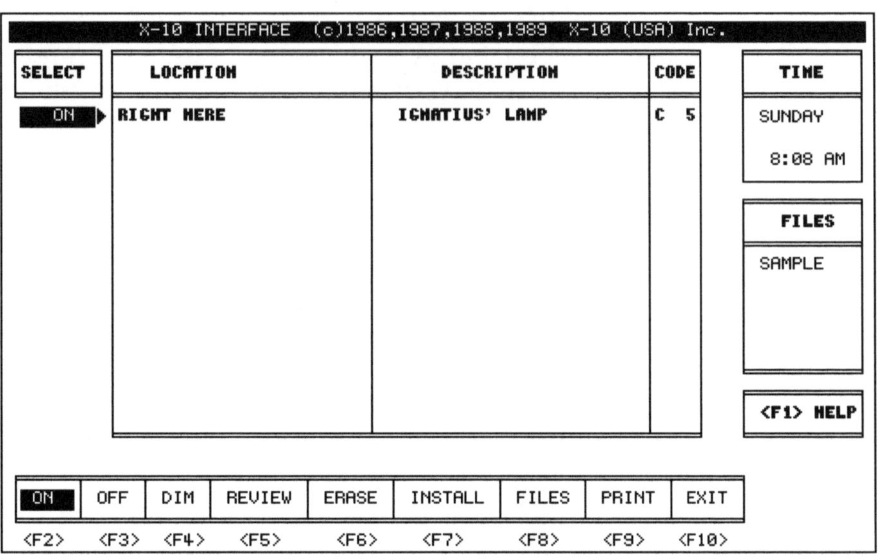

This will be a reminder that you have programmed one or more events for that module. This may not seem like a big deal now, because you've installed only a single module. But in the future, after you've installed a screenful of modules, this will be a useful visual clue to show you which ones have been programmed with timed events.

Now you'll watch the time on your screen. In five minutes, when the interface clock reaches the time that you set for the lamp to turn off, the lamp should, indeed, turn off. If it doesn't, check all the usual possibilities:

- Make sure that the Housecode and the Unit Code on the module are set correctly.
- Make sure that you have correctly set the time for AM or PM.
- Make sure that the interface is still plugged into the outlet.

If the lamp still doesn't turn off, there's a chance that you set the time incorrectly. For example, if it was 8:08 AM when you set the Off time, then five minutes later would be 8:13 AM. But what if you typed 9:13 AM? Either you'd have to wait an hour for the lamp to go off, or you'd have to change the timed event. You'll learn how to modify existing events now.

Reviewing and Deleting Timed Events

Looking at the mode indicators at the bottom of your screen, you've probably already figured out that you'll use Review mode to review timed events.

Press F5 to enter Review mode.

You'll be presented with another screen that allows you to review the timed events that you've set for the selected module. At the top of the screen, in boldface, will be the location, description, and address of the module that you're reviewing. Below that are four columns that contain the function, time, mode, and "when" for each of the timed events that you've set. There is one line for each timed event. At the bottom of the screen will be three options for you to choose from.

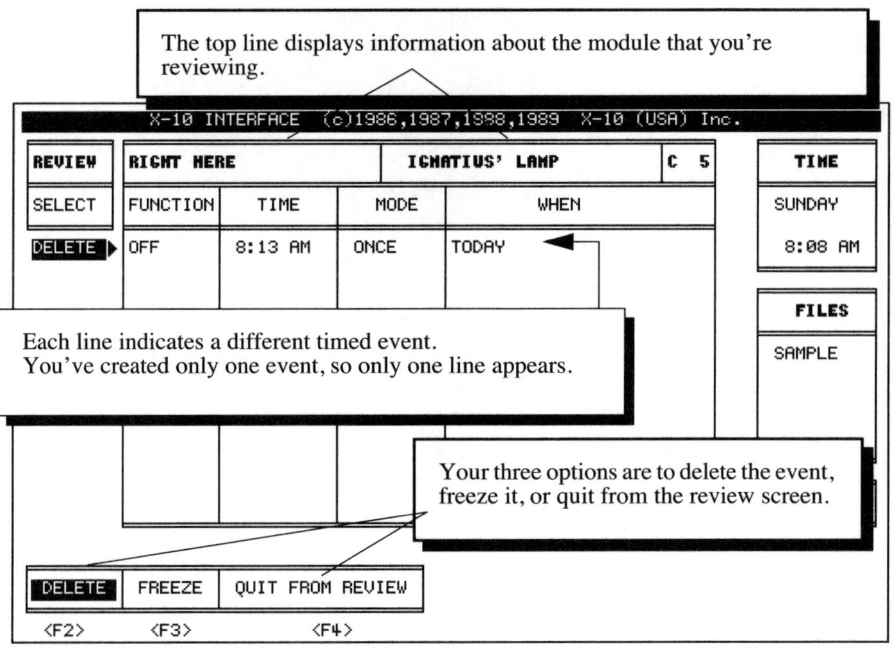

DELETE Allows you to delete the timed event; the function key equivalent is F2.

FREEZE Stops an event from occurring until you unfreeze it. You unfreeze an event by selecting it with the up or down arrow keys and then selecting FREEZE again. The function key equivalent is F3.

QUIT FROM REVIEW Returns you to the main screen; the function key equivalent is F4.

Tip: When you are in Review mode, you can review timed events for other modules without first returning to the main screen. To do this, hold down the Shift key and press the up or down arrow keys to scroll through the list of events for all of your modules.

If you make a mistake, press F2 to delete the timed event. Then follow the instructions in the previous section to re-create the timed event. If you have not made a mistake, and everything is OK, press F4 to return to the main screen.

Saving, Printing, Exiting, and Other Activities

Saving Timed Events in a File

Now you're almost ready to enter information for all of the modules that you've installed in your home and create timed events for everything in sight. Already probably can think of occasions when you'll want to change your timed events. For example, during the summer months, you'll want the lights to come on later in the evening, and if you're controlling a heater, you probably won't want it to come on at all. Likewise, in the winter, you'll want to turn on the lights earlier in the evening, have the heater on most of the time, and leave the air conditioner off.

One solution is to change the timed events you've programmed each time the seasons change. This is somewhat inefficient, though, because you end up retyping things over and over. Fortunately, there's a better way. You can save a list of timed events to use at a later time. For example, you can save one set of events called "SUMMER" and another called "WINTER" that you swap from season to season.

To create a file, you'll first select the Files mode.

Press F8 to select Files mode.

A new screen will appear.

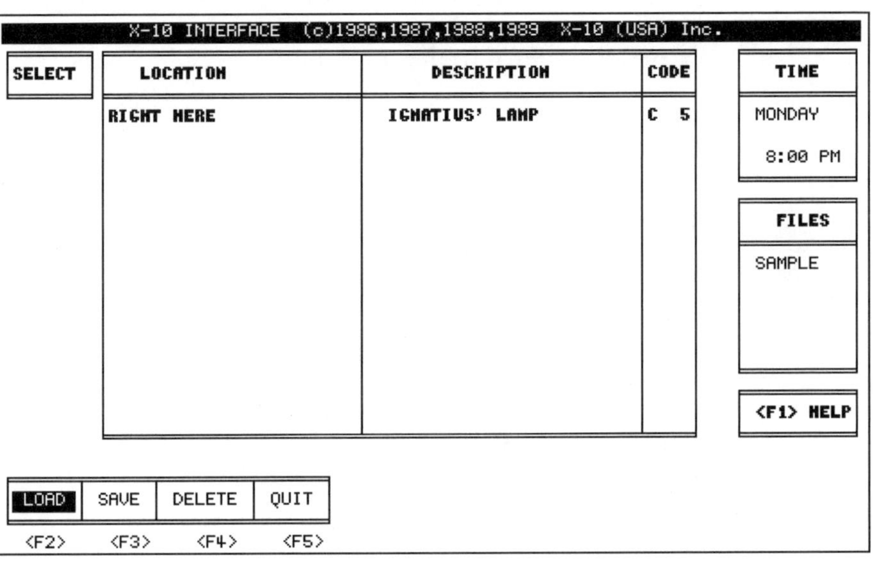

You'll be given the following options:

LOAD Load a file from disk. You'll be asked to enter the name of the file that you want to load. Type the name and press Enter. Note that when you load a file, the contents completely replace everything that is stored in the interface. So, for example, if you've just created a long list of timed events, you won't want to load a new file until you save the current events in a file, or you'll have to retype them. The function key equivalent is F2.

SAVE Save the current set of timed events. You'll be asked for a file name. Type the name and press Enter. For example, you might type FIRST as a file name for the timed event you just created. Note that your files will be saved with the extension ".X10." For example, if you save a file and type "FIRST" for the name, the complete file name will be "FIRST.X10". The function key equivalent is F3.

DELETE Delete a file. You'll be asked for the name of the file to delete. You'll type the name and press Enter. The function key equivalent is F4.

QUIT Return to the main program screen. The function key equivalent is F5.

Now let's return to the main menu.

Press F5.

Printing Files

You can print the current file by choosing PRINT. This gives you a printed list of all of the modules that you've defined and all of the timed events that you've created for each module. A printed list can be very useful when you're creating files for different seasons of the year, or if you want to quickly review all the timed events that you've programmed before going on vacation, to see if you should make any changes before you leave.

Press F9 to print the current file.

Your printout should look like the one shown below.

```
 X-10 INTERFACE
-----------------------------------------------------
-----------------------------------------------------
RIGHT HERE            IGNATIUS' LAMP          C  5
 OFF   8:13 AM  ONCE     TODAY
-----------------------------------------------------
```

Exiting from the Program

You'll exit from the program by choosing EXIT from the main screen or by pressing F10.

Press F10 to exit from the program.

You'll return to the familiar DOS C> prompt (or the A> prompt, if you don't have a fixed disk).

Clearing the Interface

If you ever want to completely clear the interface of all timed events, you'll simply remove the battery and unplug the interface for a few seconds. This clears all the memory.

Moving the Interface

Once you've opened a file, the timed events contained in the file automatically will be loaded into the interface. Then you can move the interface anywhere, and it still will execute your timed events. That is, you don't have to leave it connected to your computer. The only time that you need to connect the interface to your PC is when you want to update the timed events in the interface or control devices immediately.

Where To Go From Here

Now you should know everything that you need to build a complete home-automation system around the X-10 Home Automation Interface. As you add module information to the system and create timed events, you should be able to find all of the information that you need in the sections that you've just read.

As always, if you have problems, see Appendix B, "Troubleshooting," on page 233.

A Technical Overview

Overview

You don't need to refer to this appendix when designing, installing, and using X-10 systems. It's for the curious, who can't merely plug something in without wondering how it works (like us). If you're an electrical engineer, you'll be severely disappointed by the depth of the information, but for weekend soldering-iron jockeys, the appendix should provide a general understanding of how X-10 works.

How It Works

X-10 is based on a technology broadly called **Power Line Carrier.** As you have seen, this design is based on the concept of using the existing transport mechanism for electricity— the **AC power lines** in your home—to carry the commands that controllers send and modules receive. The most obvious benefit of this technology is that there's no need for additional wiring, which can be a huge obstacle in automating existing homes. Power Line Carrier systems also draw the power necessary for the signal—a tiny amount— directly from the power line that is used as the transport mechanism. No alternate power or transformer is required.

All of this takes place with no noticeable effect on the power line itself. The signals are sent back and forth at a **frequency** that's much higher than that of the electrical current. Appliances and lights that are not connected to X-10 modules will never know the difference. The exceptions are other devices that use the same system to transmit signals, such as certain home intercom systems. Problems can occur if the intercom uses frequencies in the same **bandwidth** as X-10. Most manufacturers attempt to avoid this problem because the X-10 standard is so well-established.

Household wiring is subject to **noise** on the line from appliances, fluorescent lights, electric motors, televisions, and other items that create electrical noise while operating. This limits the amount of information that can be transmitted effectively in this manner.

For systems such as X-10, the amount of data sent is actually quite small. The signal is sent in one-millisecond bursts of 120 kHz. The information is sent at the **zero crossing point** of the 60-Hz frequency of electrical power (see the figure on the next page). A 120-kHz signal at the zero crossing point represents a **binary** "1," and the lack of a signal at the zero crossing point represents a binary "0."

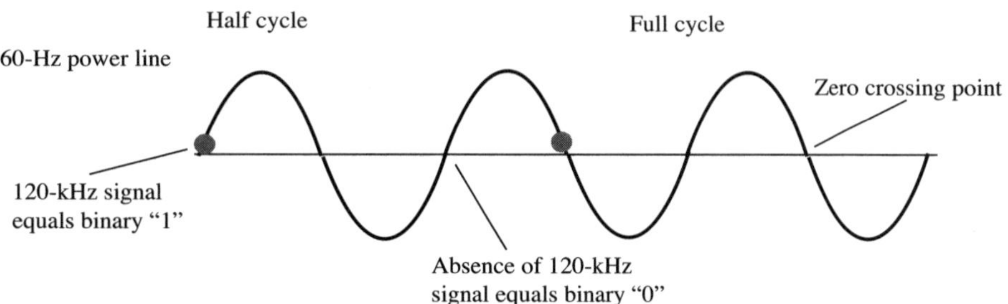

You might think of this as an inaudible Morse code signal traveling across your electrical wires.

When a module "hears" the **Start Code**—1110—come across the line, it knows that the next signal will be the Housecode. If the next thing that the module hears is its own preset Housecode, it listens to the next four signals, or bits, to find out if its unique Unit Code is being sent. If it hears that code (represented by Unit Code 1 through 16 on each module), it is ready to act on the next code sent, which is the five-bit Function Code. If another Housecode or Unit Code comes across the line at any point in the sequence, the module recognizes that the message is meant for another module and stops.

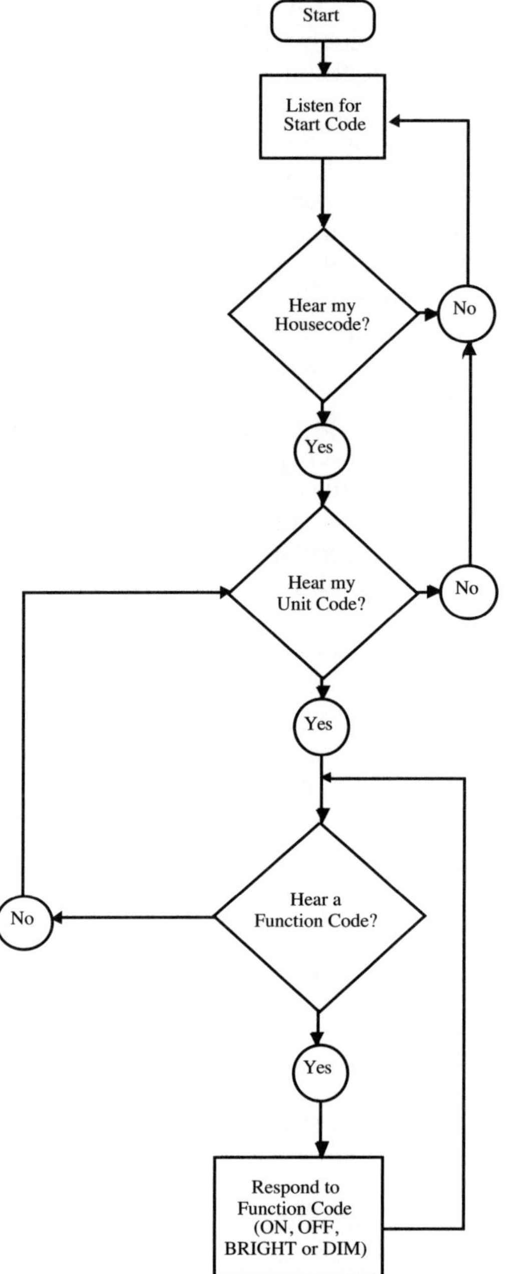

The complete transmission of the X-10 code requires 11 cycles of the power line. The first two cycles represent the Start Code, the next four cycles represent the Housecode, and the last five represent either a Unit Code (1 through 16) or a Function Code (ON, OFF, DIM, and so on). Modules listen to Function Codes only if they have received a correct Housecode and Unit Code. The order is critical—a complete code block with the Unit Code first, followed by a complete code block including the Function Code.

Each complete code block is transmitted twice, with three clear (no signal) power-line cycles between pairs. BRIGHT and DIM Function Codes are sent continuously, with no cycles separating them, because they are, in effect, "increasing" or "decreasing" commands instead of single ON or OFF commands. For example, if BRIGHT is sent and the next code is DIM or Unit Code 1, then a three-power-line-cycle gap will be left.

Each bit or signal is actually transmitted twice—once in its true form and once in its **complement**, or opposite, form on the next half of the cycle of the power line. This helps ensure the accuracy of the signals. If any signal on the first half of the power cycle is not followed by its complement on the next half of the power signal, it's ignored. This is a very simple method of error checking that helps ensure that your modules don't respond to line noise.

The entire code sequence, including complements, is as follows:

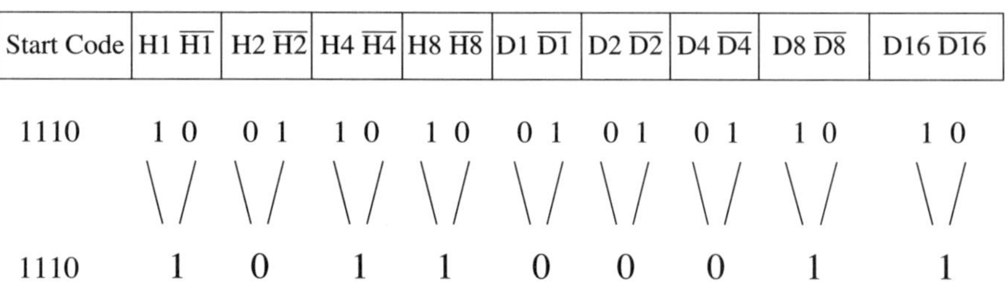

Each signal, such as H1, is followed by its complement, $\overline{H1}$. If H1=1—meaning that a 120-kHz signal was detected at the crossing point of the 60-Hz power line, and on the next half cycle another 120-kHz signal was detected—a transmission error (no complement) would be detected, and the entire code sequence would be ignored. The exception to this rule is the Start Code, which is always the unique 1110. Because no complement is necessary for the Start Code, four bits of information can be sent in two cycles of the power line (one bit per half cycle, with no complement). The next bit requires a full cycle for the signal on the first half and the complement on the second half.

Each complete 11-cycle code block (Start Code, Housecode, and Function or Address Code) is sent twice to double the chances that the code is received correctly. The two types of redundancy (sending the complement bit and sending the complete code block twice) are a simple yet effective way of ensuring signal accuracy and transmission without requiring a "return signal" from the modules, which would require additional hardware and dramatically increase cost.

The code sequences for address commands are shown below.

Housecodes					Unit Codes					
	H1	H2	H4	H8		D1	D2	D4	D8	D16
A	0	1	1	0	**1**	0	1	1	0	0
B	1	1	1	0	**2**	1	1	1	0	0
C	0	0	1	0	**3**	0	0	1	0	0
D	1	0	1	0	**4**	1	0	1	0	0
E	0	0	0	1	**5**	0	0	0	1	0
F	1	0	0	1	**6**	1	0	0	1	0
G	0	1	0	1	**7**	0	1	0	1	0
H	1	1	0	1	**8**	1	1	0	1	0
I	0	1	1	1	**9**	0	1	1	1	0
J	1	1	1	1	**10**	1	1	1	1	0
K	0	0	1	1	**11**	0	0	1	1	0
L	1	0	1	1	**12**	1	0	1	1	0
M	0	0	0	0	**13**	0	0	0	0	0
N	1	0	0	0	**14**	1	0	0	0	0
O	0	1	0	0	**15**	0	1	0	0	0
P	1	1	0	0	**16**	1	1	0	0	0

And the code sequences for Function Commands are shown in the table below.

Function Command	Code Sequence				
Table 1: ALL UNITS OFF	0	0	0	0	1
Table 2: ALL LIGHTS ON	0	0	0	1	1
Table 3: ON	0	0	1	1	1
Table 4: OFF	0	0	1	1	1
Table 5: DIM	0	1	0	0	1
Table 6: BRIGHT	0	1	0	1	1
Table 7: ALL LIGHTS OFF	0	1	1	0	1

The X-10 code format is patented, but there are ways to use the technology for your own product ideas without dealing with complicated licensing issues. If you're interested in developing your own X-10–compatible products, we suggest that you investigate two products available from X-10 (USA), Inc. for OEM manufacturers and hobbyists: the PL513 transmitter and the TW523 transmitter/receiver. Both products plug into regular AC outlets and use a standard telephone RJ-11 interface to connect to your product or experiment. This method eliminates the need to connect directly to 110 AC current and makes implementation safer and easier.

If you want more information about the technical aspects of X-10 technology and more sophisticated aspects of home automation, you can refer to *Circuit Cellar* magazine or call X-10 (USA).

B Troubleshooting

Overview

In general, X-10 Home Automation products are extremely easy to install and use. Like any electronic equipment, however, they require proper setup and configuration to function properly. Occasionally, you may have a problem with an X-10 system. When you do, this appendix is the first place you should look for a solution.

If you can't find the answer here, you should consider consulting a **gearhead** at your local electronics store. These people are generally more than happy to help you solve your problem.

We've divided all the problems we think you'll ever experience into two categories: things don't work at all, and things don't work correctly. In the following pages, we provide troubleshooting tips for both types of problems.

Things Don't Work at All

If you can't get anything to work—that is, you can't turn modules on or off with your controller, then try these solutions.

Is the controller plugged in?

Shame on you if this is the problem. Please consult pages 18, 22, 28, and 41.

Is the outlet a working outlet (not controlled by a wall switch)?

If the electrical outlet is controlled by a wall switch, and the wall switch is off, the controller won't be able to send commands, and the system will not work properly. Make sure you've plugged the controller into a functioning electrical outlet.

Is the Housecode the same on the controller and on the Module that you're trying to control?

The Housecode on the controller must match the Housecode on the module, or the module will not respond to the function commands that the controller sends. Check again, even if you think you've set the Housecode correctly—sometimes the dials don't line up perfectly.

Is the appliance or light you're trying to control turned on?

After you plug the appliance into the X-10 module, make sure that the appliance is turned on. The X-10 module works by regulating the amount of power that the device receives. That is, the X-10 module can prevent a device that's switched on from turning on, but it can't turn on a device that's switched off.

If you're controlling a light, does the light work? Does it have a working light bulb?

Make sure that the light functions without the X-10 module attached. If it doesn't, you've found your culprit.

Are you sure you're using the right Unit Code for the module?

If you don't press the correct rocker button or Unit Code button on the controller, the light or appliance will not turn on or off.

If you're using a Mini Controller, a Mini Timer, or a Remote Control, also be sure that the SELECTOR switch is set correctly for the module you're trying to control.

If you're controlling a Two-way Wall Switch Module or a Three-way Wall Switch Module, is the slide switch in the On position?

If the slide switch on the bottom of the module is to the left, the module cannot be controlled. Make sure that the slide switch is in the right position before you try to control the module.

Does the module work?

X-10 products are well-built and reliable. But if you suspect that a module may be defective, swap it with another module, preferably one that you know works properly. If this solves the problem, contact X-10 (USA), Inc. about its in-warranty replacement policy. Here is contact information:

X-10 (USA), Inc.
91 Ruckman Road
Closter, NJ 07624-0420

(201) 784-9700

Does the controller work?

If you have two or more controllers, first try swapping the one you're using for another. Although it's unlikely, the controller may not be functioning properly.

If you're using a Mini Timer, be sure that the MODE switch is set to RUN, or you won't be able to control anything.

Try moving the controller and the module to the same electrical outlet (if you can). It's possible that the X-10 commands are not reaching the module because they are traveling over too long a distance. Note that even if you have a small house, or you've plugged the module and controller into outlets that are reasonably close together, you still could run into a distance problem. Here's why.

When you send an X-10 command by pressing a button on the controller, the command must travel from the outlet the controller is plugged into to the outlet that the module is plugged into. In a standard two-phase wiring system (used in most homes), that signal might have to travel the entire length of the house back to the **circuit breaker.** From there, it would need to run out to the local power source, back along the trunk to the circuit breaker, and then through some of your home's wiring before reaching the module. This distance might be more than a quarter mile! Moving the controller and module to the same outlet will help you rule out this problem. In addition, some companies sell "signal bridges," which could help you solve these problems. For information on vendors of X-10-compatible products, see the Compatible Products section at the end of each chapter.

Things Don't Work Right

Check this section when things aren't working as well as they should be—for example, if devices turn on or off when they shouldn't.

Could someone else (a neighbor or family member, for example) be controlling the module with an X-10 controller?

That light that seems to come on by itself might be turned on by someone who has discovered an X-10 controller.

Could a Mini Timer or Home Automation Interface be sending the signals?

Did you set up automatic commands to be sent from one of these controllers? They'll continue to send those signals until you program them to stop.

Does your neighbor have an X-10 system?

X-10 controllers send signals over the power line, and those signals continue to travel until they reach a pole transformer or lose strength. Four or five homes may be supplied through the same pole transformer. If you suspect that this is the problem, try switching Housecodes until the problem stops. Or better yet, talk to your neighbors about their systems and decide which Housecodes each of you will use.

Do you have a wireless intercom system or baby monitor?

Some intercoms also use the power line to transmit signals. These devices "broadcast" their signal continuously in order to transit sounds, and can wreak havoc on the X-10 signals that are trying to travel on the same wires. Changing Housecodes may help, but it's best to turn off the intercoms except when necessary, or the erratic behavior will continue.

C Troubleshooting Equipment

Overview

If the previous section still leaves your X-10 not X-10ing, then more serious analysis is required. Leviton, a manufacturer of X-10-compatible equipment, has created special test equipment that quickly can track down difficult-to-diagnose problems.

You've already gone through the basic checks for faulty controllers or modules by process of elimination. The more difficult problems often show themselves as intermittent malfunctions that generally are caused by weak X-10 signals or "noise" on the AC line. To more precisely determine the solution to the problem, use a a Signal Test Transmitter and a Signal Strength Indicator.

Testing Controllers

The Signal Test Indicator gives a visual reading of the strength of the X-10 signal via four light-emitting diodes. As the X-10 signal travels along the power line, it can be read by the Signal Strength Meter as the signals pass by the electrical outlet being tested.

Make sure that the controller to be tested is plugged into an electrical wall outlet.

Set the controller to Housecode P.

Refer to Chapter 2, "Controllers," on page 17, if you don't know how to set the Housecode. It must be set to P because the Signal Strength Meter receives only signals transmitted on this Housecode.

Plug the Signal Strength Meter into the other half of the electrical outlet into which you just plugged the controller.

The Signal Strength Meter can be plugged into any outlet that is on the same circuit as the one used by the controller—the closer the better to begin with.

Press 1 and the ON button.

The Housecode P and the 1 ON signal are sent.

Press "1" and the OFF button.

The Signal Strength Meter should indicate a signal strength of two volts of signal as a minimum. If the reading is less than two volts, the controller is faulty and must be replaced. If the yellow indicator marked ERROR CONTIDITON is lit, there is electrical noise on the line that won't allow a clean X-10 signal to be sent.

If the yellow ERROR CONDTION light is lit, make sure that all appliances are shut off and test it again. Objects that could cause electrical interference include wireless intercoms, baby monitors, electric motors, fluorescent lights, grinders, razors, and some stereo and computer equipment. If the ERROR CONDITION cannot be traced directly to any light or appliance, try the Plug-in Noise Filter, produced by Leviton. It is plugged in between the problem light or appliance and the electrical outlet. This device doesn't interfere with the electrical current needed to run the device, but will filter out electrical noise being transmitted.

Set the controller back to the original Housecode.

Testing Modules

The Signal Test Transmitter transmits a continuous P Housecode, Unit Code 1 ON and OFF signal that can be used in conjunction with the Signal Strength Meter to determine the integrity of modules.

Plug the Signal Test Transmitter into the same electrical outlet that you normally use for the controller.

If you have multiple controllers, you'll have to do this for each of them.

Plug the Signal Strength Indicator into the electrical outlet where the module you are testing is normally plugged in.

If the module and the controller are not close together, you may need a friend to help.

The Signal strength must be 100 millivolts (mv) or more for a module to hear the signal. If the Signal Strength Meter reads less than 100mv, then signal strength is the problem. If the ERROR CONDITION indicator lights up, there is electrical noise on the line.

Phase Coupling

Problems with signal strength are common when the controller is on one "phase"' or side of the electrical circuit and the module is on the other. Even though they may be very close to each other, even in the same room, the electrical signal has to travel all the way to the electrical transformer and back again to reach from the controller to the module. The distance may be too far, and by the time that the signal has made its way to the module, it may be too weak to be heard.

Leviton makes a device called the Signal Bridge that can solve this problem. It connects the two halves of a residential electrical system so that the commands can travel between them via a much shorter path, resulting in a stronger signal that is more easily heard by the module.

Because installation of the Signal Bridge is best done in the main circuit breaker box, leave the job to a qualified electrician.

Once the Signal Bridge is in place, repeat the module test from above to see whether the signal is in excess of 100 mv. If you still receive a weak signal, try signal amplification. The Signal Bridge is a "passive" bridge, meaning that the signal is passed from one side to the other unaffected. If the signal is too weak, even with the Signal Bridge in place, you can try signal amplification.

Signal Amplification

Assuming that the Signal Bridge was functioning properly, but the signal still didn't have enough strength to reach the module, the Signal Bridge can be replaced by a Leviton System Amplifier that not only "connects" the two phases of the electrical systems so that commands can cross over, but it also boosts the signal to the full five-volt specification of an X-10 controller.

The System Amplifier, just like a module, requires a minimum of a 100mv signal at the point where it's connected in order to properly receive and reiterate the command.

The System Amplifier also connects in the circuit breaker box and should be installed only by a qualified electrician.

Glossary

address
The combination of a module's Housecode and Unit Code—for example, A1.

address command
A command that a controller sends to identify modules before sending function commands. The address command consists of a Housecode and a Unit Code. After receiving the address command, modules with that Housecode and Unit Code listen for subsequent function commands, which they execute.

alarm
A device that creates a sound or other signal based on the status of a receiver.

arrow keys
Keys on the keyboard of IBM personal computers that allow you to navigate through the Home Automation software for the IBM PC.

Base Housecode
The default Housecode for the Home Automation Interface. It determines which modules are controlled by the rocker buttons on the interface.

binary
A numbering system made up of only 1s and 0s that is used by computer systems and electrical devices.

circuit breaker
A safety switch in your wiring that will turn off the electricity to a certain portion of your home if a problem occurs that increases the amount of current beyond its rated capacity.

command
A message that a controller sends to a module to control it. See also **address command** and **function command.**

Control Area
In the Home Automation software for the Macintosh computer, the area on the screen that includes the interface clock, the Events Meter, and the ON, OFF, and DIM buttons. The other portion of the screen is called the Module Map.

controller
A device that sends address commands and function commands telling a module what function to perform. Many types of controllers are available, including the Maxi Controller, the Mini Controller, the programmable Mini Timer, and the Home Automation Interface, which work in conjunction with a computer. They all have special features that provide a variety of ways to send address and function commands to modules.

decibel (dB)
A measurement of sound. 85 dB is loud; 120 dB is painfully loud.

desk accessory
Software for the Macintosh that can be used while other software is running.

device
A generic term for an entity controlled by an X-10 module—for example, a lamp or an appliance.

Diet Coke
A source of nutrition and caffeine for aspiring authors.

Dimmer Control
In the Home Automation software for Macintosh, a control in the Edit Module Program dialog box that allows you to create a timed event that will dim a light.

electric valve
A device that opens and closes when an electrical current is passed through it. Used to start and stop the flow of water.

Events Meter
In the Home Automation software for Macintosh, an icon or picture that represents the number of events that have been defined relative to the total number available.

fluorescent
A bulb that creates light by exciting a gas contained in a pressurized tube. Fluorescent bulbs are usually long and thin and produce very little heat. They can be turned on and off by an Appliance Module, but never should be used with a Lamp Module. Fluorescent lights cannot be dimmed.

function command
A command that a controller sends to a module after it has identified the module with an address command. Modules respond to all function commands until they receive another, different address command.

gearhead
A person who's very knowledgeable about things mechanical or electronic. Also known as a nerd or, less often, a techie.

Housecode
A letter from A through O that's used to identify groups of modules. The Housecode and the Unit Code of a module together make up the module's address. Housecodes provide a useful way of grouping modules; for example, all modules with the same Housecode respond to the ALL LIGHTS ON and ALL UNITS OFF commands.

icon
A small picture that represents an item in the Macintosh environment, such as a hard disk, a folder, a module, and so on.

incandescent
A bulb that creates light by forcing electricity through a filament. Incandescent bulbs produce heat. They can be controlled by a Lamp Module, turned on and off, and dimmed.

infrared
A transmission method that uses infrared light for signaling. Infrared signals cannot penetrate walls and glass and therefore require that the receiver be within the line of sight.

Install mode
In the Home Automation software for the IBM PC and compatibles, the mode used to enter module information.

Instant X-10
A desk accessory for the Macintosh that's used to control X-10 modules via the Home Automation Interface.

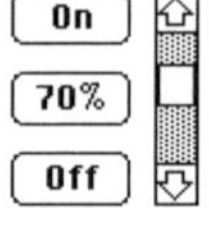

Intensity button
A button that sends a DIM or BRIGHT command to a Lamp Module or Wall Switch Module. The intensity button is labeled with a percentage that represents the intensity of the lamp.

Jones, Chuck
The greatest director of animation ever. Creator of the Road Runner, Wile E. Coyote, Pepe LePew, Marvin the Martian, the best Bugs Bunny cartoons, and many, many others. What does he have to do with home automation? Probably nothing, but he's our hero and it's our book.

low voltage
Less than 30 volts.

magnetic contact switch
A device that uses a magnet to open and close a circuit.

mode
One of a number of states of a software program. The mode determines which actions you can take at a particular time. For example, the home automation software has a mode for entering information and a mode for editing information.

module
An interface box that you connect to lamps, appliances, or other devices to control them. Every module has an address, not necessarily unique, that consists of a Housecode and a Unit Code. Controllers communicate with modules by sending addresses and commands to them.

module icon
In the Home Automation software for Macintosh, an icon that represents a module. You control the module by selecting the module icon and choosing a command to send to it.

Module Map
In the Home Automation software for Macintosh, the area on the screen where you create, manipulate, and view module icons.

momentary switch
A switch that closes an electrical circuit when activated and opens the circuit when released.

normally closed
A switch that's typically connected and whose attached circuit is complete.

normally open
A switch that's typically disconnected and whose attached circuit is not complete.

open-loop system
A design that relies on one-way communication for signaling. In an open-loop system, no confirmation or return signal is used to acknowledge that a signal has been received. X-10 is an open-loop system.

INSTALL **pointer**
In the Home Automation software for the IBM PC, an on-screen indicator that identifies which module you are controlling and specifies which mode the software is in.

Power Line Carrier
A system that uses existing AC power lines for the transmission of control signals from controllers to remote modules. Power Line Carrier systems superimpose signals in a frequency that doesn't interfere with the transmission of power, and they don't require additional wiring.

radio frequency
A transmission method that uses high-frequency waves for signaling. Radio frequency signals can penetrate walls and glass (depending on power levels) and don't require the receiver to be within the line of sight.

receiver
A device that monitors a sensor and can trigger actions, such as sounding an alarm or turning on a light.

rocker button
One of a group of buttons on some X-10 controllers that are used to send address commands and function commands.

scene
When using the Lighthouse for Windows software, a group of modules set to be on, off, or dimmed to create a certain environment. Scenes make it easier to program large groups of devices together.

schedule
When using the Lighthouse for Windows software, a listing of what scenes should be active at what times. By defining a schedule, you easily can specify that groups of modules should be controlled together to achieve a desired effect.

sensor
A device that detects a change from the standard state. For instance, a magnetic contact switch is a type of sensor that can detect the opening of a door or a window.

sounder
A device that creates a sound when electricity is passed through it.

Start Code
The special signal that lets a module know that the next signal coming is the Housecode. The X-10 Start Code is 1110.

techno-speak
A dialect of English most often spoken by gearheads.

timed event
A command that's stored in the controller and sent to modules at a specified time. Timed events can take place just once or can recur on certain days of the week.

Unit Code
A number from 1 through 16 that is used to differentiate modules. The Housecode and the Unit Code of a module together make up the module's address. Housecodes provide a useful way of grouping modules because all modules with the same Housecode respond to the same ALL LIGHTS ON and ALL UNITS OFF commands.

Unit Code button
One of a group of buttons on some X-10 controllers. The Unit Code button is used to send an address command.

watt
A measurement of the quantity of electrical current that flows through a circuit.

X-10 Home Automation
Home-automation technology that uses controllers and modules that communicate over existing electrical wiring. X-10 technology is inexpensive, flexible, and easy to use.

zero crossing point
The midpoint of the amplitude of an AC sine wave. This is where X-10 signals are sent.

Index

Numerics

3-Way Wall Switch Module 71–74
- installation 71

A

Appliance Modules 91–94

B

burglar alarm systems *see* home security

C

commands
- ALL LIGHTS ON 12, 13, 20–21
- ALL UNITS OFF 12, 13, 20
- BRIGHT 12
- DIM 12
- OFF 12
- ON 12

compatibility 15

compatible products
- Appliance Modules 110
- controllers 54
- Home Security 137
- Lamp Modules 86
- Windows software 165–166

controllers 9–10, 17–62
- overview 17

controlling appliances
- overview 91

controlling lights
- applications 85
- overview 63

G

gearhead 233

H

Heavy Duty Appliance Module 100

Home Automation Interface 36–38
- comparison with other controllers 38
- for IBM PC, *see* IBM PC
- for Macintosh, *see* Macintosh
- overview 36–37
- using for manual control 37
- using for timed events 37

home security 113–134
- basics 113–116
- Burglar Alarm Interface 116–120
- Door/Window Sensors 126–129
- Miniature Remote Control 125–126
- options 130–134
  - Powerhorn 130–131
  - Wireless Motion Detector 131–134
- overview 113
- Remote Control 123–125
- Supervised Home Security System 120–129
  - Base Receiver 121–123
- using the system 134–137

Housecodes 13–14

I

IBM PC 203–225
- arrow keys 210
- connecting the interface 204–205
- controlling modules 213–218
- entering module information 209–212
- erasing module information 213
- exiting from the program 224
- function keys 216
- overview 203
- preparing the software 205–206
- printing 224
- reviewing and deleting timed events 221–222
- saving files 222–224
- setting up the interface 204–205
- setting up timed events 218–220
- starting the program 206–208

Instant X-10 200–202
- installing 200
- using 200–202

K

Key Chain Remote 45–46

L

Lamp Module 63–66

M

Macintosh 167–202
- changing module setup information 189–190
- changing the background 194–197
- checking the Events Meter 188
- creating and using module icons 174–180
- deleting module icons 192
- getting started 170–174
- Instant X-10 desk accessory 200–202
- overview 167
- printing 197–198
- removing timed events 186

reviewing timed events 187–188
saving files 198
setting the Base Housecode 190–192
setting the interface clock 193–194
setting up the interface 168–169
setting up timed events 180–186
testing the interface 172–174
Maxi Controller 18–21
comparison with other controllers 21
overview 18
using 18–21
Mini Controller 21–24
comparison with other controllers 24
overview 21
using 22–24
Mini Timer 26–35
comparison with other controllers 35
installing the backup battery 35
overview 26
using for manual control 27–28
using for timed events 28–34
clearing events 34
one-time timed events 32
overview 28
reviewing timed events 33
Security mode 32
setting the clock 28
setting the Wake-Up Alarm 31–32
setting timed events 29–30
Sleep mode 33
modules 9–11
setting addresses 12–14

P

PL513 transmitter 232
Power Line Carrier 227
Powerflash Burglar Alarm Interface 116–120
problems, troubleshooting 233–236

R

radio frequency signal transmission 50
Remote Control and Wireless Transceiver 44–54
comparison with other controllers 54
overview 44
rocker buttons 22, 23, 25

S

security *see* home security
Supervised Home Security System *see* home security

T

technical overview 227–232
techno-speak 41
Telephone Transponder 38–43
comparison with other controllers 43
overview 38–39
using for manual control 39–40
using for remote control 40–43
remote operation 42
setting the ANSWERING MACHINE switch 42
setting the security code 40–41
setting up the transponder 41
3-Way Wall Switch Module 71–74
installation 71
timed events 26
timed events *see also* IBM PC, Macintosh
troubleshooting problems 233–236
TW523 transmitter/receiver 232
Two-Way Wall Switch Module 68–70
installation 69

U

Unit Code buttons 18
Unit Codes 13

W

Wall Receptacle Module 94
Windows 139–164
compatible products 165
connecting the interface 140
creating a scene list 150
creating a schedule 156
creating a unit list 147
exiting from the program 164
help system 163
overview 139
setting up the interface 140
Wireless Motion Detector 131–134
Wireless Transceiver 44
Wireless Wall Switch 46–48

X

X-10–compatible products 15

Z

zero crossing point 227